W9-BSI-737

BEETHOVEN'S
PIANOFORTE SONATAS
DISCUSSED

Da Capo Press Music Reprint Series
GENERAL EDITOR
FREDERICK FREEDMAN
VASSAR COLLEGE

BEETHOVEN'S PIANOFORTE SONATAS DISCUSSED

BY ERIC BLOM

DA CAPO PRESS · NEW YORK · 1968

A Da Capo Press Reprint Edition

This Da Capo Press edition of *Beethoven's Pianoforte Sonatas Discussed* is an unabridged republication of the first edition published in 1938. It is reprinted by special arrangement with E. P. Dutton & Co., New York, and J. M. Dent & Sons, London.

Library of Congress Catalog Card No. 68-21092

Da Capo Press
A Division of Plenum Publishing Corporation
227 West 17th Street
New York, N. Y. 10011

Printed in the United States of America

BEETHOVEN'S PIANOFORTE SONATAS DISCUSSED

BEETHOVEN'S PIANOFORTE SONATAS DISCUSSED

BY ERIC BLOM

NEW YORK
E. P. DUTTON & CO. INC.

Made in Great Britain
at The Temple Press Letchworth
for
J. M. Dent & Sons Ltd
Aldine House Bedford St London
First Published 1938

FOREWORD

THIS book was written, so to speak, inadvertently: it is, in fact, a republication of a series of annotations and essays contributed by degrees to the albums of records published by the Beethoven Sonata Society under the auspices of 'His Master's Voice.' As that society was formed in March 1932, the present effort was spread over a period of more than five years, and I doubt whether I should ever have found the time, the energy and the courage to undertake it as a continuous and independent task. However, here it is, and somehow it does look like a book now—or so my publishers tell me, and I must leave it to my readers and critics to decide whether they share that view.

The material appears here in a slightly different form, with some improvements (I hope) and numerous minor changes necessitated by the new arrangement of the annotations in chronological sequence. The records made by Artur Schnabel for the Beethoven Sonata Society appear in no sort of order except that of the artist's choice. But now that the twelve albums of records are available as a complete series there is, of course, no reason why the sonatas should not be played in the order in which Beethoven wrote them; and, it follows, no reason either why this work should not still be used in conjunction with the admirable gramophone reproductions for which it was originally designed. While I hope that in its new form it may appeal to a wider circle of music lovers than the subscribers to the Beethoven Sonata Society, I shall not forget how much Mr Schnabel's performances did to stimulate it.

But this is not the only tribute I wish to pay: above all I should like to express here my gratitude to the Beethoven Sonata Society and to 'His Master's Voice' for the generous way in which they have allowed me to reissue a mass of material which, although my own copyright, must be regarded as at any rate morally their property, and for their courtesy in giving the publishers permission to reproduce the vast number of musical quotations from the pamphlets accompanying the albums of records.

I have no illusion that this book will be found acceptable for continuous reading, and indeed no wish that it should be so read; but I hope that it may be dipped into here and there with some profit, that the analyses it contains will elucidate some points for those who study Beethoven's sonatas, whether as performers or as listeners, and that the essays and incidental observations scattered through these pages will serve to enliven what must at first sight look like a forbiddingly dry treatise.

E. B.

June 1938.

CONTENTS

PAGE

PRELUDE: THE PLACE IN HISTORY 1
- Op. 2 No. 1, F minor 4
- Op. 2 No. 2, A major 10
- Op. 2 No. 3, C major 15

INTERLUDE I: THE CONTEMPORARIES 21
- Op. 7, E flat major 25
- Op. 10 No. 1, C minor 32
- Op. 10 No. 2, F major 39
- Op. 10 No. 3, D major 44

INTERLUDE II: CONCERNING REPEATS 52
- Op. 13, C minor (*Pathétique*) 56

INTERLUDE III: BEETHOVEN'S KEYBOARD MANNER 63
- Op. 14 No. 1, E major 67
- Op. 14 No. 2, G major 74

INTERLUDE IV: THE TURN OF THE CENTURY 79
- Op. 22, B flat major 81

INTERLUDE V: NEW WAYS AND MEANS 90
- Op. 26, A flat major 93
- Op. 27 No. 1, E flat major 102
- Op. 27 No. 2, C sharp minor (*Moonlight*) 107
- Op. 28, D major (*Pastoral*) 112

INTERLUDE VI: ON THE PLAYING OF BEETHOVEN 119
- Op. 31 No. 1, G major 123
- Op. 31 No. 2, D minor 131
- Op. 31 No. 3, E flat major 136
- Op. 49 No. 1, G minor and major 141
- Op. 49 No. 2, G major 144
- Op. 53, C major (*Waldstein*) 147

INTERLUDE VII: LURID LIGHT ON BEETHOVEN 155
- Op. 54, F major 159
- Op. 57, F minor (*Appassionata*) 163

INTERLUDE VIII: THE THREE STYLES 168
Op. 78, F sharp major 172
Op. 79, G major 177

INTERLUDE IX: THE PROGRAMME SONATA 181
Op. 81a, E flat major (*Farewell, Absence and Return*) 183
Op. 90, E minor 190
Op. 101, A major 194

INTERLUDE X: 'HAMMERCLAVIER' 202
Op. 106, B flat major (*Hammerclavier*) 205
Op. 109, E major 224
Op. 110, A flat major 229
Op. 111, C minor 236

POSTLUDE: SUMMING-UP 240

BIBLIOGRAPHY 246
INDEX 247

PRELUDE

THE PLACE IN HISTORY

MUSICAL historians are fond of attributing the important junctures in the evolution of the art they deal with to its outstanding creative exponents. It is tempting, of course, thus to fix the responsibility for theoretical changes as well as for consummate practice on a few great figures, not only because it enhances their fame, but because it simplifies the historian's task by narrowing his field of investigation.

This process, however, leads often to utterly erroneous conclusions. One of these is that it was Beethoven, chiefly, who effected the change from the old style of keyboard sonata writing to the new style called for by the instrument that gradually took the place of harpsichord and clavichord—the pianoforte. The truth is that the greatest creators are generally content to leave the glory of such purely technical discoveries to smaller men, and indeed, considering the little attention their inferiors are likely to receive even from experts, they can well afford to do so. But it is not by any such mean calculation that they forgo the chance of being celebrated as innovators: they are too engrossed by the enthusiasm of creation to trouble themselves with the prospect of posthumous appreciation of whatsoever they may be contributing to the purely mechanical evolution of their art. A superb egotism makes genius take little interest in the mere material with which he builds his structures. He cares nothing whether he finds it ready to his hand, made and trimmed by another craftsman, whether he has to forge some of it himself as he goes along, or whether he may possibly leave some over for such newcomers as may be quick enough to use a chance discovery.

If we are asked who wrote the finest keyboard music round about the early years of the eighteenth century, we at once say Bach. But when we try to call to mind the typical exponents of the harpsichord style of that period, we do not thinkof this universal figure, but of François Couperin and Domenico Scarlatti. It is significant that Bach's preludes and fugues in *The Well-tempered Clavier*, for example, lose nothing by being played on the modern piano, while to the delicate impressions of Couperin and the lightly-sprung sonatas of Scarlatti we can only do the fullest justice on a harpsichord.

It is much the same with the period of transition during which composers gradually made up their minds to abandon the older instruments for the piano, the many advantages of which—fuller tone, the possibility of gradation, a greater sustaining power, and so on—were not to be gainsaid, though it is a pity that the piano should ever have been regarded as a substitute for the harpsichord and clavichord instead of as an entirely different instrument that could not replace their own characteristic qualities. In the keyboard sonatas of the great men of the time, Haydn and Mozart, very little evidence is to be found that they were aware of the desirability of a different treatment. They simply concerned themselves with writing as good music as they could and cared so little what instrument it was played on that it will never be clearly understood from their sonatas where the piano actually parts company with the harpsichord. There is scarcely the smallest sign of a struggle for supremacy. A conscious effort to disentangle the styles appropriate to the different instruments was again made by lesser men, such as two sons of Bach's, one of whom, it is true, is a historically important figure, but whose music is all but unknown to-day. It was Carl Philipp Emanuel Bach who defended the harpsichord, and his brother, Johann Christian, in London, who championed the new instrument.

And once more, in Beethoven's time, when the pianoforte was firmly established, the most characteristic writers for it are the comparatively unimportant composers Clementi and Dussek. The true piano style—or let us say *a* true piano style, for so resourceful an instrument is infinitely adaptable—had been worked out by them before Beethoven was ready to tackle the piano sonata as a vehicle of his much more vital thought and his much suppler form.

That he possessed the essential creative qualities in vastly greater abundance than his pianistic forerunners no critic in his senses would dispute. But it does him no harm if we give their due to Clementi and Dussek, whom he has overshadowed almost to extinction after profiting by their example; on the contrary, it proves his overwhelming genius that he was able to match with so much significant matter of his own a new manner the handling of which he had learnt from others. It was fortunate for him that a congenial pianistic style was ready, for he was too absorbed in his own problems to make innovations of a purely executive order for the benefit of music at large. He never wrote so well for the keyboard, as far as sheer pianistry went, as the two pioneers just mentioned. The elegance and lucidity of Clementi, the variety and abundance of tone-colour attained by Dussek, were not within his reach; but then, he never cared enough for manner as distinct from matter to cultivate pianistic writing for its own sake.

Now as to the matter. How much of that was wholly Beethoven's own? Probably as much as any composer ever brought forth independently—and none was ever entirely independent. Certain idiomatic turns are in the air at a given period and find their way into every composer's work, how far by unconscious association and how far by deliberate adoption it is impossible to decide except in definitely documented cases. There are passages in Beethoven which seem directly suggested by Clementi, and Dussek wrote a Sonata in C minor, some five years before Beethoven's *Pathétique*, which contains some startling likenesses to that work.

A much more powerful influence was that of Haydn, whose piano sonatas seem often linked up in a direct line with Beethoven's earliest works in that form. Occasionally, indeed, they throw out hints of the mature Beethoven, almost as though the influence had worked by some mysterious backward process that disregarded time. The finale of a Sonata in D major written by Haydn in London (where the best and most expressive pianos were made at that time), is extraordinarily Beethovenian with its explosive accents and its premonitions of the romantic scherzo type.

All the same, Beethoven was a magnificently independent creator. Like all other great masters, he did not merely assimilate influences: he converted them by the unfathomable secret of genius into assets of his own. His emancipation is to be demonstrated most convincingly by a study of his attitude towards Mozart, his most embarrassingly gifted precursor. Until all too recently it was a commonplace estimate among musicians that Mozart was a kind of infant Beethoven, as though, forsooth, any one could have improved on Mozart at his own particular best. This view was not only fatuous, but grossly unfair to both composers, making the one appear as if he had never matured and the other as if he had brought nothing of his own into music.

The plain truth is that Beethoven could never have been a grown-up Mozart, but only a second-hand Mozart, and fortunately for music he had far too much of a mind of his own to consent to hold such a position, even if he had been temperamentally in greater sympathy with his immediate predecessor than he was. It is interesting to look at what is perhaps the most Mozartian movement in Beethoven's sonatas, the finale in the A major Sonata, Op. 2 No. 2, and to observe the difference which his individuality makes. The intention was obviously to write a smooth Mozartian rondo, and the composer deliberately marked it *grazioso*; but the very first bar is a gesture of impatience (see Ex. 14, page 14), and the passage becomes more violent at each repetition. A movement that is meant to have a character of kittenish playfulness shows the lion's claw almost before Beethoven is aware of the self-betrayal. And so it goes on throughout even the early sonatas: first movements full of impetuosity, splenetic scherzos, adagios and andantes whose calm beauty clearly covers up suppressed fires, and rondos that let us suspect the whims and sudden gusts of temper that we find in Beethoven's letters. Never was such tell-tale, such autobiographical music written before.

Beethoven, we all know, was an impossible man to live with; but though that intractable personality peeps out everywhere from the sonatas, they have not only proved endurable: they have endured. Their greatness has softened the composer's asperities and rudenesses and made them for us, over and above their purely musical wonders, into an intensely individual expression of the most irresistible fascination. Though we could not, any of us, have lived with Beethoven for a week, we still live with his sonatas, and the world will go on doing so as long as it has such civilization of the mind as it managed to keep in spite of its failure to attain to that universal brotherhood of mankind that was Beethoven's delusion.

He lived at a time that believed in a new heaven and a new earth. A revolution was supposed to have brought them about. Democracy, which in art was the assertion of personality, and republicanism, which meant music's deliverance from empty courtly formality, were not to be shown up until much later as but another road to enslavement by human greed and opportunism, in spite of many later revolutions, new democracies and new republics. But even now that they *are* thus exposed, Beethoven, their chief musical champion, remains great by reason of his unfailing power of individual expression and his self-controlled independence in the matter of form. His individuality, grasped at once on hearing any representative work of his, is not to be laid hold of by analysis; his form can be theoretically seized easily enough, and the descriptions that follow may reveal something of Beethoven's mastery over its adjustment to invention. Here only two points need be raised: his new power of managing the art of transition, which his contemporary, Stendhal, said was the essence of artistic structure, and the unprecedented significance with which he invested the coda.

The brilliant fillings-in between first and second subjects with which the eighteenth century contented itself, compared by Wagner to the rattling of plates between the courses of some princely dinner, would not do for Beethoven, though of course there is more to be said for them, from the point of view of eighteenth-century aesthetics, than Wagner could fit in with his own theories. Neither could Beethoven content himself with perorations that merely informed the listener of the approaching close of a movement; he wanted to bring down his fist at the end of a discourse with a weighty oratorical statement, a logical summing-up.

But of all this more anon, so far as a literary commentary and its writer's experience can make anything of it. That is never enough, however. Beethoven's sonatas must be known to be read about with profit. Their possessions as a living experience is indispensable. Walter Bagehot once said about Greek and Latin that, while a knowledge of these languages was not necessary to a writer of English, he should at least have a firm conviction that they existed. Well, we all have this conviction about the Beethoven sonatas, but not many of us know them intimately enough, for most of the later ones at any rate are not often heard in public and can be adequately played by few people at home. Fortunately the gramophone can do much to help, and particularly the Beethoven Sonata Society's records of the complete series, for which these essays and notes were originally written in a slightly different form. At any rate, if some sort of performance is accessible, the sooner the music-lover passes from information to knowledge by leaving off reading in favour of listening the better.

SONATA IN F MINOR, Op. 2 No. 1 (1795)
(BEETHOVEN SONATA SOCIETY RECORDS, VOL. VII)

AT the end of 1792 Beethoven, who had just settled down in Vienna, became a pupil of Haydn. He was twenty-two and already very sure of himself, so that it would have been something of a miracle if the lessons had been a success. They were not. Haydn, just back from England, where he had enjoyed an immense success, was not perhaps disposed to take the ambitious and self-assured young man quite at his own valuation, while Beethoven's suspicious nature exaggerated the negligence he ascribed to the master who was his senior by nearly forty years. In any case Beethoven, who was afterwards to study counterpoint with Albrechtsberger, for the moment transferred himself to Schenk, the composer of *Der Dorfbarbier* and other harmless *Singspiele* for the lighter Viennese operatic stage.

More than that, there was a threat of a definite estrangement. Beethoven suspected Haydn of wishing to suppress him when the older master advised him to withhold one of the Trios, Op. 1, from publication on account of its boldness —and needless to say, the one for which Beethoven cared most. However, like all Beethoven's quarrels and incipient quarrels, this blew over, and in 1796 he published the three piano Sonatas, Op. 2, with a dedication to Haydn. The date of publication is 9th March; that of composition is not known. As Haydn did not return from his second visit to England until August 1795, and Beethoven played the three Sonatas for the first time in the presence of the dedicatee at one of Prince Lichnowsky's Friday concerts, we may take the turn of the years 1795–6 as the approximate time at which they were committed to paper. If the chronology of the three works, as it now stands, may be taken as a guide, the F minor Sonata is to be assigned with fair certainty to the year 1795, with the observation, however, that the slow movement was an adaptation from a piano Quartet in D major, written at Bonn ten years earlier, at the age of fifteen.

Although now always published as Beethoven's first three piano sonatas, Op. 2 was not his first attempt in this medium and form. He dedicated a set of three Sonatas, in E flat major, F minor and D major, to Maximilian Friedrich, Elector of Cologne, nearly ten years before he left Bonn for Vienna. There are also an unfinished Sonata in C major and two Sonatinas in G and F major, all dating from 1792. The exclusion of these early works from the published collection of the Sonatas is, of course, justified by Beethoven's own refusal to dignify them with the sanction of an opus number.

We do not know what Haydn thought of Beethoven's sonatas. No such enthusiastic testimony to the young genius came from him as that which he so spontaneously offered to Leopold Mozart about the greatness of his son. On the other hand, no such affectionate and respectful preface as Mozart addressed to Haydn is prefixed to Beethoven's sonatas; but if no love was lost between the hot-headed young man and the older master, they respected each other in spite of the fact that the former had very quickly discontinued his lessons. The Sonatas, Op. 2, are Beethoven's very convincing expression of that respect, and there can be no doubt that Haydn must have been impressed by the assurance of their mastery, even if he found them here and there too subversive in method and violent in expression for his taste.

Allegro.—The first-subject group of the Sonata No. 1 opens at once with the following theme:

Ex. 1

the rising figure (*a*) of which is identical (except for the difference of key) with the opening of the finale in Mozart's G minor Symphony (K. 550). But here the resemblance to Mozart begins and ends. It cannot be often enough emphasized that the music of Beethoven, even at its earliest stages, is anything but Mozartian, and that it is no tribute to either master to pretend to find any traces of such an influence in the younger one's work. That Beethoven learnt a great deal from Mozart in the matter of the sheer management of the *materia* of music is too evident to be talked about, and the talking becomes futile directly it is recognized that temperamentally the two composers have so little in common that even had Beethoven by accident worked with Mozart's own themes without being aware of the fact, the music he would have constructed on them could not have failed to be entirely different in spirit from what their owner made of them. One musician may teach another, in a technical sense, how to compose—or much more likely how not to set about composing—but no two creative minds can ever think alike, and when master and pupil both happen to be as great as a Mozart and a Beethoven, the chances of any sort of close approach in style and manner become infinitely more remote than they would be between two relatively uninspired craftsmen. When, moreover, two composers are spiritually so utterly unlike each other as these two, there is simply no possibility of their meeting on common ground in their works, which are carriers of messages from their disparate worlds of the spirit.

Ex. 1 is continued by means of harmonic changes, the figure (*b*) being insistently drawn together three times. After a pause (*a*) starts in the dominant (minor) and in the bass, rather as though Beethoven, who was brought up on Bach's *Well-tempered Clavier*, had subconsciously thought of a fugal answer and then, very properly in a work in sonata form, resisted the impulse to carry out the idea.

A new sequential treatment of (*b*) provides the modulations necessary to lead to the new key (A flat major) for the second-subject group, which is approached very early and with scarcely any transitional material. It is for some time poised firmly on a dominant bass, and the minor ninth (F flat) gives it a darker colouring than the second subject in works in minor keys generally took on in the exposition at that time, although the custom was to set it definitely in the tonic minor in the recapitulation:

Ex. 2

Another theme follows in which a descending figure akin to that in Ex. 2 appears in the bass, and then an expressive phrase, into which, although it is still in A flat major, a minor third repeatedly introduces its plaintive note, concludes the exposition.

The working-out begins with Ex. 1 in A flat major, but very soon passes on to Ex. 2, which before long is heard modulating in the left hand. The music then becomes thematically more featureless, but the interest is sustained by a series of emphatic syncopations and later by broken figures that keep up the tension by suggesting some tentative approach to a new event. What happens is that the figure 1*b* returns in a new succession of sequences and suddenly brings the music back to F minor, leading it the more unexpectedly into the recapitulation because the upbeat of 1*a* is omitted. The recapitulation proceeds normally, with an interesting new modulation provided where the transition to the second subject has now to be so managed that everything continues to be heard in the tonic key of F minor. The few clinching bars at the end are perhaps hardly enough to be called a coda in the full Beethovenian sense of the term, but already they show how well aware the composer is that this feature of the sonata form is going to be of the utmost significance to him later on. Nothing in this movement, which has both the elegance and the passion of youthful genius, is more telling than the sudden divergence of the plaintive clinching theme into an unexpected cadence, which makes the addition of a few extra bars imperatively necessary before the final tonic chord can be reached.

Adagio.—The slow movement, in F major, is so simple in expression and form as to need no detailed analysis. At the same time it will not do to let our knowledge that it is a much earlier composition than the rest of the Sonata mislead us into listening to it patronizingly. It may not be especially interesting; but it is certainly filled with a truly Beethovenian melodic nobility, and a highly finished piece of craftsmanship, in spite of its somewhat rudimentary form. This defect, if it be a defect, is easily explicable: Beethoven sets out to write an *adagio* in sonata form, with two groups of subjects, which inevitably means excessive length compared with the size of a fast first movement in that form. Thus he discovers that he must give up the idea of inserting a working-out section of any sort, and he accordingly proceeds straight from the exposition to the recapitulation. However, he feels that there should be some sort of development, and so hits upon the notion of varying his themes as they come round again. The result is a sonata movement which is incomplete in form, but for compensation has an interestingly elaborated lay-out of its material. Another evidence of how keenly Beethoven's sense of balance was developed, even at the very early age at which he wrote this movement (1785, *aet.* 15), is his cutting out from the recapitulation of the transitional theme between the two subject groups and then making up for his omission by adding a few bars, partly derivative and partly new, by way of a coda.

Minuetto : Allegretto.—This is not a dancing minuet like that in *Don Giovanni*, for example, or, to speak of purely instrumental music, that in . . . But here the pen is unexpectedly arrested. Where, indeed, in classical music that has got past the suite stage to that of the sonata is there a minuet to be found which actually goes as slowly as that in Mozart's opera? In a Quintet by Boccherini, which has preserved that amiable but neglected composer's name from oblivion precisely because of its appealing minuet. Where else? After a little reflection that in Haydn's 'Military' Symphony comes to mind, and I have no doubt that I could look up examples in the same master's string quartets and in Mozart's serenades and divertimenti. But I am not going to do so for the present purpose, the point here being that the minuet in classical sonata-form music came, even before Beethoven's days, much nearer to the scherzo which he was to evolve out of it than musicians usually choose to remember. It is not surprising, therefore, that this early sonata minuet of Beethoven's should approach his later scherzo manner, for all that its pace is still too leisurely for a real scherzo. There is a touch of the spleen about it already, as will be gathered from the opening bars:

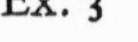
Ex. 3

and it will become more and more evident as the music proceeds to an irascible outburst of octave unison passages and several explosive accents, some of them off the place where the strong beat would naturally be expected.

The trio section, in the major, runs on quite smoothly by way of contrast:

Ex. 4

The hands exchange their figures in a way that seems to have been suggested to Beethoven by some exercise in double counterpoint, but here the principle of that device is not carried out strictly. The impulse to yield to free musical invention is too strong for a young composer who has not yet discovered the secret of finding inspiration in rigorous discipline.

The minuet, needless to say, is repeated.

Prestissimo.—The precipitous finale is in sonata form. The following first-subject figure is the most important feature in the structure:

Ex. 5

It has the curious effect of shifting the accent which would seem most obvious to the ear by beginning its accompaniment on the first beat of the bar, for the three chords in the right hand look very much as though they were a half-bar upbeat followed by a strong accent on the third chord. Thus a certain ambiguity of accentuation prevails throughout the first-subject group, which includes a more melodious episode.

The first idea of the second subject need be given only in skeleton form for the sake of identification:

Ex. 6

It is laid out in triplets throughout and frequently combines two quavers in the left hand with the three in the right. There is another strain later that also belongs to the second subject, a descending melodic phrase played by the right hand in octaves on various degrees of the scale of C minor—the key in which the whole of this group stands, with incidental modulations, of course.

The exposition is repeated. Upon it follows a working-out section with a distinctly Mozartian feature, though it is not in the least like Mozart in character. The earlier master often begins a working-out with an entirely new thematic notion, generally purely melodic, as though he were much too innocent to know what to do with the themes he has brought forward in the exposition. That is, of course, only his sly way of deceiving his hearers and suddenly surprising them by tying up his material in such intricate knots of development that he and they enjoy the ingenuity all the more for the teasing in which he has indulged for a while. This is more or less what Beethoven does in this finale of his, except that the knots later on are not going to be forbiddingly Gordian. He introduces a surprisingly long independent episode in A flat major, which almost necessitates a kind of development of its own. At last the rhythmic beat of Ex. 5 returns stealthily and makes itself heard almost continuously for the rest of the working-out section, which thus merges naturally into a recapitulation that is perfectly regular and has a few bars of brilliant triplet arpeggios tacked on to it as a coda.

SONATA IN A MAJOR, Op. 2 No. 2 (1796)
(B.S.S. RECORDS, VOL. IV)

Allegro vivace.—With a characteristic gesture of defiance Beethoven at once falls to one of the brief thematic snatches that group themselves together as his first subject:

Ex. 7

It is played by both hands in unison and leads through a descending chord of the dominant seventh back again to the tonic, in which this more extended phrase appears:

Ex. 8

The easily-woven polyphonic texture of this passage should be noticed: such things came naturally to the young composer and were as readily abandoned again for a different lay-out. The studies with Albrechtsberger had borne fruit, but none of his pedantry had passed to the pupil of genius. A third idea, still in A major, because still belonging to the first-subject group, appears a little later:

Ex. 9

The approach to the second subject is made with great subtlety, emphasized by a slight retarding of the pace for an instant. The orthodox key for the second subject was, of course, E major in a movement in A major, but Beethoven boldly makes for E minor. Not only that, but his subject passes through a series of extremely daring modulations that take it to G major and B flat major:

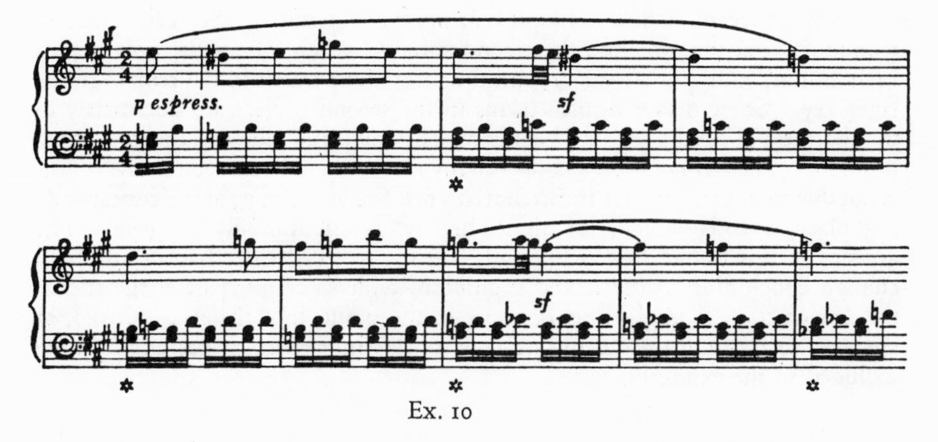

Ex. 10

At that time a subject in a sonata or symphony was supposed not only to start in its proper key, but to remain in it for at least a reasonable time. To make it do neither was a drastic new departure. Beethoven had spent his youth in a period that witnessed a tremendous political revolution, and it was he who expressed its tendencies most openly in music, as far as that art can reflect outward events. But his time was not ripe for artistic insurrections of the most rabid kind. Note that in the bass of the preceding example there was a glorious opportunity to defy the authorities by writing consecutive triads—a chance which Debussy or Puccini or dozens of other composers of a century later would have welcomed. But Beethoven is seen, at the places marked * under the bass stave, to go out of his way to avoid what would then have been an unpardonable solecism.

In the end the second-subject group does arrive at E major, in which key it asserts itself triumphantly. A peroration to the expository section of the movement is made up from the theme of which Ex. 9 is a fragment, and there is a very quiet close in E major. This whole section is repeated.

A link from the exposition to the working-out is made by a suggestion of E minor, from which, with the fifth of the chord left out, it is only a step into C major. In that key the opening theme (Ex. 7) at first asserts itself vigorously, and it passes through the dominant of C major as it had previously gone through that of A major. But it jerks with dramatic suddenness into A flat major, and the theme now alternately presents itself below and above a regularly moving semiquaver accompaniment, returning by way of F minor to C major. This, however, soon reveals itself as being merely the dominant of F major this time, and it is in F major that the second strain of the first subject (Ex. 8) now presents itself. Having insisted on that tonality just long enough for us to fancy that it was meant to be more than episodic, there is a sudden contraction of the rhythmic periods, which now go through a variety of keys, with D minor tending to be uppermost, producing an effect of restlessness, as though the composer were anxious to resume the main argument. But there are digressions of some length, loosely based on the main material.

When the recapitulation comes, it is as normal as possible. Scarcely anything is modified but the turn into the second subject, which, of course, now begins in A minor, ending in A major, and the peroration, which has to remain in the latter key. Some octave displacements in the second subject are due merely to the shortness of Beethoven's keyboard, which would not allow of upward transposition. There is not even a coda—at any rate so the schools would say. This is not due to immaturity, for in Beethoven's first Sonata there is, at the corresponding place, a coda which, for all its brevity, is astonishingly eloquent. The absence of this feature here is due rather to the fact that there has already been enough concluding matter in the exposition, with its counterpart at the end of the movement. It might thus be more to the point, though less academic, to say that, so far from there being no coda to this movement, it has already been included in the exposition.

Largo appassionato.—The principle of the slow movement is the very emphatic statement of one important theme with comparatively little modification, its solidity being thus insisted upon while at the same time monotony is avoided by a variety of episodes. The theme in its whole extent is much too long to quote, and to show a mere fragment of it in music type would be useless, since it is its deployment as a whole, not the presentation of any single feature, that makes the structure of this movement remarkable. The theme lasts for eighteen and a half bars of very deliberate time. It is in D major, with an A major middle section and a return to the tonic. The muffled staccato bass under the sustained upper notes is characteristic and was novel in its time. The A major section is written in parts, like a string quartet, details repeating themselves above and below.

There has been little change of key in the theme. For compensation Beethoven modulates very freely in the first episode, which begins in B minor, but goes on thus:

Ex. 11

The first restatement of the theme is substantially unaltered; but the hearer who does not read music—which is understandable—or who, doing so, does not happen to have a copy of Beethoven's piano sonatas—which is inexcusable—would do well to memorize the first statement of the theme from a gramophone record for comparison with the second. The small changes which occur will serve as well as anything to give him an insight into a great composer's carefully weighed procedures.

For the second episode, which is quite short, Beethoven never departs from the key of D major. This may seem contrary to an original intention to throw variety of key mainly into the episodes. But we shall discover in a moment that it is precisely an astonishing sense of balance that made the composer so reticent here. For now it is at the third return of the theme that he chooses to go in for vigorous modulation. With a startling loudness the theme suddenly bursts in, not as before, but in D minor, whence it makes an even more surprising excursion into B flat major. The former A major section is cut out to make way for a bridge passage that leads back to D major, in which the theme is concluded over a new inner accompaniment figure of gently purling semiquavers. There is a short coda—nothing more than two slightly extended and decorated cadences, but quite enough to round off a movement that has contained so much significance.

Allegretto.—After a movement built on extended melodic phrases comes a scherzo that depends for its pouncing effect upon short figures. Here are three of the scraps from which a tasty dish is made with remarkable economy:

Ex. 12

The hearer who does not seek the assistance of the printed page may amuse himself by trying to trace by ear the derivatives they engender. In this way the music may piece itself together in his mind much as it did in Beethoven's when it was composed, one phrase giving rise to another until the pattern is complete. Note, for instance, how the third of the fragments quoted (Ex. 12*c*) at first opens a short melodic phrase in G sharp minor, the only sustained melody in this section of the scherzo, and how it afterwards makes up this modulatory bridge:

Ex. 13

This leads to the return of the opening themelet (Ex. 12*a*).

The trio, by way of a change, is a smoothly flowing piece in A minor, distinctly melodic in character, without however producing a memorable tune. This again, whether instinctive or deliberate, is a wonderfully ingenious contrivance:

what was wanted here was a mild contrast, not an arresting one. To provide that is the function of the preceding and following movements.

The scherzo is restated without repeats.

Grazioso.—This rondo has already been described as perhaps the most Mozartian movement in Beethoven's sonatas, though with a warning not to regard even this as anything but characteristically Beethovenian, with that 'impatient gesture' at the beginning, which grows more emphatic with each repetition.

Here is the opening of the piece, which at once states the main rondo theme:

Ex. 14

To us, who have Wagnerian thunderstorms and Straussian fretfulness behind us, this sounds mild enough, and we must remember that after all the *grazioso* direction was uppermost in Beethoven's mind. All the same, things are smouldering in this music of which the eighteenth century had no notion. Not only that upward arpeggio in the first bar, but the leap in the second and the *sforzando* in the fourth are symptomatic of Beethoven's later manner—and also, we may say, of his manners. There is a certain gruffness even about a piece of his in which he sets out to be gracious.

After the first eight bars of the rondo theme, which is a melody—a distinctly instrumental melody—with an Alberti bass accompaniment, come another four bars containing a contrasting strain with some polyphonic imitations that make for a pleasing variety of the musical fabric. The four concluding bars are based on the four opening ones.

The first episode, which occurs after some subsidiary matter of a mainly ornamental character, is in the nature of a second sonata-movement subject, for it is in the key of the dominant and held in reserve for another appearance later. It spins itself out with perfect naturalness into another transition, which leads to the first restatement of the main theme. The opening arpeggio now spreads itself over four and a half octaves instead of three and a half, as before, and the figuration is slightly altered later on.

The next episode is entirely different in key (A minor) and character, so much so, in fact, as to have almost the effect of an intrusion. It is true that such independent incidents were exactly what was expected in a rondo, but it is impossible not to feel that the young Beethoven, with his exuberant faculty of developing any thematic idea at length and without loss of interest, was here in danger of letting his chief topic out of sight and writing a piece complete in itself.

When at last the rondo theme reappears, it is preceded by an uprushing scale instead of an arpeggio, and again the pianistic figures are changed, those of the intermediate strain being converted into semiquavers, still treated in contrapuntal imitation. The bridge passage leading to what has been described as the second subject then recurs, followed by that subject itself, now of course in the tonic key. This enables the main theme to glide back quite unostentatiously. But it makes an interesting display after a few bars of simply varied restatement by suddenly modulating into the remote key of F major and back again, by a short cut, to A major, where the opening figure becomes unexpectedly active in a dialogue between bass and treble. Then, just as we expect to have heard the last of it in this intensified form, which seems to forecast the end, the music takes another surprising turn and makes, of all things, a reference to the long A minor episode which has seemed before as though it could have no possible organic connection with the structure of the rondo. Beethoven's instinct for form after all gets the better of his inventive exuberance; he cannot forbear to make his earlier digression relevant to the whole on the last page but one. The rondo concludes with a final statement of the principal theme, which is pleasantly diverted into a short closing period.

SONATA IN C MAJOR Op. 2 No. 3 (1796)

(B.S.S. RECORDS, VOL. VIII)

Allegro con brio.—The first movement shows a sonata-form scheme of the greatest clarity: two immediately distinguishable groups of subjects, including one feature that is interchangeable between them. The opening theme is structurally important:

Ex. 15

The semiquaver groups at once assert their significance by taking part in the development, appearing very soon in the bass. It is all very demure at first and kept strictly in four parts, like a string quartet; but suddenly the music breaks loudly into a passage that could not be anything but keyboard music:

Ex. 16

This is the incident which is to return in the second-subject group. It is extended by modulation towards G major and followed by a brief new idea ending with an emphatic insistence on that key, thus clinching the first subject in the manner of the eighteenth century, which liked to have the formal landmarks of a sonata or symphony movement clearly pointed out. Very ingeniously, however, Beethoven does not wholly dispel the impression that G here is still the dominant of C major, for reasons that will reveal themselves later.

The second subject, however, has to be definitely in the key of the dominant, and it begins thus with a strain in G minor, a relic from the Piano Quartet written at Bonn at the age of fifteen which had already yielded him the slow movement of the Sonata, Op. 2 No. 1:

Ex. 17

It modulates smoothly to D minor and A minor, a new notion with a descending scale appearing in the latter key. Further modulations lead at last to what is a more normal key for the second subject in a C major sonata—G major, in which a beautiful melody arises, treated in imitation, one phrase acting as an accompaniment for the other:

Ex. 18

After some extension of this, Ex. 16 returns, slightly modified but in its original key of C major at first. It reverts to G, however, and leads into a descending passage of syncopations in which Beethoven shows that disregard for harmonic clashes of which there is a familiar and notorious example in the *Leonore* Overture No. 3 (bars 360–77, if any one wishes to look it up). Three rising arpeggios that follow include an augmented triad—a considerable audacity for the end of the eighteenth century, and this concluding phrase is important:

Ex. 19

The actual close of the exposition, though, is made by unharmonized broken octaves, more akin to Ex. 16. This whole section is repeated from the beginning.

The long and interesting working-out section begins with a development of Ex. 19, modulating successively into C minor, F minor and the dominant of E flat major. At that point all thematic allusion disappears for a while to give way to sharp, glittering chords, broken into semiquavers. They are played by the right hand to patternless basses with gradually changing harmony in the left. Thus, over a sudden *diminuendo*, we arrive at D major, in which key the opening strain of the first subject (Ex. 15) returns. Its two initial phrases are almost unchanged, save that the key has risen by a whole tone. But now two of its figures, *a* and *b*, detach themselves, to be independently developed at some length, the former unaccompanied, the latter in bold octave formations in which fierce clashes of semitones are conspicuous. After three alternations in various keys, these two elements are brought together again, but still spun out in new ways, and then a chain formed of 15*a* and descending over dominant harmony leads back to Ex. 15 in its original form and key: in other words to the recapitulation.

This is remarkable for its ruthless omission of Ex. 16, made perhaps because this incident has already been twice used in the exposition. A new thematic formation based on the concluding cadence of Ex. 15 (not shown in music type above) is substituted, and then the music proceeds straight to the theme previously used to clinch the first-subject group. This is done in exactly the same way as before, and again the impression is created that the key of G reached here is really still the dominant of C. The reason for this now becomes perfectly clear: the second subject is, of course, not to be allowed to turn to G again, but must remain in the principal key of the Sonata. Ex. 17, which is the first theme of the second-subject group, accordingly turns up in C minor, and Ex. 18 is led up to without any other change than that of tonality, to reappear in C major.

When the concluding figure, Ex. 19, has been reached and the movement appears to come to its inevitable end, Beethoven springs his surprise: for the first time in a piano sonata he ventures on a large coda. It is approached in the most original manner. There is a sudden leap of an interrupted cadence from C major into A flat major, a tonal region the composer has so far avoided, and here a free fantasy begins which eschews every thematic reference and confines itself solely to broken chords—mainly diminished sevenths. When the music is arrested on a conventional $\frac{6}{4}$ chord, we cannot fail to gather, from the experience of countless musical precedents, that we are in for a cadenza. And so it proves. This ornamental feature is for a moment concerned with figure 15*a*, but dissolves into a shake and, with a rapid chromatic descent, comes back to Ex. 15 again, with which the coda continues. There is still some new development to come, but eventually the music turns back to the broken octave figures with which the exposition had concluded.

Adagio.—The slow movement is in E major—a long way from the main key of the Sonata. If we choose to think of Schubert on seeing such a bold departure, we are entitled to some astonishment at Beethoven's making it before that master was born, and very early in his own career; but it is worth remembering that Haydn had already been partial to such enterprising key distributions between a group of movements within one single work.

There is a recurrent theme with intervening episodes, which are themselves recurrent; in other words, we have here a slow rondo with strong leanings towards sonata form.

The principal theme needs no quotation in music type. It is heard at the very beginning. Very soon the key changes to E minor, and the right hand plays continuous murmuring figures with the break of a pause on each beat. There is much crossing of hands, as in this characteristic passage:

Ex. 20

The music has arrived at the first restatement of the main theme, which recurs at first without any modification. The reason is an exceedingly subtle one, and none the less so if one likes to consider the result due to unconscious promptings rather than to deliberation. Beethoven, by refraining from developing his theme at once, makes a change the more dramatic when it does come, quite unexpectedly. It is nothing less than a sudden explosive restatement of the initial thematic figure in a new key, or rather in an old and almost forgotten key, for the Sonata remembers all at once its distant home tonality of C major and drops into it without the slightest preparation. But the flowing right-hand figures return and quickly lead back to E major, in which key, instead of G major, the crossed-hand figures shown in Ex. 20 return.

At its final appearance the main theme is beautifully elaborated and kept for the most part higher up on the keyboard. An extension in which its predominant melodic motif is played quietly in the bass, as though on two discreet bassoons, under a single repeated B in the treble, is exquisitely poetical, and so is the questioning pause that follows and finds its answer in one of the most curious and characteristically pianistic final cadences Beethoven ever devised. It had better be quoted, together with the preceding interrogation:

Ex. 21

Allegro.—As we have already seen, the first Sonata of the Op. 2 group still adhered to the minuet form for its third movement, though it made a more than tentative approach towards Beethoven's scherzo manner. In the third Sonata, as in the second, there is, on the other hand, a real scherzo, explicitly so called by the composer. It begins in this lightly polyphonic, gracefully imitative manner:

Ex. 22

There are two sections, each repeated, and the second one is more than three times as long as the first. Almost the whole is based strictly on Ex. 22, but with great resourcefulness of development. The only extraneous feature is this rhythm, introduced occasionally either singly or in pairs:

3/4 sf

Ex. 23

It is this which provides the concluding bars, which are rounded off by an abrupt drop of Cs in bare octaves.

The trio, in A minor, consists entirely of rapid arpeggios for the right hand which let no distinct thematic material arise—itself a contrast to the sharp-featured music from which it provides relief. It leads back, over a descending dominant-seventh arpeggio of C major, to the scherzo, which is played right through again. More than right through, in fact, for this time the octave drop does not conclude it: there is a short coda. The octaves are twice repeated, each time a minor third lower (A and F ♯), and then chords in the right hand are accompanied by rigid basses with a semitonal growl, based on the scherzo theme. Once more Beethoven contrives a most original conclusion.

Assai allegro.—The finale is a rondo in very rapid 6–8 time. The chief thematic landmark is exposed at once:

Ex. 24

Having driven towards the dominant, it is repeated in that position, only to turn back to the tonic—in the naïvely spontaneous manner that is common to innumerable classical themes and derives, of course, ultimately from the people's songs and dances. (Which may or may not be accepted as a hint not to take the classics more seriously than they took themselves.) There is a not very clearly thematic continuation in semiquavers, making for a return of Ex. 24, this time with a modulatory twist that brings us to the first episode, in G major, a strongly accentuated melody over a broken-chord accompaniment and a bass descending in three consecutive steps. When it is repeated an octave higher it soon turns into G minor, and its attendant figures are much extended until detached upward runs in the manner of the chief theme herald its return.

The subject remains unaltered at first, but presently the runs are transferred to the bass, and in this way the music modulates three times. Broken figures in contrary motion then act as a transition to the new key of F major, in which the second episode, a gentle, sustained melody laid out in right-hand chords, rises and falls. It passes into bass octaves accompanied by fluttering treble groups of two notes that come in off the beat, and after a brief subsidiary idea these are given to the left hand while the right resumes the chord treatment of the melody. This kind of development is carried on for a surprisingly long time, with the subsidiary theme returning twice, ingeniously turned the second time into another display of rising detached notes.

The second return of the main theme is thus prepared, and we now find ourselves in a regular sonata recapitulation, with the second rondo episode returning, in the key of the tonic, as a definite second subject. A new approach is made to yet another appearance of the main rondo theme, which actually comes back to form an important coda. It begins where a high shake becomes conspicuous, below which Ex. 24 is played by the left hand. A free development of it follows which is in the nature of a cadenza rather than in that of a coda closely worked to form a structural climax. For some thirty or forty bars we seem to be listening to a concerto at a moment when the orchestra happens to be silent rather than to a sonata. But thoughtfulness returns when the subject, once more in the bass, is heard slowly and softly just before the end, which comes with a last outburst of energy.

INTERLUDE I

THE CONTEMPORARIES

It may not be uninteresting to cast an eye over Beethoven's contemporaries round about the period of the Op. 2 Sonatas. He had been in Vienna since November 1792. Haydn had come across him at Bonn on his way to and from London and later agreed to teach him counterpoint. But Haydn was sixty, rather spoilt by his success in England, perhaps, and not too anxious to exert himself over a young man of twenty-two who was already more than commonly wilful, to say the least. We have seen that as artists the two did not get on any too well together, and so Beethoven went to Johann Schenk, who suited him better, not only because he was a much younger man, but doubtless also because he was less eminent. One cannot imagine a composer of thirty-two, whose fame rested upon little more than some light operettas, laying down the law too rigorously and uncomfortably for a Beethoven.

But perhaps Schenk insisted too little on discipline; at any rate in 1794 Beethoven sought yet another master, finding him in Albrechtsberger, who had two years before been appointed musical director to the cathedral of St Stephen. Albrechtsberger was very little younger than Haydn, and he was something of a pedant; but then he was not a strong enough creative personality to hinder his pupil's flights of fancy. He simply exercised him in technical matters and left aesthetic questions alone. But even for technical instruction the insatiable student went elsewhere when he wanted the expert advice of some specialist. Thus he submitted studies in Italian vocal composition to Salieri and exercises in string quartet writing to Aloys Förster, who were both in their middle forties. He also took violin lessons from young Schuppanzigh, who later became a great friend and the first to lead the early performances of his string quartets.

Salieri, in spite of the unenviable reputation he has made for himself by his intrigues against Mozart (whom, however, he certainly did not poison, as the legend goes), was an eminent figure in the half-Italianized Vienna of the period, and he was by no means universally disliked. His most eminent pupil, Schubert, even came to respect and love him later on, and in 1799 Beethoven dedicated three violin Sonatas, Op. 12, to him. In 1792, when the Emperor Leopold II died, and was succeeded by Francis II, Salieri was reinstated in the office of musical director to the court which Leopold had withdrawn from him in favour of Cimarosa. Altogether, the year of the accession of Francis and of Beethoven's arrival in the Austrian capital, was a great one for musical appointments there. Not only was Albrechtsberger given his post at St Stephen's, but Kozeluch, aged thirty-eight, succeeded Mozart in the purely honorary post of composer to the Emperor, and Weigl, aged twenty-six, became composer to the court opera. About the same time, too, Anton Tayber, who was one of the minor Viennese composers along with Süssmayr, Wranitzky, Wenzel Müller and Marie Therese von Paradis, was appointed composer to the imperial chapel. Süssmayr, by the way, who had been Mozart's favourite pupil, that year took over the completion of his master's unfinished Requiem from Eybler, to whom it had at first been entrusted by Constanze Mozart—a fact that is not generally known. Like Schenk and Müller, Süssmayr was mainly a composer of operettas (*Singspiele*), with which he supplied Emanuel Schikaneder, the part-librettist and producer of Mozart's *Magic Flute*. Kozeluch was first associated with Beethoven in the publication, in 1794, of arrangements of some Welsh airs in London, for which the two composers had been recommended by Haydn, who himself took a share in this task—a curious one for Viennese musicians to undertake. (One can hardly imagine Cecil Sharp entrusting settings of English folk-songs discovered by him to Alban Berg, Julius Bittner, Erich Korngold and Franz Léhar.)

Looking more particularly at the year 1795, we are naturally curious to see which of Beethoven's contemporaries occupied themselves with composition for the pianoforte, and more especially with sonatas for that instrument, still sufficiently novel, one would have thought, to attract many creative musicians. Actually, however, very few addressed themselves to such a problem at that time. There were only three outstanding masters of keyboard composition left after the death of Mozart, and one of them—Haydn—had almost entirely ceased to write sonatas. The two chief figures, therefore (if we agree to place ourselves for the moment at the point of view of the period, which could not regard Beethoven as anything but a beginner), were Clementi and Dussek, both of whom lived in London. The Italian master, then forty-three years old, also wrote much symphonic music for the orchestra, and indeed many of his works now known as piano sonatas were at first symphonies; the Bohemian, who was thirty-four, had reached his three Sonatas Op. 39, which brought his catalogue up to his nineteenth work in that form. But at Clementi's pianoforte warehouse in London there was also an Irish boy of thirteen, John Field, who was uncommonly clever at showing off the instruments with improvisations, and was before long to blossom into the most congenial specialist in composition for it the musical world was to know before Chopin, whom indeed he influenced considerably.

Field, though, was not the only youth who took to the new instrument at that time. Much nearer to Beethoven, in fact in Vienna itself, was a lad of seventeen, Johann Nepomuk Hummel, who had been a pupil of Mozart's and was to become one of those intimate friends of Beethoven's who could withstand even his most insulting fits of bad temper and unworthy suspicion. Hummel was an admirable pianist; he also began to grow into a composer who understood his instrument intimately and wrote better music for it than the world is nowadays willing to recognize. Then there was a young man named Woelfl, not much over twenty, who had already come forward as a pianist-composer and that year produced his first opera—so called: it was no doubt more of a *Singspiel*, for it came out at Schikaneder's popular theatre. Woelfl dedicated three piano Sonatas to Beethoven after having met him in 1798. Another keyboard virtuoso who composed for his instrument was Daniel Steibelt; nor must those elegant eighteenth-century relics, the worldly, piano-playing, improvising abbés Stadler, Gelinek and Vogler (Browning's rather unduly ennobled 'Abt Vogler') be forgotten.

As for the rest of the musical life in Vienna at the end of the eighteenth century, it was still largely Italian and Italianate. The church music, not excluding even Haydn's and Mozart's masses, was rather mundane and southern, with the emptily festive works by Reutter still leading and those by Michael Haydn, who worked at Salzburg, being much favoured. The instrumental composers, among the more distinguished of whom were Gyrowetz and Wanhal, were people only too easily eclipsed, before long, by Beethoven, who joined Haydn and Mozart right over their heads. The operas by Umlauf, Weigl, Winter, not to repeat the names of smaller native composers, could compete with the more dazzling Italian repertory only by their greater appeal to the populace. There was, however, a growing taste for serious French opera, especially the works of Méhul and Cherubini, with their ethical, humane post-revolution librettos, in which virtue triumphed at the last moment after the most perilous trials, and which thus became known as the species of 'rescue opera.' A work of this type that was to prove of particular importance to Beethoven was *Léonore, ou l'amour conjugal* by Pierre Gaveaux, produced in 1798, which, as may be gathered from the title alone, is the direct source of *Fidelio*. Indeed, the first version of the libretto for Beethoven's opera is simply a German translation of Bouilly's French book written for Gaveaux (*Lonore, oder die eheliche Liebe*).

Coming to the year of the two Sonatas Op. 14, and the last of the seventeen-hundreds, it may perhaps be useful to survey the four chief musical countries of Europe and to compile a short list of the leading composers, showing their ages in brackets, with such brief remarks as may be illuminating. Germany, the country of Beethoven's birth, and Austria, that of his adoption, must come first.

His instructors were still in Vienna: Haydn (67), Albrechtsberger (63), Salieri (49) and Schenk (38). His rivals were as active as ever: Stadler (51), Vogler (50), Gelinek (41), Steibelt (34) and Woelfl (27). Hummel (21), too, was now well to the fore. On the other hand a distinguished composer of orchestral and chamber music as well as of operettas, Dittersdorf (60), died that year. A last offshoot of the old Mannheim school of early symphonists, Carl Stamitz (53), was becoming unfashionable. In Vienna church and instrumental composers like Kozeluch (45), Gyrowetz (36), Eybler (34) and Eberl (33) were still active, and Seyfried (23) was coming on, while Wanhal (60) was losing ground. Winter (44), Süssmayr (33) and Weigl (33) were in their prime as operatic composers. In Germany Schubert's forerunners, Reichardt (47), Zelter (41) and Zumsteeg (39) cultivated a still somewhat primitive art of German song. Schubert (2) himself was still a baby, and other coming German composers at various stages of childhood were Spohr (15), Weber (13), Meyerbeer (8), Marschner (4) and Loewe (3). There were also two children who were destined to become pupils of Beethoven's: Ferdinand Ries (15) and Carl Czerny (8).

Most closely allied to Vienna, next to the Germanic contemporaries, were the Italians. Of the older operatic school Piccinni (71), who had once been forced into becoming Gluck's rival, was still alive, and so were Guglielmi (*c.* 72) and Sarti (70). Among the ageing and middle-aged were Paisiello (58), who had composed the first *Barber of Seville*, Gazzaniga (56), who had written a *Don Giovanni* opera before Mozart, Cimarosa (50), Zingarelli (47), Righini (43), on whose air, *Venni* (*sic*) *amore*, Beethoven wrote variations in 1790, Simone Mayr (36) and Fioravanti (35). The only non-operatic composers of distinction were Boccherini (56), Clementi (47) and Viotti (46). Among the young men were Paer (28) and Spontini (25), while Raimondi (13), Rossini (7), Mercadante (4) and Donizetti (2) were growing up.

In France the veterans were Monsigny (70), a tune from whose Opera, *Le Déserteur*, Beethoven as a child had daily heard ringing from the belfry of the electoral palace at Bonn, Gossec (65), whose bold instrumental experiments anticipated those of Berlioz, and Grétry (58). Composers still in full activity were Dalayrac (46), Pleyel (42), Cherubini (39), Lesueur (39), Gaveaux (38) and Méhul (36). There was also Rodolphe Kreutzer (33), the violinist-composer to whom Beethoven was to dedicate his most famous violin sonata. The rising composers were Catel (26), Boieldieu (24) and Auber (17); Hérold (8) was a child and Halévy was born in 1799.

England was the musical country most remote from Vienna, both geographically and culturally, although it was to seek a closer connection than any other with Beethoven towards the end of his life. Meanwhile the two masters of the pianoforte, Clementi (47) and Dussek (36), were still active there as composers, although the former retired that year from his public appearances as pianist and conductor. Field (17) was by this time ready as a performer and played a concerto of his own that year. For the rest England, although vigorously active on the executive side and always hospitable to foreign composers, had little indigenous music to boast of at that time. Not a single universally famous name will be found among those that follow. Jackson of Exeter (69), Attwood (34) and Samuel Wesley (33) represented the church; Arnold (59), Dibdin (54), Shield (51), Reeve (42) and Michael Kelly (37) the stage; and there were glee composers, unique in their cult but not greatly inspired, like Webbe (59), John Stafford Smith (49) and Callcott (33). A young man of prodigious promise that was never adequately fulfilled was Crotch (24), and among the coming generation were Bishop (13) and Cipriani Potter (7), the latter a future friend of Beethoven's.

Passing to 1816, when the musicians born in the earliest year here dealt with (1795) came of age—and the year of Beethoven's Op. 101 Sonata—we find the musical situation of Europe greatly changed, and changed very largely through the influence of Beethoven, or at any rate through the influences that influenced him. But the scope of this essay happens to extend only to outward events, a few of which may be set forth here, taking the composers concerned in order of age. Salieri (66) celebrated the fiftieth anniversary of his arrival in Vienna from Italy and received a gold medal and chain from the municipality. Clementi (64) published the first volume of his *Gradus ad Parnassum*. Cherubini (56) composed his Masses in C major and E flat major, and his Requiem in D minor. Spontini (42), with Berton (49), R. Kreutzer (50) and Persuis (47), brought out an opera, *Les Dieux rivaux*, for the marriage of the Duc de Berry in Paris. Hummel (38) left Vienna for Stuttgart, where he was appointed musical director to the court. Spohr (32) produced his violin Concerto *in modo d' una scena cantante* in Italy. Weber (30) was appointed conductor to the court opera of Dresden, a post later occupied by Wagner. Meyerbeer (25) substituted that name for the original Beer and became completely Italianized. Rossini (24) produced *The Barber of Seville* in Rome and *Othello* in Naples. Schubert (19) composed his fourth and fifth Symphonies and the song *Der Wanderer*. To all this may be added that E. T. A. Hoffmann (40), although first and foremost a literary man, brought out the Opera, *Undine*, composed by himself, which was one of the earliest purely romantic musical works.

The three composers who came of age in 1816 were a German, an Italian and an Englishman: Marschner, Mercadante and Pearsall. Paisiello died on 5th June at the age of seventy-five. Sterndale Bennett was born on 13th April. But what is of far greater significance is that a young generation was emerging which included seven of the great names in musical history within the space of ten years: Berlioz (13), Mendelssohn (7), Chopin (6), Schumann (6), Liszt (5), Verdi (3) and Wagner (3). Nor is this all: nearly a score of other composers of greater or lesser importance had been born in the early years of the nineteenth century: Bellini (15), Lanner (15), Adolphe Adam (13), Glinka (14), Lortzing (13), Johann Strauss the elder (12), Balfe (8), Félicien David (6), Nicolai (6), Ferdinand Hiller (5), Flotow (4), Vincent Wallace (4), Dargomizhsky (3) Macfarren (3), Henselt (2), Robert Franz (1) and Stephen Heller (1). It is almost as if Beethoven, who always longed to marry, yet could never bring himself to face the material responsibilities of such a venture, were giving a host of spiritual children to the world.

SONATA IN E FLAT MAJOR, Op. 7 (1796)

(B.S.S. RECORDS, VOL. XI)

THIS was the first of Beethoven's piano sonatas issued under a separate opus number: i.e. not published in a group of two or three similar works. This may perhaps be taken to indicate that the composer was aware of its being a work of greater dimensions than those of the three Op. 2 Sonatas, and of the growing importance of his contributions to the species. The work was written about 1796 and published by Artaria in Vienna on 7th October 1797. The dedication is to Countess Babette von Keglevics, a young lady of no particular physical attractions with whom Beethoven was nevertheless said to have been in love. Whether this is true or not is of no significance whatever, though if we had any reason for supposing that this aristocratic girl had any tender regard for him, we should at least have an explanation of the curious fact that this Sonata was in its own time known under the nickname of *Die Verliebte* (*The Lovelorn Maiden*). However, we may be thankful in any case that this fancy title has long ago been discarded, as that of the *Moonlight* Sonata ought to have been, and it would be impertinent to attempt to read any sort of 'programme' or 'confession' into this work, which, whatever prompted it originally, speaks more than eloquently enough for itself considered simply as music. Let it therefore be examined as such.

Molto allegro e con brio.—The group of motifs that form the first subject is headed by four bars of rhetorical chords:

Ex. 25

They are simply the call to attention with which composers of the eighteenth century had found it advisable as a rule to open their symphonies, written for patrons who did not listen to music at concerts, but had it performed at social gatherings and often during dinner. Beethoven no longer needed this device. He was quite capable of silencing conversation and demanding attention by less polite and less musical means, if necessary. But such conventions often linger on in art when their original purpose is forgotten. The 'trio' of the minuet or scherzo, for instance, was so called long after composers had given up writing it actually in three parts. Here we have no doubt an unconscious use of such a convention, but a use that shows the original treatment of a wilful genius who could turn classical tags into a living language of his own.

The right-hand quaver figures (Ex. 25*a*) that follow are repeated three times in rising steps, then transferred to the bass and a moment later dissolved into scale passages. They are suddenly and dramatically interrupted by the opening chords, very emphatically given out with a new harmonic distortion and answered softly by a new staccato figure. The chords with falling thirds are twice re-echoed with changing harmony (oblique instead of direct chord formations, so to speak), and on this follow six bars of transition to the second subject.

The group devoted to this opens, very unconventionally, with music which still appears to be derived from, or at any rate to belong to, the first subject:

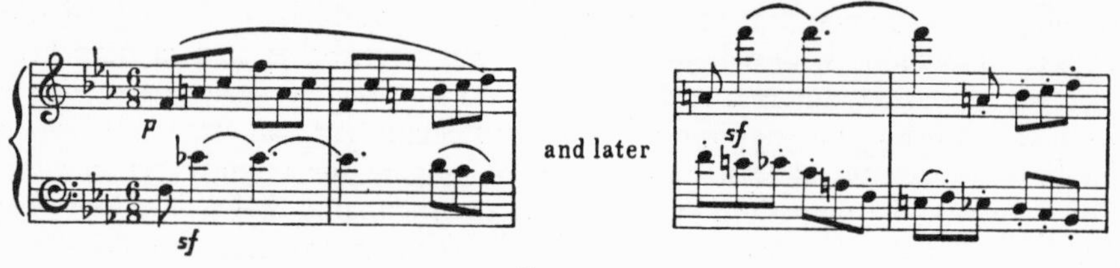

Ex. 26

But as the music is now definitely in the key of the dominant (B flat major), we are bound to take it that the second subject begins with Ex. 26 and not with the following:

Ex. 27

which is much more in the nature of the contrasting, songful theme tradition demands as a true second subject. However, Ex. 27 certainly is part of that subject, though it appears too late to mark the stage at which that feature begins. It is repeated with the top part broken up into quavers, which pass into the bass and are developed into a new and powerful cadential passage leading to C major. In that key yet another idea arises that has evidently been suggested by the rhythm, though not the melody, of Ex. 27. Its expansion leads straight back into B flat major, and here yet another theme, of which this fanfare-like figure is the dominant idea:

Ex. 28

has every appearance of heralding the immediate close of the exposition. But no: there is still more to come. Beethoven is determined to clear as large a building-site as possible for the future of the sonata form. Naturally enough, he does not do it quite convincingly at so early a stage of his career. In later years he would not have led the hearer to believe that he had said all his say when, in fact, he had still a page and a half of exposition to write; he would have avoided the effect of an afterthought or of an unforeseen appendage. But even great masters do not often solve a new problem all round at one and the same time—at any rate not at the age of twenty-six—and it is quite remarkable enough that Beethoven made such plans for the enlargement of the sonata form of Haydn and Mozart so early, even if he did not carry them out quite persuasively at once.

After an upward run which for the first time brings semiquavers into the composer's scheme, Ex. 28 is continued in broken octaves, and the semi-quaverage then continues without any thematic feature over a pedal bass broken up into slow syncopated groups. The concluding theme is structurally important:

Ex. 29

The beginning of the working-out section is based on the first subject, Ex. 25, and its scale continuations; but the chords are now in dominant instead of tonic harmony, and the key is not E flat major but C minor. Then, out of all the material Beethoven might have used to thicken his plot, he brings back the theme that has hardly had time to get off the stage, namely Ex. 29. It goes through a series of modulations that lead us from F minor as far afield as A minor, in which key Ex. 29 is resumed and followed by a new melodic phrase. For, as Mozart had shown Beethoven, a working-out can be made just as effective by making use of new matter that is subtly relevant to the exposition as of material from that exposition itself. The same process, beginning with Ex. 25, is repeated in D minor, and then the music leads by two simple but surprising modulatory steps of the main theme to the recapitulation. The working-out has been brief and thematically not very elaborate; but, by instinct or design, Beethoven has hit upon exactly the right dimensions. His expansion of the exposition after an apparent rapid approach towards the closing key of the dominant demanded a corresponding concentration of the working-out.

The curious event of the recapitulation is the omission of the dramatic incident that had led to the second subject the first time. The latter is much more smoothly approached this time by a mere extension of the quaver passages derived from Ex. 25*a*. The second-subject group is now, of course, in the tonic key (E flat major). Everything proceeds normally until we have reached the clinching figure (Ex. 29) once more. It might close the movement quite as easily into the tonic as it had previously closed it into the dominant; but Beethoven now gives us a large coda, for the first time in a piano sonata. The bass is suddenly jerked up by a semitone, and so the falling chords of Ex. 25 are brought back in C minor. The second subject returns in E flat major and is followed once more by a new presentation of Ex. 29; but the music finally returns to Ex. 25, the chords of which are in the end diminished into half-time.

Largo, con gran espressione.—The slow movement begins with a noble, long-drawn tune—so long that it suffices as a clause for half of Beethoven's main sentence:

Ex. 30

In the fifth bar we have an early example of that rising figure Ernest Newman has called a characteristic Beethovenian 'fingerprint,' other specimens of which are referred to in the notes on the Sonatas Opp. 31 No. 1 and 109 (pages 129 and 228). The second clause of the melody opens as follows, and as one of the formal principles on which this movement is based is that of variation, it will be interesting to show the different forms which the ornamental figures in the second bar take in the course of this piece:

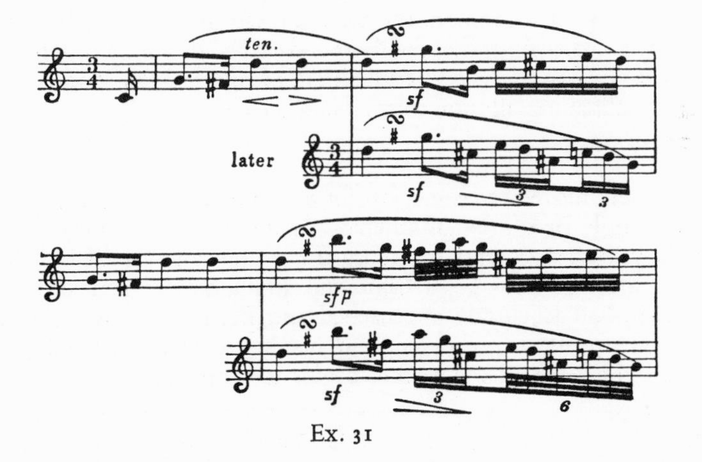

Ex. 31

When Ex. 30 returns it is carried on from the third bar by modulation and thematic allusion, subsides into an apparently normal C major cadence, is dramatically interrupted by a chord of the diminished seventh and reverts to the cadence by a broken rhythm of loud, detached chords, closing this time in

C major. But almost immediately the key turns sharply into A flat major, and here a new section begins thus:

Ex. 32

By way of F minor, this turns up again in D flat major and then leads to a restatement of Ex. 30 in B flat major, preceded by a curious passage of bare octaves alternating with pairs of soft little chirps in the treble. A descending broken chord of the diminished seventh leads to the return of the main theme.

Ex. 30 is restated exactly as quoted above, except for a slight and subtle change of harmony in the last bar but one. Then come the ornamental variants already shown in Ex. 31, and the movement proceeds for a while as before, though there are several small elaborations. When the abrupt chords have been heard again, the second theme, Ex. 32, unexpectedly appears in the bass, but the key of C major is retained. After that the short coda proceeds with a new development of figure *a* in Ex. 30, a twice-stated phrase of one bar that had not occurred before, and a clinching allusion to the main theme.

Allegro.—This movement is too fast for a minuet and too sunny and friendly in tone for a truly Beethovenian scherzo. It is, in fact, a kind of intermediate stage between these two types, retaining the courtly tone of the old dance and introducing the capricious key-scheme and ample development of the scherzo, which Haydn had tentatively approached and Beethoven was to bring to full maturity. The gentle main theme need not be quoted, but the canon in the octave with which the second section begins is worth showing:

Ex. 33

That second section, significantly enough, is much longer than the first. Beethoven cannot resist leading the music round on an excursion through various keys which takes it as far as C flat major (seven flats)—quite a long way off, seeing that the key might just as well have been B major (five sharps). The movement is further extended by some byplay with a figure detached from the main theme for the purpose.

The trio section is in the tonic minor and appears melodically featureless on paper, being almost wholly made up of quaver triplets of this kind:

Ex. 34

Actually, however, the top and bottom notes of the right hand make a continuous melody in octaves which the ear perceives much more readily than the eye. A pathetic phrase, heard twice at the end of the trio, leads to the repetition of the first part.

Poco allegretto e grazioso.—The finale is a rondo on a large scale, with one of the episodes as a second sonata subject. The main theme keeps to the amiable tone of the third movement, but is otherwise quite different in character:

Ex. 35

The following incidental figure is important:

Ex. 36

It is presently transferred to the left hand, which crosses over the right to echo the tail-end of Ex. 36. This appears in the following two forms, plain at first and then decorated:

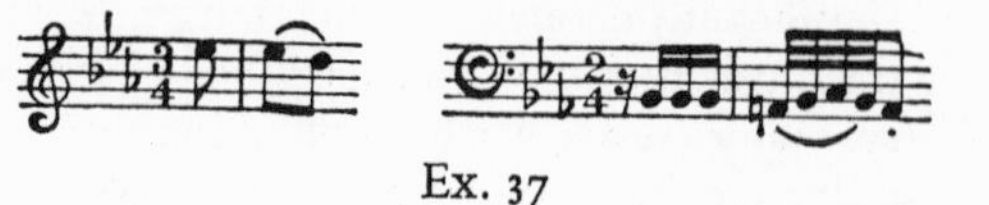

Ex. 37

In the latter form it carries on the music until it is time for the first episode to appear in B flat major:

Ex. 38

After some ornamental development this leads to the first return of the chief rondo theme, which is only slightly altered in the last bar.

The energetic second episode in C minor derives its accompaniment from Ex. 36, but nevertheless acts as a complete contrast. The demi-semiquavers are alternately in the left and the right hand. This episode is in itself much longer than the first, and still more extended by the repetition of its two sections.

The main theme is once more approached, slightly elaborated, and this time restated complete with the transition to the first episode (Ex. 38), which now returns in the tonic key, thus restoring the balance which would otherwise have been upset by the disproportionately long second episode.

A final return to the chief subject, although this time varied by syncopation and chromatic harmony, still keeps admirably to the point, which is to present nothing too unexpected. For the surprise is to come after the subject has reached its pause as before. That surprise takes the form of a coda, in which the bare B ♭ of the pause suddenly slides a semitone upwards and thus introduces the dominant of E major. In that quite unforeseen key the subject is once more stated, softly and with an effect of mystery which the change of key alone produces without any sort of strain. Then, with a touch of his abrupt humour, Beethoven as suddenly jerks back into E flat major again. But almost at once the laugh gives way to a smile: the movement is rounded off by a suave, peaceful page based on the accompaniment of the second episode, which is thematically new, yet relevant to what has gone before.

SONATA IN C MINOR, Op. 10 No. 1 (? 1796)
(B.S.S. RECORDS, VOL. XII)

THE three Sonatas, Op. 10, published in 1798, may have been composed at any time between the summer of that year and 1796. The end of 1796 may perhaps be suggested as not improbably correct for No. 1 and 1797 for No. 2, while No. 3 is likely to belong to the year of publication. That is as far as one may safely go, however, and the reader should bear in mind that the supposition is subject to every reservation. These three Sonatas cannot be dated by any mention of them in Beethoven's extant letters.

They are dedicated to the Countess von Browne, to whose husband Beethoven had already inscribed the three string Trios, Op. 9, with the following words, at once grateful and self-congratulatory: '*Au premier Mécène de sa Muse la meilleure de ses œuvres.*' It is clear that already at this time Beethoven had a very good notion of his own worth, and if he thought his Op. 9 his best work up to the time of its dedication, it by no means follows that he did not soon afterwards regard Op. 10 as better still. Indeed he had good reason to be proud of it. The passionate first Sonata of the set, in C minor, was a considerable advance in personal expressiveness, and the third, in D major, blends character and maturity of presentation in a way that makes it the most lastingly interesting of the earlier piano Sonatas.

The epithet 'passionate' applies most obviously to the first movement of the C minor Sonata, with its far-flung opening gesture, its melodic suspensions, suggestive of suppressed agitation, and its dramatic, breathless pauses; but passion is also disclosed by some of the quick, almost violent figuration in the slow movement and by the abrupt, short-tempered first subject of the finale.

Allegro molto e con brio.—Here is the opening gesture referred to above:

Ex. 39

It is followed by that gentle answer which is so characteristic of Beethoven's first subjects: they are a kind of reflection in miniature of the thematic duality that is, on the larger scale of a whole movement, the guiding principle of the classical sonata form. The theme repeats the same procedure in dominant harmony, and then comes a second strain of the first-subject group:

Ex. 40

Note the threefold repetitions of the phrase with their subtle changes and the melodic suspensions already mentioned which extend it the third time. Next come the pauses, intersecting a small triplet figure which at its third recurrence leads back to Ex. 39. But now only the energetic dotted figures are heard—again three times—and the gentle answering chords are omitted. A character has left the stage and a dialogue has become a soliloquy, if we like to give a dramatic interpretation to a movement that is quite histrionic enough to warrant such an expedient.

Now comes a very striking rhetorical device: three abrupt ejaculations, a moment's pause for reflection, and then an entirely new thought:

Ex. 41

Technically (for one must abandon metaphor before it gets out of hand) Beethoven operates in a very curious manner here. He uses in fact the effective trick of first doing the expected and then following it up with a complete surprise. The first three bars of Ex. 41 conclude the first subject in no uncertain manner. It is not only dispatched, but three nails are very emphatically knocked into its coffin, which is perfectly in keeping with the habits of the eighteenth century, when the sonata was a new toy and composers made a point of showing its inner workings as clearly as possible. But the eighteenth-century mind would now have expected the contrasting second subject to follow immediately, and of course in the key of the relative major in a work cast in a minor key. Here we have, from the fifth bar of Ex. 41 onward, what sounds ideally like a second subject, at any rate in relation to our particular first-subject material. But it is in A flat major, the wrong key for the purpose, and moreover it repeats itself immediately in F minor and in D flat major. Only when this last key has been traversed does the music settle on the dominant of E flat major, thus:

Ex. 42

(The right-hand figures, which afterwards have an ornamental variant, are structurally more important than they look at the moment, as we shall see presently.) And now the second subject is at last ready to appear in its orthodox key:

Ex. 43

It too has a more elaborate extension and it diverges to other matter with dramatic accents off the first beat, until the quaver accompaniment affects the right hand, which for four bars plays in unison with the left in a powerful *crescendo*. Then the figure *a* of Ex. 39 is used as an approach to a last-moment idea that is in a way new, yet has a strong rhythmic affinity with the right-hand motif of Ex. 42:

Ex. 44

Thus the exposition ends in E flat major.

The working-out can be so called only because it begins with a new version of Ex. 39 which, with its C major and diminished-seventh harmony, leads to a new theme in F minor. From here onward none of the material is, properly speaking, 'worked out,' so that this section might more aptly be called a 'working towards' the recapitulation. But though not thematically allusive, it is certainly thematically relevant. The music passes through keys that have not been touched by the exposition and eventually turns on the dominant of C minor, in which key the recapitulation begins in the normal way.

It does not remain normal for long. The restatement of what we may call the sham second subject (Ex. 41, bars 5 ff.) surprisingly follows immediately after the triplet figures intersected by pauses, the earlier resumption of Ex. 39 being omitted. But even more unexpected than this elision is the fact that the transitional theme enters in the key of G flat major, for which the close of the triplets in C major has left us quite unprepared. The immediate effect of this is that the true second subject (Ex. 43) is now brought into the key of F major, whereas according to the rules it ought to stand in the tonic minor. Beethoven's way out of this unusual situation, which he has of course purposely created in order to show both his independence and his unabashed resourcefulness, is to modulate to C minor next (which is easy enough, since F is the subdominant) and to reiterate the second subject, at full length and with some changes of figuration, in the proper key. After that he has simply to transpose the whole material of his previous E flat close into C minor, including the allusions to Ex. 39*a* and the figures of Ex. 44. A coda would, he may have felt, have overweighted this section of the movement in view of the F major interpolation; at any rate he dispenses with that feature.

Molto adagio.—The slow movement has the first and second subjects and the coda of a sonata, but no working-out section, which is omitted no doubt partly to avoid excessive length and partly because three movements in regular sonata form in a single work would have been too much—for the finale is also in that form. But Beethoven does not deprive a highly organized movement of an important structural feature without making some sort of compensation. We have just seen this in the first movement, where a redundant section was in retrospect made to appear justified by the omission of a coda. Here the compensation for the missing development is made by letting the principle of variation assume an important function. The opening strain of the first subject must be quoted:

Ex. 45

If the reader will look at this original form of it again when it recurs later on, he will at once notice the many changes it undergoes. It is in fact heard in a modified form as soon as the passage shown above has been completed.

A bridge to the second subject is formed by violent arpeggio figures, followed by a sharply rhythmic formation of chords. This occurs three times, and I quote the third instance, for a reason that will appear before long:

Ex. 46

The second subject, in E flat major, follows immediately:

Ex. 47

This too is varied, in turn by precipitately rapid, by jerky and by restless, broken figuration which discloses the passionate feeling that was said to underlie even the slow movement of this Sonata.

The return to the first subject is made in the simplest way, by a detached dominant chord of A flat major following on the tonic of E flat. There is on the face of it no more art in this than in the change from one section to the next in a Johann Strauss waltz or an operatic potpourri; but as we know that Beethoven was capable of effecting the most cunning modulations when he chose, we realize that here his art reveals itself precisely in the decision not to use a complex device when a simple one happens to be perfectly suitable. The variants of the first subject should now be noted by comparison with Ex. 45, and they need no detailed explanation; but I will show why I have quoted an incident from the bridge-passage in Ex. 46, a conjunction which has now to lead to A flat major instead of E flat and presents itself thus:

(Ex. 46)

Here we have a striking example of that Beethovenian ingenuity in modulation to which I have just referred. The bass behaves at first almost exactly as before, except that the E ♭ in the arpeggio has become F ♭. The bass C ♭ remains static for a moment: it refuses to sink down as before, as though it were waiting for the raised top harmony to descend with it. What happens is that the top harmony comes down first, which is just the opposite of what occurred earlier, and now the bass decides that it may as well follow, whereupon the harmonic situation is exactly as before (Ex. 46*a*). But that would bring the second subject back in E flat again, which is what must on no account happen; so the top harmony sinks down yet another degree of the scale, from which the next natural step is for treble and bass to converge together on a dominant seventh of A flat.

The way is now open for the second subject (Ex. 47) to re-enter in that key, and so to lead to a conclusion. But something else than the second subject is wanted to round off the movement, and this is done by a coda based on yet another variant of the first theme. This, however, would only seem to lead the music into a kind of endless pendulum swing between first and second subject if it took the same turn as before, and Beethoven now drastically alters not only the figuration of the theme, but, after the first four bars, its whole melodic deportment. It loses its distinction as a tune and becomes more and more purely harmonic, thus making an admirable peroration suggestive of a gradual vanishing.

Prestissimo.—It has already been said that the finale, like the other movements, is in sonata form. As is to be expected of Beethoven, however, he guards against a feeling of monotony not only by producing great contrasts of character, pace and mood between the movements, but by contriving a structural climax to compensate for sameness of shape. As usual, he hits on a surprisingly simple expedient. He has had no coda in the first movement and no working-out in the second. Very well, there shall be both a coda and a working-out in the finale, and behold, short as the movement is, especially in view of its extremely fast tempo, the impression of a heightening in constructive power is most convincingly made, more especially as the working-out really is a thematic development this time. The fact that it is extremely condensed only seems to give it a more forceful structural function.

The first subject begins as follows, in octave unison:

Ex. 48

The second opens like this:

Ex. 49

and its continuation is delightfully underpainted by a bass derived from figure 49*a*. But 48*a* almost at once reasserts itself in the left hand and then, rising for one single flash into the right, calls forth a succession of small themes which, in the highest of spirits and with the nimblest wit, bring about the close of the exposition in E flat major.

When that section has been repeated, the very concise working-out makes use exclusively of figure 48*a*, which eventually comes to a halt, with the comic effect of some disgruntled character in an *opera buffa*, on a series of dropping diminished sevenths. The recapitulation is regular, with the second subject in the tonic major. The close seems to come quite naturally in C minor, but the bass suddenly falls a major third to A ♭, which reveals itself as the dominant of D flat major. In that key the second subject (Ex. 49) is once more alluded to, but in a halting, timid manner that seems to belie the boisterous character of the whole piece and to introduce a touch of sentiment. But that character reasserts itself in a few closing bars based on the main theme.

SONATA IN F MAJOR, Op. 10 No. 2 (? 1797)
(B.S.S. RECORDS, VOL. VI)

THE F major Sonata is the least considerable of the Op. 10, though it was much favoured by the composer himself. The prevalent mood is humour—the typically Beethovenian humour which shows itself in abrupt statements of short sentences and in a habit of twisting and turning them, very much as he twisted words into puns and nonsense rhymes in his letters. In the F minor middle movement there are moments of suppressed anger which alternate with bouts of tenderness and little outbursts of temper. Emotionally this is the maturest of the three movements; it foreshadows the splenetic mood of many of Beethoven's later scherzos.

Allegro.—The first movement opens with the pithy remark shown here without harmony:

Ex. 50

A syncopated melody follows, which quickly leads back to the opening motif, still in F major, but immediately turned by means of a cadence suggested by the triplet figure (Ex. 50*a*) into the dominant of A. Having led us to wonder whether A major or A minor will ensue, Beethoven, with comic abruptness, goes to C major, the proper key for the second-subject group in a movement in F major. He has thus reached this feature quite unexpectedly and much earlier than his normal procedure of spinning out a first subject would suggest.

Here is the theme with which the second-subject group begins:

Ex. 51

Compared with the first it is disproportionately long, but although C major prevails to the end of the exposition, with several new thematic ideas remaining in that key, Beethoven astutely guards against letting it predominate unduly over the main tonality of F major, which he has so far curiously neglected, by inflecting his harmony heavily towards other keys. Thus a subsidiary theme appears poised on the dominant of C major after a cadence verging on G major:

Ex. 52

and immediately afterwards, having been restated in a varied way and in the minor, it abuts momentarily on A flat major by means of an interrupted cadence:

Ex. 53

A little later C major is confirmed again by yet another theme, led up to by a cadence formed from the triplets of Ex. 50*a*. It begins:

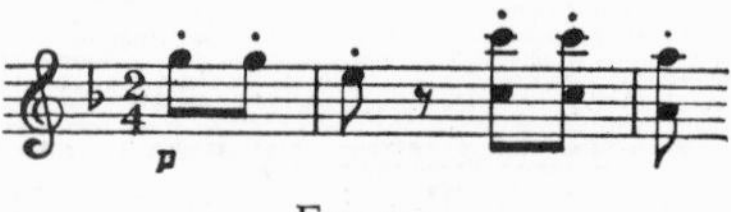

Ex. 54

and ends:

Ex. 55

After the repeat of the exposition the clinching figure, Ex. 55, is used for the opening of the working-out. It is merely due to a useful convention that this section can be so named in this case, for in actual fact it works out next to nothing. Neither the first nor the second subject is once referred to, unless the triplet motion is to be regarded as coming from Ex. 50*a*, in spite of the fact that the figuration is different. All that Beethoven develops here is the concluding phrase of the exposition (Ex. 55), and even that development is interrupted by a lengthy and wholly independent episode in the middle, which is thematically rather featureless and passes through the keys of D minor, G minor and B flat major. It should be noticed that F major is still studiously avoided, though once the music comes as near it as the tonic minor.

When a pause indicates the place at which the recapitulation is to be reached, a very curious thing happens. Here, if anywhere, we feel that the main key should at last assert itself. It does nothing of the kind, however. Beethoven has the astounding audacity to reintroduce his first subject (Ex. 50) in the alien key of D major. It takes a moment's reflection to explain his procedure, which is in fact extraordinarily subtle. We have seen that his working-out contained the permissible minimum of thematic development; but we may now regard the odd behaviour of the recapitulation as a compensation. By turning his first subject into D major and thus compelling himself to give it a new modulatory curve before it can be made to return to the principal key, Beethoven makes this juncture in his musical discourse partake in some measure of a working-out as well as a recapitulation. Small differences in the presentation are worth attentive study. It is important to note that the triplet figure (Ex. 50*a*) in the D major restatement does not descend a step with the change to the dominant harmony, as at first:

Ex. 56

a point that fails to become clear until an instant later we find that this new formation serves the composer for his long-delayed return to F major in this way:

Ex. 57

It is one of the evidences of his mastery that he can not only find such means of giving point to a transition, but that he also knows the art of hinting at it before it actually turns up.

The second strain of the first-subject group, which has already come up in that false start in D major, now returns in the main key, and from here to the end F major remains predominant, exactly as C major had done in the greater part of the exposition. The movement ends in the same way as that section, there being no coda.

Allegretto.—The second movement is a scherzo, though not so named by the composer, perhaps because of his irregular expedient of varying the return of the main theme after the contrasting trio section. The piece is in F minor, but during the stealthy first strain of eight bars it modulates quickly into the relative (A flat) major. This passage is repeated. Then comes a new idea which is imitated in canon at the fifth. Strong accents on the third beat lend the music a capricious, quick-tempered character. The opening phrase is then repeated two octaves higher up the keyboard, in the right hand alone, and when the left joins there is another brief suggestion of canon:

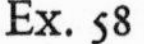
Ex. 58

Its figure (*a*) is then used as accompaniment to a cadence that leads to the concluding strains.

The trio section, in D flat major, is calm and consolatory at first. As a modulation to A flat major is approached, we come upon another instance of Beethoven's subtlety in preparing the hearer for a point that is about to arise:

Ex. 59

The interesting factor here is the G ♮ in the upbeat, which gives an A flat major implication to the passage from the start, although the first two bars are still quite distinctly in D flat major and would not by themselves indicate any impending modulation. As the opening tune of the trio is restated, the left hand adds a new figure which cuts rhythmically across it and is like the sting of angry words thrust into a suave conversation. The two contrasting ideas are then developed at considerable length.

A drop of a semitone from the concluding tonic (D ♭) brings us to the dominant of F minor, in which key the first section is now repeated with a different pianistic lay-out. The first eight bars are no longer written down with repeat signs, but twice newly set forth, the second time in syncopation. From this point on the syncopated motion continues almost throughout, save where the little theme in canon returns in an inverted form.

Presto.—We have not done with formal curiosities yet. The humorously blustering opening theme of the finale suggests a rondo:

Ex. 60

(The concluding F is the implied ending of the phrase, but it rarely arises in that form, being as a rule dovetailed with the beginning of the next statement.) When the right hand enters with the same figure while the left continues a contrapuntal course, the rondo theory may be abandoned and the development of a fugue suspected. Only by those, however, who do not know that the second entry of a fugue subject cannot, like the first, be in the tonic, as it is here. The third appears in the dominant, but by this time Beethoven has abandoned polyphony, so that the texture is no longer even suggestively fugal. Now, as we do not yet know that there is going to be no real second subject, we may decide for sonata form; and indeed, for all that such a subject fails to arise, sonata form it is—of a kind. As far as the exposition goes, Beethoven may be said to have reverted here to the form of the old Italian harpsichord sonata or, if we like, to something like that of the very first sonatas actually written for the *pianoforte* by Lodovico Giustini of Pistoia, though it is inconceivable that Beethoven can have known his work. The mock-fugal opening reminds one strongly of Domenico Scarlatti. In feeling, as distinct from form, the piece is, of course, thoroughly Beethovenian.

A new development of the theme towards the end of the exposition, with the tune in the bass, faintly suggests a second subject, but only because it is in the key of the dominant, for it does not assume a sufficiently independent character:

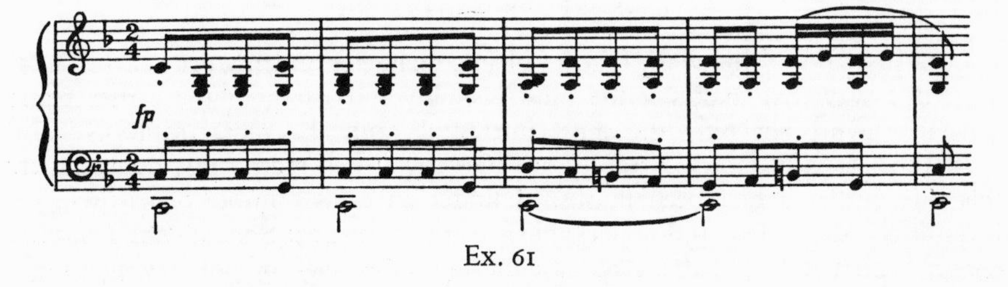

Ex. 61

In any case we soon discover that it comes too near the close of the exposition and has been set into the dominant merely because that section must end in the neighbouring key (C major).

After the repeat of the exposition the music plunges unexpectedly into A flat major, with a variant of Ex. 60 which soon resumes its normal form over a flowing semi-quaver accompaniment. Beethoven then begins to develop the tune and fragments of it with a good deal of contrapuntal elaboration, so that now we have the curious experience of a closely thematic working-out section allied to an exposition and recapitulation in a rudimentary sonata form, the exact opposite of what happened in the first movement. Here again Beethoven seems to have acted on a principle of, or more likely an instinct for, compensation, thus miraculously achieving a satisfactory balance even where he is apparently most erratic in his treatment of form. The climax of the development of his theme comes where he brings in the bass tune quoted in Ex. 61 in contrary motion:

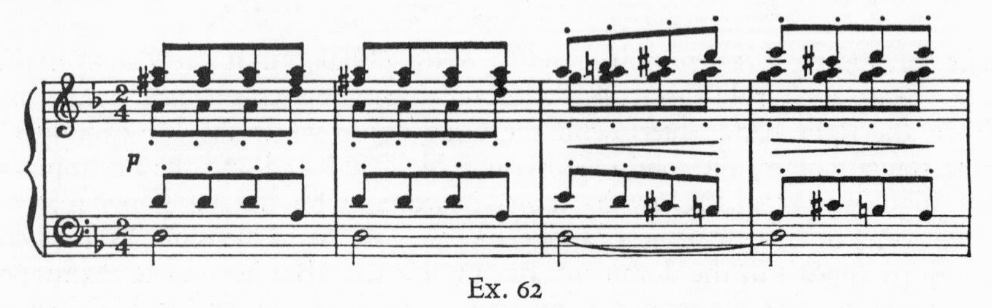

Ex. 62

He uses this again, in F major, for a brief coda; but first he deals with his material in a section that by reason of its position must be regarded as a recapitulation, though in reality it makes such free modulatory excursions and indulges in so many new elaborations as to be more in the nature of an improvisation. But Beethoven keeps to the point just as logically as if he merely repeated with the conventional modifications what had gone before, with the result that this finale of his, for all its humorous exploits, is structurally as satisfying as the most strictly formal of his sonata movements.

SONATA IN D MAJOR, Op. 10 No. 3 (1798)
(B.S.S. RECORDS, VOL. XII)

I HAVE just said of this work that it 'blends character and maturity of presentation in a way that makes it the most lastingly interesting of the earlier piano sonatas.' And not only the most interesting, but the most impressive and satisfying. It is in fact so great an advance towards a more individual mastery that one wishes it had been published under an opus number of its own. It is quite as independent and remarkable a work as the next Sonata—the *Pathétique*—over which it has at the very least the one advantage of not having caught the popular imagination by a fancy title and thus run the risk of enjoying an artificially induced preference.

Presto.—The first movement opens with this significant phrase, played by both hands in octave unison:

Ex. 63

The figure of the four initial notes, marked *a*, is exceedingly important as a thematic feature: it has almost the function of a Wagnerian *Leitmotiv*, in the sense that it is not a melodic theme but a kind of symphonic brick out of which surprisingly solid structures can be built by a piling-up process. It is used in some such way at once, thus:

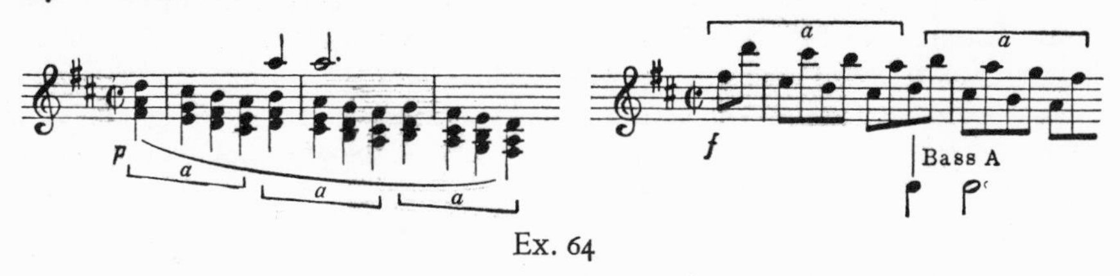

Ex. 64

Ex. 63 then returns broken up between the hands and after another pause, similar to that shown at the end of Ex. 63, but this time on F sharp. Only now does the music become melodic, if melodic treatment means the introduction of something in the nature of a cantilena:

Ex. 65

and after this B minor idea comes another in F sharp minor:

Ex. 66

Since the term *Leitmotiv* has been used, the temptation may assail the hearer to see in the groups of four descending notes I have purposely marked *x* subtle allusions to our figure *a*; but this suggestion is to be firmly resisted if it is ever encountered in an analysis of this Sonata by any scholar, whatever his eminence and qualifications. For we are still in the domain of the classical sonata, where thematic derivations of this kind are not to be looked for and even if they manifestly exist must not be regarded as consciously devised by the composer. It is always perfectly clear in Beethoven's music where thematic workmanship serves a purpose of formal design, and we shall have no doubts whatever when we see our *Leitmotiv* so applied; but the place for such ingenuities is emphatically not in passages which serve, for one thing, as transitional intermediaries between first and second subject and, for another, as a complete contrast to both.

Neither is it conceivable that a second subject should be derived from a motif belonging to the first. Beethoven had broken with that primitive habit of the earliest symphonists, though occasionally he would deliberately thrust a first-subject feature into his second theme, as we have noticed in the finale of the Sonata Op. 10 No. 1, or may remember his doing in a much more famous instance—the first movement of the fifth Symphony. The opening phrase of the second subject, then, is emphatically not a new employment of the descending motif *a*:

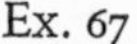
Ex. 67

though the appoggiatura is, of course, to be played as an even quaver. Indeed, if one must at all costs be clever, one might perhaps suggest that Beethoven wrote the D as a grace-note in order to avoid the appearance of any resemblance between this sequence of notes and our figures *a* and *x*. But in the enchanting new strain of the second subject we may, if we like, see another of those instances in which he does admix a first-subject element with a second-subject feature:

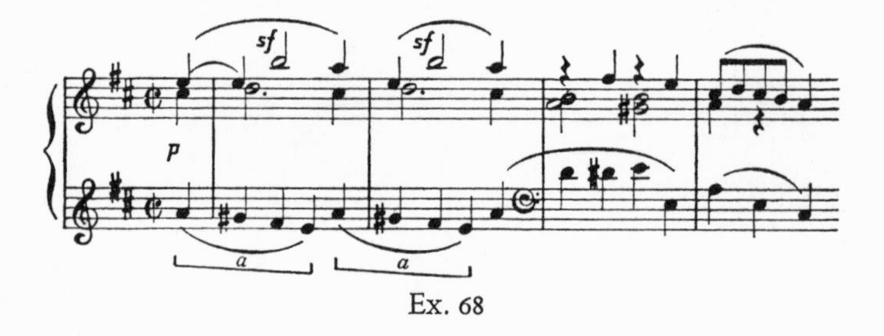

Ex. 68

The bass here is decidedly our *Leitmotiv*; in fact this passage gives rise to a very extensive use of it during practically all the rest of the exposition, and indeed beyond. Here, for instance, the motif constantly appears, right way up and upside down:

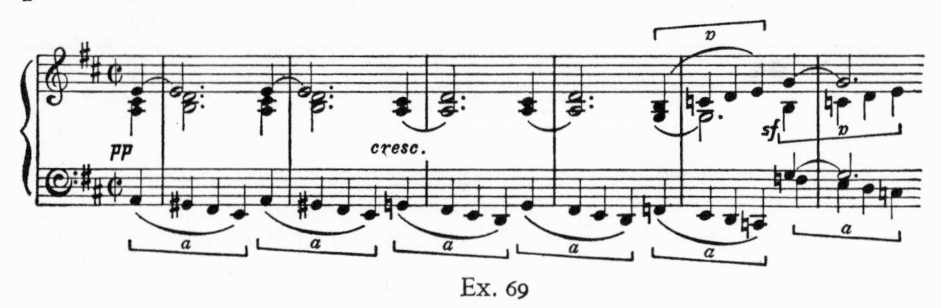

Ex. 69

and here are other instances of its ingenious use:

Ex. 70

Ex. 71

The melodic formation of Ex. 71 is presently transferred to the bass. Then come a few bars of fascinating cadential chords in minims, followed by a new treatment of 63*a*, which leads to the end of the exposition. Not a perceptible end, however: one of the most interesting phenomena of this Sonata is the astoundingly subtle transition, first to the repeat of the exposition and then to the working-out section. I cannot resist showing this in music type:

[*Continued*

Ex. 72

When the unexpected key of B flat major has been reached, it is found that the working-out adheres much less strictly to the thematic material than the greater part of the exposition had done. I have mentioned Beethoven's instinct for structural compensation before: we have seen that he sometimes gives additional weight to a section because a preceding one had been treated rather cursorily. Now we notice that he may just as well reverse the process and lighten even a development section of thematic references because an earlier page had been unusually burdened with them. Beyond rising basses which are obviously an inverted presentation of 63*a*, the working-out contains no familiar matter, in fact not very much plastic matter of any kind. Its chief interest lies in a new orientation of keys, which go far afield before the music turns towards the dominant of D major for the recapitulation, which begins after the rhetorical passage shown in Ex. I in the concluding essay (see page 244).

When this new survey of the exposition, with its disposition of keys adjusted to the changed requirements, is completed, the cadential minim chords, instead of closing symmetrically in D major, are extended until they end in G major, in which key a lengthy coda begins. It follows at first the outline of the transition between the end of the exposition and the working-out and then keeps to the rhythm, but not the shape, of 63*a*, until that motif is restored to its rightful form in a final passage that holds on grimly to an inner pedal on the tonic note D. The descending basses quite near the end may or may not be augmentations of 63*a*. The reader may here take his choice.

Largo e mesto.—The very eloquent and beautiful slow movement, in D minor, adheres to sonata form, and though it has an independent section in place of a working-out, there is a more or less thematic coda. The first subject need not be quoted, but its splendid, pathetic treble melody beginning at the ninth bar should be particularly noticed. The second subject may however be shown here:

[*Continued*

Ex. 73

It is, of course, in the dominant, A minor, and will recur in due course in the key of the tonic. The striking phrase marked *a* should be kept in mind, as it is used to build up a short climax.

A full close is made with a downward arpeggio on the A minor triad.

An entirely new idea now comes in place of a development. It is in F major, but soon turns into other keys, and an accompanying figure of broken demi-semiquavers should be noted as well as the loud, heavily groaning short phrases with their oppressive and closely spaced diminished-seventh harmony, made to sound the more bitter by the admixture of minor seconds.

The return to the first subject is made by a kind of broken but metrically regular cadenza. The subject is differently laid out and half of the pathetic melody is ruthlessly omitted. The second subject then leads to a return of the first in the bass. It is heard below an arpeggio accompaniment; and this is the beginning of the coda. The thematic reference soon becomes vague, and presently the broken demi-semiquavers of the middle episode take its place. But at the end the music once more alludes to the main theme before it dies away over one of the most original closes Beethoven ever devised.

Allegro.—The minuet, which restores the major key, begins with a sunny melody that seems all the brighter by contrast with the seriousness and the gloomy tonality of the *largo*. The second part, which is much longer than the first, begins with an imitative passage ending in a shake, below which the main theme is gaily resumed. It rises this time to a higher melodic climax and is rounded off by a short and very soft peroration. Both parts are, of course, repeated.

After such a riot of blossoming tunefulness, the trio, in G major, is melodically uneventful, the contrast being thus admirably and effortlessly heightened. With the single exception of four bars in the middle, it is merely a succession of chordal triplet figures for the right hand, above and below which the left, crossing over and returning to position, adds simple two-note basses and tiny fragments of tune.

Allegro.—Here, after two excursions in the preceding sonatas of this opus, Beethoven returns to the rondo form, which he treats with a new splendour and resourcefulness, and also with a peculiar humour that gives this finale a mood all its own. Charm and abruptness contend with each other in giving us the impression of a wilful and quick-tempered but warm-hearted personality.

Once again we have something like a *Leitmotiv*—this all-important figure:

Ex. 74

with which the movement begins in a curiously hesitating, questioning fashion, and which permeates the whole of it more or less persistently. It is in fact remarkable that the episodes are short and of no particular thematic significance, whereas these three notes assert themselves strikingly whenever they are present and indulge in all kinds of acrobatic pranks. The first episode, for instance, could hardly be identified as such if it were not in the dominant key prescribed for its appearance, A major:

Ex. 75

and the second, which turns up after a verbatim return of the main theme:

Ex. 76

has little more intrinsic distinction and is given hardly more space to remain wholly itself, for the *Leitmotiv* thrusts itself impertinently into it. The third return makes a little more of Ex. 74 by overlapping imitations, but remains otherwise unchanged. The few bars of the last episode are wholly dominated by the three-note figure, though it sometimes changes its intervals:

Ex. 77

The final return of the rondo subject again shows but small modifications; a real development is reserved for the magnificent coda, in which Ex. 74 first blossoms out more melodically, then gives way for a moment to a purely harmonic passage of syncopated chords which introduces a touch of mystery as fascinating almost as the famous intrusion of sudden seriousness into the finale of the second Symphony, and finally it concludes the Sonata with muttering allusions in the bass.

INTERLUDE II

CONCERNING REPEATS

THE question frequently arises in the performance of Beethoven's music—or, to narrow the issue down to what happens to be relevant, of Beethoven's piano sonatas—what ought to be done with his repeats. Since this is not quite as simple a question as it looks, it may perhaps be worth discussing here.

It is not only in connection with Beethoven that this subject becomes important enough to deserve detailed examination, though he must of necessity remain uppermost in this brief essay. There are cases in earlier music where it is more than a matter of mere convention whether a repeat should be observed or not. The slow movement of Mozart's so-called 'Prague' Symphony (No. 38, K. 504) always seems to me an outstanding case for a debate of this kind. The reader may remember that at the very end of the first part of this *andante* Mozart finds a last-moment inspiration in a lovely new melody that brings this section to a close in the key of the dominant (D major, the movement being in G major). Now his second section begins straightway with a new version of this theme in B minor; but the point loses more than half its value if that arises immediately after the melody has been heard *for the first time*. What Mozart reckoned with was, of course, that the whole first part should be repeated and that this striking modulation should not make itself heard until the tune in question had come round *the second time*. Only then does its new development take on the right significance, because only then does it arise in its proper place in the course of the music. But unfortunately that repeat makes the whole movement much too long, not only for our present-day feeling, but in proportion to the rest of the Symphony, and so the predicament arises, for any conductor who is sensitive enough to be aware of it, that either it must draw itself out too much or else what is a particularly subtle feature of Mozart's construction must be suffered to turn into something very nearly like a blemish.

Generally, however, in pre-Beethovenian music any doubts that arise over repeats may be settled by an application of common sense. Mozart's two piano sonatas which contain variation movements are interesting in this connection. In the first-movement variations of the A major Sonata (K. 331) Mozart gives repeat marks at every section, which means that the slow variation becomes about twice as long as the others if all repeats are observed. A good plan, then, is to make all repeats except those in the slow variation, where the alternative interlocking bars at the end of each section, the first of which has to be omitted, do not happen to be of any particular interest.

In the D major Sonata (K. 284), which has variations for its finale, the case is different, however. Here the one thing that is obvious is that the repeats of the quick variations must on no account be disregarded, for it is to be observed that in the *adagio* variation Mozart does not give any repeat signs, but writes out each section fully in its all double length, with a different ornamental treatment for each repeat. This slow section is therefore bound to be disproportionately long in any case, but almost ridiculously so if the fast variations are played through without repeats. It is bound to be at least twice as long; to make it four times the duration of the theme itself would be preposterous.

As a rule the problem in the pre-Beethovenian piano sonata is even simpler than that. It generally resolves itself merely into the question of how long it is desired that this or that movement should last, and the usual solution is to repeat the exposition of a fast movement in sonata form, but not that of a slow one, and never to restate the working-out and recapitulation. But no repeats are really obligatory in such music, nor do difficulties often arise similar to that to which no satisfactory solution is to be found in the 'Prague' Symphony. For it is to be noticed that interlocking repeats (i.e., alternative endings for the first and second time of playing) are seldom found in Haydn's sonatas and more rarely still in Mozart's. Moreover, where they do happen to occur, they cannot be said to have any function in the support of the musical structure, as they often have in Beethoven's case. They are almost invariably coping-stones, not key-stones.

It must be remembered that repeats in the eighteenth century had a much more superficial purpose than they came to assume later on. Music at that time was the prerogative of a society of hedonists who, even when they were genuinely attached to it, regarded it by tradition as an adjunct to the rest of their diversions. Public concerts were few, and people did not visit them in the same serious, almost dutiful frame of mind as they began to do once music had become democratized.

Repeats in sonata movements were doubtless taken over from the dance forms that preceded them, largely because the composer's work was rarely listened to in complete silence and with great concentration; and since it was necessary to the comprehension of a symphony or sonata that its thematic material should be impressed on the hearers before they could appreciate its treatment by the composer, the expedient of repetition was resorted to as the most natural way of ensuring understanding. It then grew into a convention, and all conventions are apt to linger on long after the conditions which gave rise to them have disappeared and ceased to justify them. Thus, for instance, did keyboard suites continue to keep all their dance movements in the same key, though the original reason for this was that suites for the lute had to be so written because that instrument had to be retuned for changes of key. Thus, too, did composers go on indicating repeats in symphonic and sonata movements when the century of inattentive hearers was past and the new habit of careful listening had taken hold of audiences.

Even Beethoven, impatient as he was with tradition for mere tradition's sake, did not altogether escape this particular one. It would be too much to say that all repeats indicated by him must be respected as a matter of course. In fact it becomes imperatively necessary in his case to determine where the observing of repeats may enhance the structural significance of his music or their neglect impair the balance of a work, and where his indication of repeat signs may be safely regarded as a mere habit contracted by the study of his predecessors.

Some performers observe all Beethoven's repeats most scrupulously, even that almost monstrously disproportionate one in the finale of Op. 57—the *Appassionata*—to which I shall refer again on page 167. But although this scrupulousness is more than justified in a set of model interpretations, such as those recorded by Artur Schnabel for the Beethoven Sonata Society, it need not be allowed to degenerate into pedantry, and does not, for instance, in the case of Schnabel's performance of the F major Sonata, Op. 10 No. 2. Beethoven there not only desires the exposition to be repeated, but also the working-out and recapitulation; but this second wish of the composer's is as a rule disregarded. At the same time the reader may be reminded that here, as in Op. 57, is a clear case of Beethoven's asking for a repeat for the sake of a particular point he wishes to make and ignoring the fact that the performance becomes excessively long if his direction is respected. Perhaps I may be allowed to quote a sentence from Sir Donald Tovey's *Companion to Beethoven's Pianoforte Sonatas* in connection with Op. 57: 'Beethoven has unquestionably overlooked the difficulty ordinary mortals must feel in enjoying such a crisis . . . (lasting forty-three bars) . . . twice in one performance.'

The case of Op. 10 No. 2 is not altogether analogous, though. Here, it may be said, is not enough crisis for this long section to bear repetition, at any rate *in a public performance*. Mark the words I have italicized: they are suggested by the following passage in Sir Donald's book, which I cannot forbear to quote, since he, as usual, sees all round the question and puts the matter in its proper perspective:

> . . . *in private playing* [my italics] it is worth while trying the effect of repeating the second part. Beethoven certainly saw the point of the tag (*c*) [see Ex. 55, page 40] rising from F to A as contrasted with its former fall; and, if we are not impatient, the contrast of the episodic development and the novel strokes of genius in the recapitulation will gain by repetition, welding the total diversity into a more lyric unity. At all events, Beethoven never wrote a repeat mark without thought of its effect at the moment when the repetition begins and its effect on what follows upon its end; though he may forget the effect of its total length, or may disagree with our opinion on that point.

But now it becomes important to show briefly that in many cases the effect of a Beethoven sonata movement as a whole, or at least of a cardinal point in it, is completely ruined if the repeat is disregarded. I will not attempt to draw a hard and fast rule; but roughly speaking it may be taken that this happens wherever the music overlaps at the junction between the exposition and the working-out, to mention only the most vulnerable region in his musical territory, where repeats are concerned. In other words, the player must look out for those alternative endings, marked |1 :|| and |2 , which are found comparatively rarely in Haydn and Mozart, but very frequently in Beethoven. If the reader will refer to page 186, he will find a striking instance quoted there as Ex. 227. The passage occurs in the first movement of the Sonata Op. 81*a*, which simply cannot be thought of without the repeat, as it would suffer most grievously from the omission of that admirable new turn into the working-out, which owes its beauty to its difference from the earlier modulatory turn into the repeat of the exposition.

A very similar point in the *Sonate pathétique*, Op. 13, is mentioned in the description of that work which follows this essay. I will show here how Beethoven contrives by means of the utmost simplicity, combined with the greatest possible forcefulness, first to lead back to the principal key (C minor) for the repeat of the exposition:

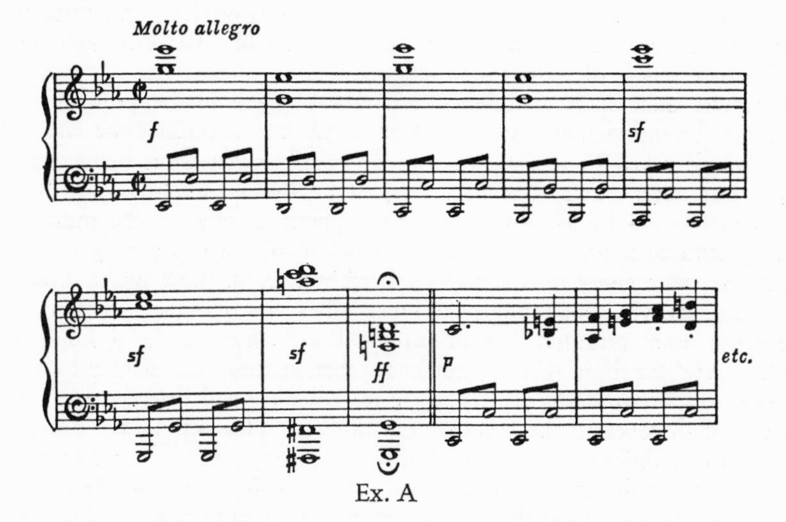

Ex. A

and then to the key of the dominant (G minor) for the working-out section:

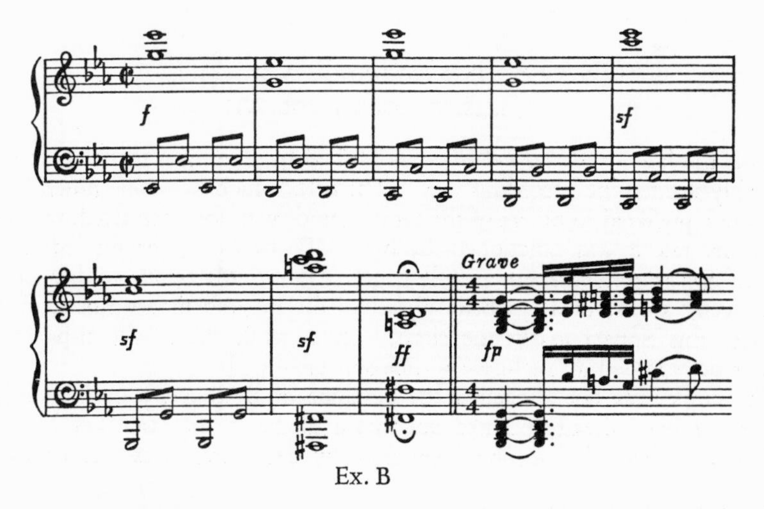

Ex. B

I would also ask the reader to look at the similar passage in the finale of the

Sonata Op. 31 No. 3 (see page 141), where a case very like that of the 'Prague' Symphony arises. Beethoven here uses a new motif at the end of the exposition and finishes on a dominant-seventh chord, which is the first time resolved into the tonic (E flat major) for the repeat, but afterwards suddenly made to give way to a remote key (G flat major). There is a heightening of the effect here which loses half its surprise if it is not first prepared by the less unexpected turn of events. One of the great secrets of Beethoven's art is that he not only makes striking points, but often foreshadows them in astonishingly cunning ways, and as he does this frequently by means of repeats, it is obvious that these should never be omitted without the closest consideration of what their sacrifice may involve in the way of formal destruction.

However, once such consideration has been given to the problem, it will sometimes be found that a section without any overlapping at the end, which the player is asked to repeat, will not necessarily suffer from being passed in review but once. Only this may be said finally: no exposition of a sonata movement should be left unrepeated by a player so long as the music is not perfectly familiar to him. Once the work is known, the repeat may occasionally become as unnecessary in a sonata by Beethoven as in those by his precursors. For in his sonatas, too, though the repeat often has a higher function, it still retains the more primitive one of driving the thematic material home to the hearer. And for those who do not know that material well it may be as fascinating to listen twice over as it may be to reread a good detective story for the pleasure of discovering the second time how the plot was laid. But there is this important difference: once we know the detective story from two perusals, we lay it aside for ever; a Beethoven sonata with which we have become thoroughly familiar we shall for that very reason want to hear or play over and over again—though not always with repeats.

SONATA IN C MINOR, Op. 13 (? 1798)
(B.S.S. RECORDS, VOL. VI)

THIS is the famous *Sonate pathétique*, published by Eder of Vienna in 1799, and probably written the preceding year. The title, which has done much to make this work preferred to others of the same period, was for once Beethoven's own, or at any rate it was sanctioned by him. To be exact, the first edition bore *Grande Sonate pathétique* on its title-page. Marion M. Scott, in her book on Beethoven,[1] speaks of a 'pathetic phase' in the master's piano music, of which she says this Sonata marks the close. Thus, while the title is appropriate, it cannot be regarded as exclusive to one sonata.

The work was not altogether the outcome of Beethoven's own moods and fancies. I have already pointed out that a sonata in the same key by Dussek which, as I was able to show conclusively elsewhere,[2] was written earlier—

[1] Master Musicians Series (Dent, 1934).
[2] 'The Prophecies of Dussek' (*Musical Opinion*, December 1927–August 1928).

probably as much as five years earlier—than the work by Beethoven, resembles it very strikingly in several respects. What may be regarded as significant, apart from musical affinities, is the fact that Dussek's direction for his slow movement is *patetico*. It would be useless to speculate whether Beethoven really did know Dussek's Sonata, and his admirers are quite at liberty to regard such coincidences as being due merely to certain currents of common influence that are often in the air at particular junctures of artistic history and have had to account for similar cases where mutual influence is known to be out of the question. At the same time nobody need regard it as in the least derogatory to the greater master if he is suspected to have allowed himself to be influenced by the smaller, whether consciously or unconsciously. It has in fact always been one of the evidences of great mastery that it could accept suggestions from smaller artists and absorb them into its own style, thus transmuting them into a nobler metal.

The fascination which this Sonata has always exercised over lovers of music, and even over people who care more for the romantic in all its forms than for music as such, is accounted for by Miss Scott in a few lines of penetrating criticism which are well worth quoting:

> In poetic content Beethoven's *Pathétique* is tragedy as the young feel it, with the glamour, urgency, even exaltation, of a *Romeo and Juliet*. And few southern love-scenes could be more softly glowing than Beethoven's slow movement with its almost unbelievable melodic loveliness and velvety tone.

The Sonata is dedicated to Prince Carl von Lichnowsky, Beethoven's friend and patron from the early Vienna days onward. The composer, aged twenty-three and almost unknown when he first lodged under the roof of Lichnowsky's house, as any poor person might in those days live in the attics of the Viennese nobles' town residences, so long as he had some respectable recommendation, was very soon discovered by his music-loving landlord to be worth cultivating, and before long he was taken into the princely household. This did not last, however, for all that Lichnowsky offered Beethoven a salary as well as a horse and groom of his own, of whose services he characteristically forgot to make use. It was not in Beethoven's nature to live with anybody on a familiar footing without before long losing his patience. He seems to have desired to set up house for himself mainly because he was expected to dress and shave for the Lichnowskys' dinner every day. At any rate, there was no serious quarrel, as quarrels went with Beethoven, and of all the aristocratic patrons who were so loyally attached to a genius for the sake of whose art they were large-minded enough to overlook a great deal, Lichnowsky was perhaps the most faithful and the most constantly attentive.

Grave—Molto allegro e con brio.—The optional slow introduction of the classical symphony and sonata form occurs remarkably rarely in Beethoven's piano sonatas. In his symphonies he followed the precedent of Haydn and Mozart, more or less, so far as the frequency of such introductions went. Four symphonies out of his nine have them. But among the thirty-two sonatas only three have introductions prefixed to them, the present work, Op. 81*a* and Op. 111. The three and a half bars of *adagio cantabile* which introduce Op. 78 are too rudimentary to count, and the *largo* incident in Op. 31 No. 2 is not an introduction at all, but a thematic feature of the first movement itself.

As regards the treatment of the introduction in the *Pathetic Sonata*, it is very curious, if not quite unique,[1] for Beethoven not only uses it as a preface to his quick-paced first movement, but inserts two reminiscences of it into that movement itself—between the exposition and the working-out and again between the recapitulation and coda. The intention is quite plainly a dramatic one. These interruptions of the impassioned *allegro* are not merely pathetic; they hint at some tragedy that may well have been actually before Beethoven in a concrete form, so unbridled does this movement seem in its urgent expressiveness. Whether he had some written drama before him, and if so what, may be left to be revealed by Arnold Schering, with whose fantastic 'discoveries' of the alleged programmes for several of Beethoven's string quartets and piano sonatas I shall deal in a special essay later. The ordinary lover of Beethoven who has no far-fetched theories to impose on an ungratefully sceptical world will be content to use his own imagination about the possible sources of inspiration which may have caused the composer to regard this Sonata as more pathetic than others.

The following opening figure:

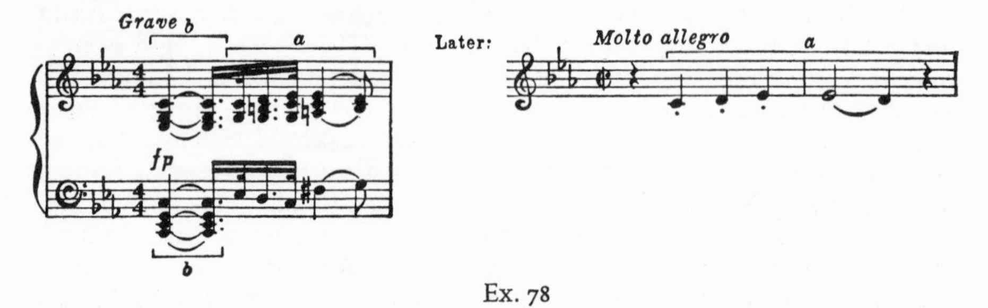

Ex. 78

dominates the introduction at first. In the third bar it is crowded together with an effect of heightening the eloquence, and two bars later, after an ornamental incident, it appears softly in E flat major, only to be rudely interrupted and tossed from one key into another. Restless and broken, it resigns itself to being lost in the freer passages that follow. A descending chromatic scale is like a ruthless tearing up of this introductory page, and after a moment's hesitation the music is precipitated into the fiery *allegro*.

Sonata form now asserts itself. The main theme of the first-subject group is this:

[1] See the reference to Clementi on p. 183. Beethoven himself had anticipated the practice in the F minor Sonata of his boyhood (see 'Postlude,' p. 242).

Ex. 79

but another motif must be quoted, as it is important that it should be recognized in the later development:

Ex. 80

The music glides gently into the second subject, the chief melody of which is first stated in E flat minor:

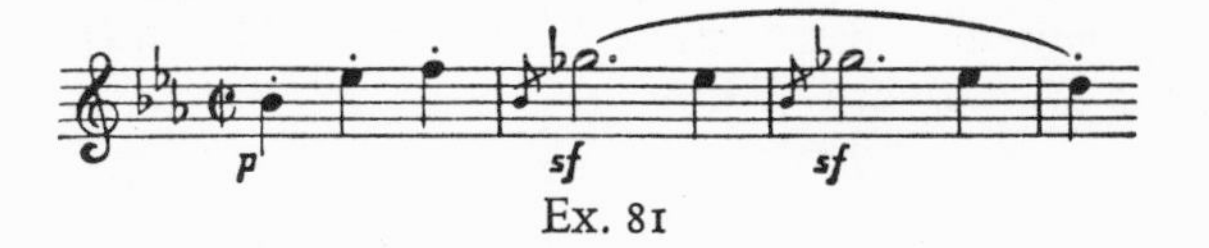

Ex. 81

The usual classical procedure in a sonata movement in a minor key was to make the first statement of the second subject in the relative major. But Beethoven is here obviously intent on avoiding a major contrast in so conspicuous a position. Only in the course of letting the second subject modulate through various keys does he allow it to appear in a brighter key (D flat major), and later he lets a subsidiary theme, beginning with a treble note repeated in syncopation, appear in the orthodox second-subject key of the relative (E flat) major. Another idea, distinguished by running passages in the right hand, also appears in that key, but where the first subject (Ex. 79) is again alluded to at the end of the exposition, the tonality verges once again towards C minor. The whole of the *allegro* heard so far is then repeated, and it is worth noticing how Beethoven alters the final harmony the second time in order to lead, not again into C minor, but into G minor for the working-out section. (See Exx. A and B, page 55.)

It is here that the slow introduction interposes itself, though only for the length of four bars, and here also that a drastic modulation to as remote a key as E minor is compressed into a very small space with remarkable effect. It is in E minor, surprisingly enough, that the *allegro* is resumed for the working-out. This section ignores both the main subjects and draws entirely on material previously treated as side issues. The effect, in some curious way that is more easily felt than explained, is overwhelmingly dramatic, mainly, no doubt, because the hearer is kept in suspense all through this section as to what is going to happen next, since he can hardly fail to expect the principal actors to enter at any moment and to wonder why they never do. The stage meanwhile is held by Ex. 80 and by the transformation of figure 78*a*, as already shown in Ex. 78 above. 80 passes into the left hand for a time, and later it is expanded in the treble.

At last Ex. 79 returns for the recapitulation, and a new, striking use is made of its figure *a*, which appears in three rising sequences. Beautiful as this new development is, it also has a structural reason, which gives an opportunity to say that in formal music, as in architecture, the features which are the finest in appearance are generally those which at the same time have a practical application, although needless to say this view must not be carried too far in connection with an art in which practical considerations can only serve ideal ends.

This transition makes a modulation to F minor, in which the second subject now appears, again rather irregularly, the key being that of the subdominant minor, whereas normally the second subject, having first been in the relative major, would in the recapitulation stand in the tonic minor. It passes into that, however, and not into a major key as before, the whole section being in a darker set of tonalities than the corresponding one in the exposition. The peroration, made of the matter auxiliary to the second subject, then remains in C minor. Finally the first subject (Ex. 79) returns for the coda, to be intersected once more by an allusion to the introduction (Ex. 78). It now appears broken by silences on the first beats (i.e. with the notes marked *b* cut out). The movement then ends abruptly with a last outburst of Ex. 79.

Adagio cantabile.—The slow movement needs very little description and no illustration by music type. It is filled with a flood of lyrical melody that is best responded to purely emotionally, though it may be worth attention that the form is that of a simple rondo with two episodes. The subject is a lovely eight-bar melody played without any introduction in the middle register of the keyboard and restated an octave higher with a fuller accompaniment (two moving inner parts instead of only one). The first episode is a new melody in F minor, appearing in the right hand over a simple accompaniment of evenly repeated chords. It is songful, but too ornamental and too widely spread to be sung—an ideal tune for a violin and needing the warmest sort of imitation of violin tone and phrasing a modern piano can produce. In other words Beethoven is here a long way from the harpsichord style, and it is mere pedantry to pretend, as has been done recently, that he was quite satisfied with the thin tone of the early pianoforte, or would still be if he could hear a more recent instrument.

A rather gloomier second strain concludes this episode, and the main theme is then restated exactly as at first, but without the modified repetition.

The second episode, beginning in A flat minor, is like a duet between a mezzo-soprano and a baritone, the former having a tender phrase, the latter a more lively reply. After an intersecting passage, the duet is repeated in the remote tonality of E major. An interesting modulatory bridge quickly leads back to A flat major for the second return of the chief theme, now enriched by a triplet accompaniment and again fully given out twice, the second time in the higher position, as before. A short coda for which Beethoven's inexhaustible invention finds new ideas at the last moment, but ideas by no means irrelevant to what has gone before, then brings the movement to its conclusion.

Allegro.—The finale is a more fully developed rondo. The principal theme opens thus:

Ex. 82

continues for another four bars and then begins to develop, closing with an emphatic C minor cadence. The first episode goes by sequential modulations into E flat major, in which key it presents its first, suavely flowing melodic idea, as also a passage with the following motif:

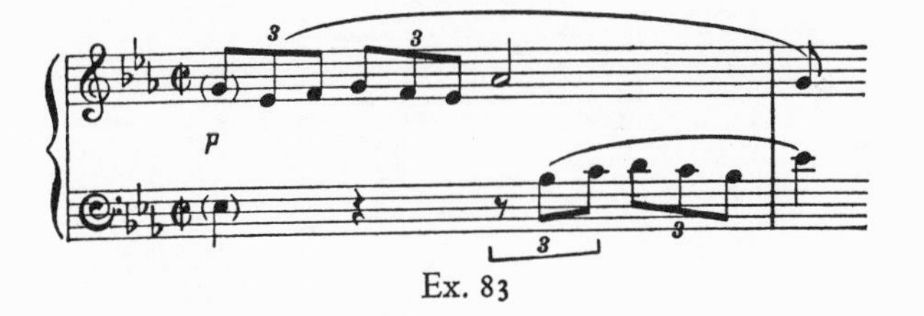

Ex. 83

which will be seen to assume some importance as a binding substance. It may be regarded as the mortar used by the composer in his structure, the themes themselves being the bricks, or rather blocks of stone. Another of these, still belonging to the first episode, is a main feature:

Ex. 84

as it will be used again, like a second sonata subject, in a later episode. Ex. 83 then provides the transition to the first return of the main theme, which reappears exactly as before, but is attended by a new episode made of two melodies proceeding by fourths and fifths in contrary motion between the two hands. They are afterwards separated, the top one being used in double counterpoint against running scale passages. A new bridge of broken chords leads to the second return, where the theme is modified by a restatement in the left hand. The suave melody then turns up in C major for the third episode, and Ex. 83 is again used for a transition to Ex. 84, also in C major, but with an F major inflection; 84 is then restated in the same key, but considerably extended by a series of wonderful modulations, which lead to the last return of 82. An extended coda follows in which figure 83 is drawn upon to a considerable extent, and the rondo closes with shy allusions to the main theme, followed by an energetic descending scale.

INTERLUDE III

BEETHOVEN'S KEYBOARD MANNER

In the introductory essay I pointed out that Beethoven did not originate the style most congenial to the instrument that was, by its own newness, so provocative of new thought in musical composition in his time. But I also made the reservation that in connection with a resource so fruitful of previously unheard-of effects it would be foolish to think of only one possible style. If the first composers who were made by their musical nature as well as their historical position to write what was, as such, ideal piano music could differ so widely from each other in their approach to the same problem, then a musician of immeasurably greater creative power could not fail to discover yet another pianistic manner for himself. That Beethoven owed something to the examples of Clementi and Dussek as far as sheer keyboard execution went is not to be denied; that he forged much more for himself is, however, at least as clearly evident.

How did he forge? Well, as one must—by hammering. The *pianoforte* was for him a *Hammerclavier* long before he explicitly called it so. There was no longer any plucking of strings, as in the harpsichord, no caressing of them, as with the tangents of a clavichord: the new method was one of an attack by blows—and how well suited to the most aggressive of composers!

It is easy to say that piano music owes everything in the first place to Beethoven, for so it looks, since he was the first great genius to write for it as an instrument with new possibilities. But it is not the whole truth. Apart from what he himself owed to the example of others, consider how much he was in his turn indebted to the new medium. It was as though invented on purpose for him. It lured from him an abundance of ripe fancies long before any other could fire him to anything to match them. He was more than half-way through the piano sonatas before he wrote the second Symphony, and the first has nothing like the significance of the contemporary piano Sonata in B flat major, Op. 22, with its thunder-laden first movement. The string quartet, too, one of the great vehicles of his middle and final periods, he handled far more conventionally in his early days, and then he left it alone for a long time. The Septet is only an eighteenth-century serenade showing an uncertain feeling for the style of the species.

The piano holds sway over the earlier concerted works in which it takes part, such as the first two concertos and the early trios; yet the other instruments will not allow it the same bold flights for which it often takes wing even in the very first solo sonatas. The young Beethoven must have it all alone if he is to be quite himself. It is clear that it helps him to find inspiration, quite as much as he helps it to display its mettlesome temper, so different from the gentle, ghostly song of the clavichord and the swaggering, elegant tinkling and rustling of the harpsichord.

Beethoven is the most dynamic nature among composers, and the outstanding quality of the piano is, of course, its peculiar way with dynamics. It is abrupt, decisive, explosive, like himself. It knows no compromise, no polite diplomatic approaches. A loud note must be loud from the start: it cannot begin quietly and gradually assert itself. Hence sharp attacks, no beating about the bush. On the other hand, there is no means of sustaining the tone evenly, for it must needs begin to tail off as soon as it has been struck, so that the most characteristic effect of the piano is the *sfp*, which produces itself again and again, even when it is not specifically asked for by the composer. The *crescendo* is possible, but not to a single note, only to a series of notes which are made to louden progressively one by one. It is an artificial product, and that too is a pianistic speciality to be exploited to good purpose.

Beethoven delights in making the fullest use of both the natural and the artificial characteristics of the piano. He knows his instrument so well that he can make the most of both its virtues and defects. While he extols the former, he would not for anything miss the latter, for he has come to love the faults as well as the good qualities of his constant companion. The *crescendo* has to serve, whether it will or no, and is made to work hard to prove its worth, if it can, and if not, at least to show that its negative merits are still a great improvement on the incapacity which the harpsichord had shown in this respect. Beethoven is especially fond of drawing attention to a passage swelling from soft to loud by letting it be suddenly followed by a *pianissimo*. The instrument, he seems to say, must simply be compelled to show what it can do in this way, now that it has acquired the power of doing it, no matter by what deception.

As for the *sforzando*, which is entirely natural to the medium, he insists on it again and again by marking it very explicitly, sometimes by a plain *sf* and often by the even more characteristic *sfp*. The device is like a new toy. Now that it is no longer necessary, as it was for the harpsichord composers, to ornament important notes in order to give them some semblance of an accentuation that was dynamically impossible, the new conquest must be exhibited again and again. The first movement of the earliest piano Sonata, Op. 2 No. 1, is literally strewn with *sf* marks.

One might be inclined to say that, had this movement been written for the harpsichord, there would be mordents and other ornaments in all the places where we now see the *sf*. But try to play the music in this way, and it will at once become apparent, even if we have no harpsichord handy to make the experiment, that this is not by any means all the difference. The music will not hark back to an earlier instrument and an earlier manner. It is something entirely different, even as the piano is an instrument wholly distinct from the harpsichord. The music is keyboard music in both cases, the instruments are both keyboard instruments; but there the resemblance ends. The piano does everything in a new way, and Beethoven, who is on such intimate terms with it, knows the way and writes as it and his inspiration between them dictate. And to all important purposes inspiration and the medium are at one from the beginning.

The early piano was looked upon as an instrument ideally made to drive home a point. All the notes played were to be heard. The harmonic backgrounds into which they can be fused are the invention of a later day, due to the improved pedal technique of such composers as Chopin and Liszt. Beethoven, so far as his markings show, resorted rarely to the sustaining pedal, not more, in fact, than to the *una corda* damper that was one of the innovations of which it was naturally tempting to make frequent use. This need not mean that he used the sustaining pedal no more than his notation shows, nor should it nowadays be restricted to his indications, for we have grown accustomed to a liberal treatment of it and demand from the piano a richer sound than it can have yielded in his time. Even in such a movement as the second of Op. 27 No. 1, where one can hardly help seeing the point of Beethoven's abstention from pedal markings, it is possible for a player to disagree with the view expressed in the notes on that work on page 104 and to take it that his harmonic implications are meant to be realized by free vibration of the strings. Still, there is in Beethoven no mere pianistic background accompaniment as there is in Chopin and Liszt, much less anything of the harmonic haze which puts colour before design in the piano music of Debussy, for instance. Where Beethoven uses accompanying patterns of a rather stiff and formal nature the player has no right to smother them by excessive pedalling: he must accept them as the remnants of a convention that, far from worrying Beethoven's contemporaries, must have been accepted by them as a matter of course.

Beethoven is outspoken in all his statements, whether important or subsidiary. What he says he is ready to stand by, and he wrote for his own world, not for the future, so far as he knew and cared. That he also wrote for all time is another matter, and because he did we need not be too anxious to gloss over what seems to us too bald nowadays in his subordinate figurations. In any case, these gradually disappear from his sonatas as his style matures. We shall find in such a specimen of his late manner as the Op. 109 no accompaniments such as may be observed in an early sonata like Op. 14 No. 1. (See Exx. 85 and 92, pages 68 and 72-3.) All the more reason for showing them frankly where they still occur, for the changes from Beethoven's earlier manner to the later are among the most fascinating subjects for study in the whole of music. There will be an opportunity to pursue this question further in an essay on the three periods—if the Lenz classification may be adhered to merely theoretically for such a purpose.

If we accept the fact that the early piano was uncompromisingly explicit, then we must also make up our minds that Beethoven meant all he wrote. From what we know of his character we may tell for certain that he must have been delighted to have an instrument to his hand through which he could express himself with perfect frankness. With evident joy he found that it could sing when he wanted it to do so. Even in the earliest sonatas, particularly the slow movements, there is a profusion of deeply expressive melody such as no keyboard instrument had ever been asked to give forth with such urgency and intimacy. But it is clear enough that he was no less glad of the instrument's capacity for making a far from ear-flattering assertion in the most downright manner, and the performer has no business to soften his harshness any more than to obliterate his occasional stereotypes of figuration. It is true that some of his asperities may be harder to bear from the modern piano than they were from his own, with its much weaker bass. The player is frequently faced with the temptation to omit the third in a major triad placed low down on the keyboard because of the thick sound it produces, and perhaps such a procedure is not altogether unjustifiable even from an historical point of view. But since the sonatas contain other things not in themselves pleasing, which yet have to be brought out without compromise for the sake of the whole truth about Beethoven's artistic outlook, one may as well interpret him quite faithfully, even at the risk of offending the ear trained to the greater subtleties of modern pianistry. These are matters of time and have nothing to do with the eternal validity of Beethoven's thought as distinct from its realization. If in the coda to the first movement of the Sonata Op. 14 No. 1 we are impressed by the manly bluntness that ruthlessly bunches together two semitonal clashes:

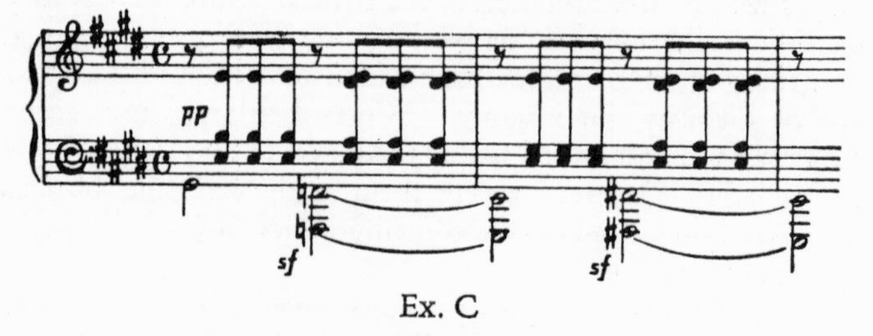

Ex. C

we must also accept the rather muddy effect created by the bass G in the final chords:

Ex. D

Whether the expression be that of a deliberate roughness or of a perhaps inadvertent clumsiness (and who is to discriminate infallibly?), it is always the man Beethoven speaking through Beethoven the artist, and speaking the truth as he sees it. That truth is worth retelling wholly and unsparingly, and never more so than when it is interpreted by the instrument that was most responsive to the genius who propounded it.

SONATA IN E MAJOR, Op. 14 No. 1 (1799)
(B.S.S. RECORDS, VOL. II)

THE date 1799 assigned to this work is not that of composition, but that of its publication, which occurred on 21st December of that year. It is not certain when the Sonata was written. Beethoven's sketches for it are found close together with those for the piano Concerto in B flat major, which he completed early in 1795; but from internal evidence one would be inclined to judge that the Sonata was probably not finished until nearer its date of publication, as it shows a good deal more maturity, both technical and spiritual. All due allowances being made for the fact that at this early stage of his career Beethoven would naturally write in a more superficial manner in a concerto and much more intimately in a sonata, we can hardly fail to notice that the difference is less strongly marked in the sonatas preceding the *Pathétique*, Op. 13, which is conjectured to belong to 1797. But even there the composer's strongly personal expression is still made in the dramatically explosive way that is at least partly due to brilliant keyboard writing. Both the Sonatas of Op. 14, on the other hand, are purged of all external effect, and No. 1 in particular turns every pianistic device to an expressive purpose. Though it may contain technical difficulties, nothing in its whole course has the appearance of being written for the sake of display. The performer's problem now is that of penetrating into the emotional significance of the music rather than that of solving digital problems. As an interpreter's task the present Sonata is vastly more difficult than the *Pathétique*, with its rather obvious dramatic and lyrical contrasts. And as Beethoven's whole life-work was an emotional intensification, a discarding of ostentatious externals, we may reasonably take it that the two Sonatas Op. 14 were written after Op. 13 (though opus numbers, in Beethoven's case, cannot be relied on to establish the chronology of his works)—that is to say, some time in or shortly after 1797.

The present work was arranged by Beethoven for a string quartet, for which purpose he transposed it into F major, for no better reason that one can see than the fact that he was thus able to use the open C string of the cello to give him the dominant as low down in the bass as possible. A glance at the original version of the first and third movements at once makes it plain that this low dominant (B in this case) is of great importance. That Beethoven did not believe in arrangements and made this one only under pressure is shown by a letter he addressed to Breitkopf & Härtel, the Leipzig publishers, in 1802. (It is interesting to find, by the way, that the tendency was evidently to arrange works away from rather than for the piano, which had not yet become the ubiquitous instrument it is to-day and had not displaced string playing in people's homes.)

> With regard to arrangements [Beethoven writes[1]], I am heartily glad that you decline them. The unnatural mania, at the present day, to wish to transfer pieces for the pianoforte to string instruments, which in every way are so different, ought to be stopped. I firmly assert that only Mozart himself could transfer his pianoforte music to other instruments, and the same of

[1] J. S. Shedlock's translation.

Haidn [*sic*]; and without placing myself on a level with these two great men, I make the same assertion with respect to my pianoforte sonatas; not only would whole passages have to be omitted or entirely rewritten, but further additions made—and herein lies the true stumbling-block—to overcome which there must be either the master himself, or at least one possessing the same skill and inventive power. I changed just one sonata of my own into a quartet for strings, which I was pressed to do, and am sure that no other man could have accomplished the task as I have done.

The Sonatas Op. 14 are dedicated to the Baroness von Braun, the wife of Baron Peter von Braun, a wealthy manufacturer raised to the rank of a nobleman, who was for a time manager of the Opera in Vienna.

Allegro.—This mere tempo indication hardly meets the case. One cannot help feeling that, had Beethoven written this movement but a very little later, he would have qualified his '*allegro*' with '*ma sempre con sentimento*,' or something else indicative of the profound feeling the music so restrainedly, yet so penetratingly suggests. No previous sonata of his begins with so utterly unrhetorical, so immediately expressive a theme as this:

Ex. 85

It is the first subject, or rather the principal strain of a first-subject group, for it is attended by other ideas that make for variety without destroying the unity of the composer's scheme, which consists mainly in keeping the whole of this material in the key of E major. First we have a semiquaver passage repeated four times, at each appearance an octave lower, then a twofold phrase the second statement of which is an octave higher, and lastly a cadence with chromatic inner parts, which is also twice stated in different octaves, the second recurrence being the lower. This merges into a new development of Ex. 85, with changing harmonies in the accompanying quavers and a new melodic development at the third bar leading to an episode built over a repeated pedal on F that serves to establish the dominant of B major, the key—itself the dominant of the main tonality—in which the second subject is to make its appearance. Before it does so, there is an energetic half-close on three chords of F sharp major.

The second subject takes this form:

Ex. 86

and has a sequential continuation a degree of the scale lower by which it returns to B major from its temporary sideslip into C sharp minor. It then coils itself into passages of imitation between treble and bass, the beginning of which may be shown here as an interesting example of the asperities from which Beethoven did not shrink when they happened to do for him what he wanted:

Ex. 87

If in his later years he had written anything like that cluster of semitones (B♯, C♯, C$^{\times}$, D♯) that cross each other so harshly, it would be universally explained as an instance of how his deafness made him insensitive to such rough places; but at the time this Sonata was written, his hearing, if not perfect, was still intact. It is much more to the point to say that he did not mind occasional harshnesses, that he even deliberately sought them now and again as—shall we say? —a relief to his tenderer feelings, just as he would storm and curse and be rude to people in order to avoid making an exhibition of the love he bore the brotherhood of man—one of his great artistic themes, when all is said and done.

An entrancing melody at once compensates us the moment this short dispute between two exponents of the same idea is over. But note that after the suave phrase there is an interruption by a passage with angry displaced accents, which in turn is followed by another conciliatory, delicate reply. Here are the three contrasts, from the end of the first soft answer to the beginning of the second, with the gruff rejoinder in the middle:

Ex. 88

Beethoven himself gives us a clue to this interpretation. He told Schindler, in a conversation regarding the desirability or otherwise of giving the public indications as to the poetic content of his music, that when he wrote his sonatas 'people were more poetical and such indications were superfluous. . . . Every one saw that the two Sonatas Op. 14 represented a struggle between two opposing principles, an argument between two persons.'

The exposition of the movement ends with a brief reference to the main theme (Ex. 85), which now appears in the bass, very softly, with the broken quaver accompaniment above it. This leads to the repeat of the exposition. When it has been heard again, the music seems once more to be taking the same turn, but now Beethoven leads it into a different channel by the simple process of depressing the C♯, F♯ figure shown in the second bar of Ex. 85 to C♮, F♮. This takes him into his working-out section, if one may use that term merely geographically, as it were. For although the music has reached the place at which the working-out ought to begin, Beethoven actually develops nothing. That this remarkable suppression of his extraordinary gift of thematic exploitation is entirely deliberate is proved, as Sir Donald Tovey reminds us, by a note in the composer's sketch for this work: '*ohne das Thema durchzuführen*.' To which Sir Donald adds in his dryly witty manner: 'Accordingly, critics who disapprove of episodic developments are not entitled to suppose that Beethoven was episodic by inadvertence.'

An entirely new tune—a melody as distinct from a theme—fills almost the whole of this section. It is played in octaves by the right hand and accompanied by chords broken into semiquavers. Beethoven evidently does not intend the episode to thrill us especially: he keeps it of set purpose on a low level of interest and restricts its eventfulness to a series of modulations which take us, with slowly shifting basses, through keys as remote from the main tonality as A minor and C major. With a sudden jerk into E minor we again come near it, however, and then, in the dominant of E major, we have once more a brief allusion to Ex. 85, alternating between bass and treble.

This leads into the recapitulation, which begins, surprisingly, with a new version of Ex. 85, the right-hand figures being now laid out in full chords and the left accompanying with ascending E major scales. The three auxiliary ideas, however, remain as before; but at the place where the first subject is due to return another surprise awaits us in the shape of an interrupted cadence that leads, not back into E major, but into C major. The transition receives a slightly different treatment and the half-close before the second subject is in B major as the dominant of the principal key, in which that subject reappears this time, according to classical precedent. Beethoven never defies an established principle for the mere fun of doing so: whenever he flouts traditions it is with a definite artistic purpose; otherwise they are good enough for him. The rest of the movement, up to the coda, also proceeds perfectly normally, with one single exception, and even that dictated by an external circumstance. It will be observed that through the transposition of the second-subject group into E major the phrase shown at the opening of Ex. 88 now lies a fourth higher, with the result that, as the piano was constructed in Beethoven's time, the phrase, repeated as it stood before, would have exceeded the range of its keyboard. It is therefore turned down thus:

Ex. 89

The brief coda of fifteen bars is, again, built on the main theme (Ex. 85), which first appears in the bass, then in the treble, and is quite freely treated though always with the characteristic figures of accompaniment with which it was associated from the first. The whole passage is of a stillness that would be perfect but for the fourfold repetition of a groaning bass that falls alternately by semitones and whole tones (see Ex. C, page 66). To the last the unquiet Beethoven must needs utter a faint note of apprehension. It is just like him.

Allegretto.—The restlessness continues. The second movement is a scherzo in motion and form, but one of those pieces filled with the hollow kind of mirth we find in Beethoven's work again and again. This is the first time that this mordant humour comes to its full expression in a piano sonata. All the same, it is, remarkably enough, already in evidence to some extent in the scherzo movements of the earlier sonatas and elsewhere in his preceding works. It is curiously noticeable that his later manner, with its characteristic touch of grimness and its almost defiant avoidance of eighteenth-century mannerliness, comes into prominence much earlier in his scherzos than in any other type of movement. One may thus fairly say that the scherzo brings out the very core of his individuality almost from the start.

The *allegretto*, which is in E minor, begins with the following strain:

Ex. 90

This is repeated, preceded by an up-beat this time, an octave higher. Then Beethoven, with great thematic economy, carries on the discourse mainly with new presentations of bars 2 and 3 in the extract quoted above (Ex. 90*a*); but, fertile as well as economical, he quickly finds a new aspect for discussion in this fragment. After a slight hesitation, he returns to the theme in its first form, emphasizes bar 4 (Ex. 90*b*) by repetition, twists its quaver figure (Ex. 90*c*) into a flowing cadence, and ends his first part by turning that figure upside down and heightening the capricious character of his music by creating a major-minor ambiguity and confusing the rhythm by cross-accents.

A trio section in C major follows, more suave, but still with a suspicion of unrest. It serves little purpose to show a portion of it in music type, as it is all one continuous melodic formation. (See, however, Ex. 91 below, the bars marked *a* of which correspond with the opening of the trio.) Formally this episode remains attached to the old dance forms, with a repeated first half ending in the key of the dominant and a second returning to the tonic. The only departure is a kind of tail-piece of six bars (Ex. 91*b*) that leads back to the scherzo by means of a half-close on the dominant of E minor:

Ex. 91

The whole scherzo is restated note for note, and then the melody of the trio begins again. But we are cheated of an expectation to hear it all over once more, aroused in us, perhaps, by our experience of the scherzo in the seventh Symphony. Beethoven here uses merely the final statement of the tune by way of a coda, with the tail-piece leading once more into the dominant of E minor. But that key is no longer insisted upon: the piece ends with a bare threefold repetition of the note E in octaves.

Allegro comodo.—The finale is a rondo with the feature of a second subject borrowed from the sonata form—in other words, a rondo with episodes highly organized. More than that, the principal subject (Ex. 92) contains a feature—a phrase 92*a* beginning with the rapid descending scale—which also lends itself to what might almost be called a symphonic development. The theme is at once stated without preliminaries:

[*Continued*

Ex. 92

It will be of interest to consider this passage for a moment as another instance of Beethoven's frequent disregard of the mere amenities of sound. To begin with, those descending consecutive 6–3 chords rather low down in the bass are not particularly agreeable, though their hardness is mitigated by the device of breaking them up into triplets; but much more noticeable are the ruthless semi-tonal clashes on the last beats of the first and second bars shown above (not counting the opening half-bar). In the first place we have E against D♯, in the second A against G♯. Beethoven, as already pointed out, was not deaf when he wrote this Sonata, so that, quite apart from the extraordinary faculty of aural imagination he must have possessed, he actually heard these clashes on playing his music. The inference is that, if he did not write them with a purpose, he at least obviously tolerated them. It is time someone made an exhaustive study of all the roughnesses of this sort to be found in his early music in order that the critical habit of making his deafness alone the explanation of his later awkwardnesses—if one likes to call them so—may be repudiated once and for all.

The passage quoted above having set the movement going, what may be called the key-phrase of the whole structure (Ex. 92*a*) is at once restated an octave lower. Then comes a repetition of the whole procedure, with the one difference that the second appearance of the descending scale is now an octave and a fourth lower, so that its further elaboration is displaced into the key of the dominant (B major). This prepares the field for the first episode, which is later to reveal itself as a true subject of the sonata type. It is a short, sustained melody in B major with a final turn and a *staccato* bass resembling that of plucked strings. After a slightly modified repetition, the final tonic chord of B major is transformed, by the addition of A♮ in the bass, into the dominant seventh of the principal key, E major, in which the main theme (Ex. 92) returns, at first unchanged, then veering towards G major, in which key the descending scales of 92*a* lead to the second episode.

This is a long, independent passage, beginning in G major and traversing a variety of keys, made only of broken triplet chords and arpeggios, with simple, conventional basses and without any clear thematic outline. The intention is doubtless to do without anything of special interest in order to heighten the contrast.

The next return of the main theme again transposes the falling scales, so that now they establish A major, in which key the second subject is brought back. In the regular sonata form this return is, of course, made in the tonic key; its resumption in that of the sub-dominant is unusual. Even more so, in this particular case, is the sudden modulation to F major, attended by a fascinating turn back to E major within the space of two bars. The final recurrence of the principal theme in the form of a coda shows considerable changes. It is in fact restated twice over in different forms, the first time running away, so to speak, to permit itself a little virtuosic excursion before it is finally dismissed with another variant. But even here it is to be observed that, as I pointed out at the beginning of this sketch, Beethoven in this Sonata always subordinates effect to an expressive aim. Here virtuosity is all very well, but the point is that a climax was wanted and that the technical display happens to supply it perfectly. The final bars, which lead to a sudden energetic close, are built on figure 92*a*.

SONATA IN G MAJOR, Op. 14 No. 2 (1799)
(B.S.S. RECORDS, VOL. VII)

THE reader who, very properly, uses this book for casual reference, not for continuous perusal, had better be reminded here that the date given above is that of publication, not of composition, of the two Sonatas Op. 14, and that the dedicatee of both these works was the Baroness von Braun (see page 68).

From the conversation reported by Anton Schindler, according to which Beethoven referred to these two Sonatas many years later, it transpires that he was by no means opposed to the idea that hearers should discover concrete meanings in his music. As we have seen, he told Schindler that at the time he composed these works people had enough poetical feeling to make any indications of this kind on the composer's part superfluous, and that every one at once saw in this music a struggle between two opposing principles or an argument between persons. The statement is offered to the reader for what it may be worth, with the warning reminder that Schindler's recollections, published thirteen years after Beethoven's death, are not unjustly suspected of having been dictated by the fancy of an author whose sentiments must at times have made him forget how far he could trust his memory. It is not clear, in any case, whether each of the two Sonatas as a whole is supposed to represent one of those opposing principles, whether the conflict arises between separate movements, or whether a new argument unfolds itself within each movement. As is so often the case with music to which we are given a supposed programmatic clue, we can here see almost anything we choose; which, duly cautioned against giving rein to mere fantasies, the reader may now be left to do for himself. Whatever temptations may assail the annotator to enliven his task with unauthorized interpretations of a picturesque order, anything more than the suggestion of a personal impression shall be duly eschewed here.

Allegro.—The opening figure of the first subject, which is the chief thematic feature of the whole of this movement, has a kind of blithe charm that is made the more enticing by the doubt which it first rouses in the hearer as to what exactly is being said. Beethoven delays the accompaniment—and with it the feeling of accent—by half a beat, so that, without looking at the music, we seem to exclaim:

O what a happy *day!*

But what it actually does say, even more delightedly, as a musical quotation will at once make clear, is:

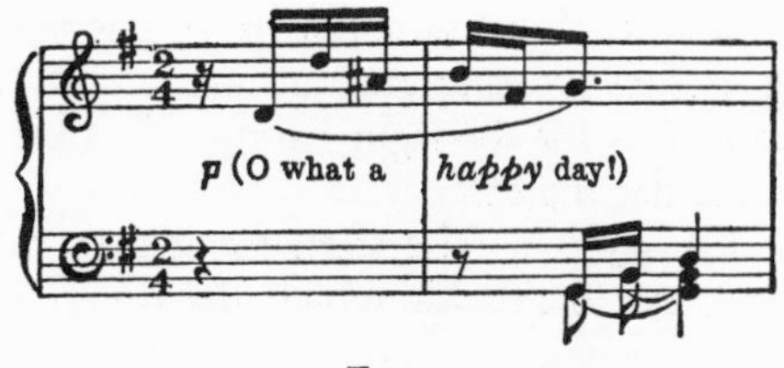

Ex. 93

(Accent on the 'happy.') A long-drawn melodic idea that follows after four statements of this fragment and a cadence closing into the tonic key—for the first-subject group is yet to be extended considerably—appears at first more significant, but is in reality episodic in comparison with the brief but not peremptory call shown above.

The second subject opens with this melody in thirds:

Ex. 94

which has an answer in the dominant. The mood remains happy: if there are two persons represented, they are not engaged, one would have said, in an argument, but combine their voices in a gentle exultation of companionship. They go on to a more emotional strain, then to some lighter chatter, and finish the exposition with a duet that strikes the gravest note yet heard, though, far from casting a shadow over the music, it only deepens the sense of bliss:

Ex. 95

A contralto and a bass exchanging tender vows, one might say, if that can be taken as a mere simile and not as a programmatic illustration.

The exposition ends unclouded. It is repeated. A hint of trouble comes at the beginning of the working-out section, where Ex. 93 appears in G minor and a moment later becomes rhythmically entangled. Ex. 94 next appears in B flat major, but the answer on the dominant has an ominously rising bass which brings the music to a sudden loud outburst in A flat major. Here Ex. 93 is expanded into a long, restless twisting and turning in the bass, below changing harmonies laid out in triplets for the right hand. This brings us to a pause on a dominant seventh of E flat major.

The restatement of Ex. 93 is a false start, for it does not occur in the right key. It is in fact the E flat major for which the dominant seventh pause has prepared us.

Very soon the music takes on a new shape again, for it now has to modulate towards the tonic key of G for the recapitulation. But this is approached in the most leisurely way over a very prolonged dominant pedal (persistent D in the bass), first with new passages and minor harmonies above it, then with allusions in the major to Ex. 93—rhythmic allusions only, not melodic. There is another pause before the initial material is resumed. Beethoven is clearly intent on blurring the metrical formation in such a way that the ear shall still be uncertain, as the recapitulation opens, whether his meaning is 'happy *day*' or '*happy* day.' It is, of course, the latter, as before, and he now goes through the process of recapitulation with little change except in the disposition of keys, which remain much nearer the tonic all the time, according to classical precedent. There is a new, extended cadence at the end of Ex. 95, however, leading to a coda of fourteen bars, based on Ex. 93 but given a new cadential conclusion.

Andante.—The slow movement is simply a theme with three variations and a coda. There are two sections, the second of which is repeated. It may appear curious that Beethoven explicitly directs the player not to repeat the first, which is only eight bars long, whereas the second runs to twelve; but his plan becomes perfectly clear on consideration, for not only does the first part contain an element of repetition in itself, but its strain reappears in the second part, thus rounding off the whole long melodic period as well as beginning it.

The first variation follows the shape of the theme exactly and retains its key-scheme throughout. But it is quite differently displayed and has a touch of greater lightness, imparted to it by luminous and soaring descants set over the tune, which is played almost wholly by the left hand.

The second variation is kept in syncopated staccato chords all the time; but while the melodic pattern is again closely adhered to, there is a new harmonic element—a complex of diminished sevenths, to single out only its most characteristic aspect.

Four extra bars treated in the same manner, but not belonging to the theme, lead to the third variation, which breaks the melody up into a gracefully flowing semiquaverage. For some reason, probably that of not wishing the even motion to become monotonous, Beethoven does not repeat the second part this time. It may also be that he wished to spring without delay the surprise of leading the music into his six-bar coda, which begins as though yet another variation were to be expected, but at once gives the melody a new twist that brings it to a final cadence of four detached chords, three of them very soft and the last aggressively loud and thick. The gentle-toned movement thus ends with an odd bout of humour—that typically Beethovenian humour which could not often be funny without at the same time hurting somebody a little.

Scherzo : Allegro assai.—The master is now fairly in one of his playful moods. He does the oddest thing, to start with: he goes and writes 'Scherzo' over a movement that is, at any rate formally speaking, not a scherzo at all, but quite plainly a rondo. Why? Nobody knows, and the fact that the music is in triple time and actually does begin in a scherzo mood explains nothing, for sonata movements were named after their form. I am not aware that an explanation of this little mystery has ever been attempted before, but it seems to me exceedingly likely that Beethoven originally contemplated a sonata in four movements and actually began to write this one with the intention of making a scherzo of it. Then, somehow or other, his first theme, though a very good one on the face of it for such a purpose, would not assume the right shape for a scherzo tune, refusing to turn into a dominant cadence at the given moment, or some perverse little obstinacy of that sort. The composer may then, in a fit of impatience, have defied it with the challenge that if it would not serve for a scherzo, very well, he would punish it by cutting out a scherzo movement altogether and making it do much harder work by dragging it into a rondo, where it would not only have to come round more often in its original form, but be made to perform all sorts of structural labours. This is pure conjecture, and may be all wrong; but the phenomenon of a rondo with a decided scherzo character is stranger than any attempt, however far-fetched, to explain it could possibly be.

Beethoven's starting joke is to practise once more a rhythmic deception, less poetic and more comic than that of the opening of the first movement. What the ear seems to catch is the beginning of a light subject in duple time:

Ex. 96

What actually happens is that the figures are set in cross-rhythm against 3–8 bars, and it is not until an extra note (C♯) followed by an emphatic accent occurs that we begin to see how the metre displays itself:

Ex. 97

But Beethoven is in no hurry to give up his game, for the next phrase is once more designed to upset our impression:

Ex. 98

The whole group of the main rondo theme closes in G major. The first episode bursts in rudely with a loud chord of the dominant of E minor, in which key a soft answer follows. This terse colloquy is repeated four times, and the return of the subject is brought about very quickly, as though there were no point in keeping up such an abrupt altercation for any length of time.

After this first return a new presentation of Ex. 98 leads to the second episode, which now is uncommonly long. It is a lyrical interlude, interrupted by some grumbling accents in the middle, but kept going at such length that one cannot help seeing the composer's reluctance to let it go. The third return is humorously frustrated at first by new modulations that make the main theme go off the rails; after a perplexed pause it is started again and proceeds normally, Ex. 98 again leading to an episode, or what at first appears to be an episode. As it turns out, it cannot properly be called that, but should rather be regarded as a very long coda, since there is no further return of the theme as a whole. Only broken allusions to it finish off the rondo when at last the episodic coda, with its entirely new material, has run its course.

INTERLUDE IV

THE TURN OF THE CENTURY

THE date 1800, which now becomes relevant as that of the next sonata to be discussed, is significant. Among the works written by Beethoven during the last year of the eighteenth century, including the first set of string quartets, the third piano Concerto, the Septet and the horn Sonata, none is so prophetic as the B flat major piano Sonata, Op. 22. This will hardly surprise the reader, to whom it has already been pointed out that Beethoven's pianistic style was always in advance of his handling of any other medium. Even the string quartet, to which he came in the end as the most congenial vehicle for his thought, after he had all but abandoned the keyboard instrument, did not express the last phase of his style nearly as early as the piano. The *Hammerclavier* Sonata, Op. 106, for instance, the finale of which is a very characteristic and mature example of his last manner, preceded the Quartet in E flat major, Op. 127, the first work in that form belonging decidedly to his third period, by no less than six years.

It is true that the discrepancy in style between the Op. 22 Sonata and the Op. 18 Quartets is not very conspicuously great. The latter have their moments of unrest, of impatience with the amiable formality of the eighteenth century, while the finale of the Sonata, for all the spikiness of some of the incidents, is on the whole bland and decorous enough. Beethoven is willing just once more to make polite conversation for aristocratic patrons here. Still, one feels that this courtly rondo is a last concession and that the composer is itching all the time to break out into some unequivocal language ('Lobkowitzian ass!' perhaps), whereas in the Quartets the outspoken passages strike one as less deliberate than the general tone of the polished writing which is evidently aimed at as, for that period, the ideal quartet style.

It is in the third piano Concerto that we see most clearly the clash between the old, pre-Revolution world and that brave new democracy which seemed to Beethoven so much preferable, though to us the choice appears far less simple to-day. That clash is reflected there in the relations between the orchestra and the solo instrument. The piano is all for new departures, while the behaviour of the body of strings, wind and percussion instruments is comparatively conventional. But if the conflict is confined mainly to matters affecting the medium in the Concerto, in the Sonata, where the piano stands alone, the struggle for freedom shows in the musical idiom itself.

It is a curious attitude in which we find Beethoven at the passing of the eighteenth century into the nineteenth. If we could only for a moment place ourselves there and obliterate all knowledge of the glories that came after, this farewell to a gracious old world—gracious on the surface at any rate—and this setting forth into another that presaged rough manners and monstrous inventions might well make us wistful. Even Beethoven did not know what was to come, though he was well enough aware of what he wanted, and for all his defiant start in the B flat major Sonata, there is something strangely, touchingly pensive about its gentler moods and about those phases of its expression which must once have been regarded as the more civilized and likable aspects of the work.

The first movement is a very determined farewell, and one admires it for its downrightness; yet it is pleasant to feel that a concession to eighteenth-century courtliness is made at the last in the finale, and made so graciously and considerately. There will be time enough, the closing movement of the Sonata seems to say, for blustering new enterprise in the new century; the faddish formality of the old one may as well be let down gently at the end, if not without a few good-natured quips which rather enhance the value of the tribute, though they make it clear enough that what is being thus humoured will never be expected to yield significant inspiration again.

For it is true, I think, that while the suavity of this rondo is still a heartfelt personal utterance, any movement in the later, nineteenth-century Beethoven which reverts to something like an earlier manner is merely atavistic. The minuets in the E flat major piano Sonata, Op. 31 No. 3, and in the eighth Symphony, for instance, are affectionate tributes to the past made without involving the emotions at all deeply, and the urbane rondo of the G major Sonata, Op. 31 No. 1, rounds off a work that is singularly disappointing. In short, once the eighteenth century was over, Beethoven's heart was never again in it, though he might occasionally be sentimental about it. But this message to it, just before it expired, was made in all sincerity with the Op. 22 Sonata.

It is almost pathetic to see how Beethoven's recollection of the musical manners he had learnt in his youth is here again and again interfered with by the creative impatience of the impulsive and progressive man of thirty. The two middle movements, especially, show him torn by the choice between intransigent expression and formal presentation. There is a kind of suppressed passion about the *adagio*, where a determination to use a strictly traditional form is at loggerheads with the romantic poetry of the language, while the minuet wavers between the smooth, amiable sociability of the similar movement in the contemporary Septet and explosive, cross-accented episodes that show contempt of the genteel composure which, by this time, Beethoven knew to be merely an outward show. There had been plenty of events in the last decade of the century to reveal the seething lava under the shapely crust, and by 1800 it was rapidly becoming clear to him that something of the inward agitation might as well be openly expressed.

The minuet of Op. 22 and its trio compress within a few bars all that the turn of the century meant, artistically speaking, to Beethoven. They are like the two hands of a signpost pointing opposite ways, to the world of serenades and divertimenti on the one side, to that of *Prometheus* and the *Eroica* and *Fidelio*—a world in which personality asserts itself at the expense of society—on the other. But as it happens, this little movement makes a close link between two other sonatas which may be usefully taken to illustrate the eighteenth-century and the nineteenth-century Beethoven respectively: the little Op. 49 No. 2, which is at least four years earlier than Op. 22, and the so-called *Sonata appassionata*, Op. 57, which is as many or more years later. I have already said that the minuet itself is akin in feeling to that in the Septet, of which the second movement in Op. 49 No. 2 is an alternative version (see Ex. 191, page 146). On the other hand the impetuous semiquaver accompaniment of the trio section in Op. 22 is built on very much the same figures as the principal theme of the precipitate finale of Op. 57 (see Ex. 210, page 166). We have here three sonatas which form a kind of interrelated triptych and at the same time, looked at from the point of view of the year 1800, perfectly represent the past, present and future of Beethoven's art.

SONATA IN B FLAT MAJOR, Op. 22 (1800)
(B.S.S. RECORDS, VOL. V)

THIS *fin-de-siècle* Sonata bears a dedication to Count Browne, who was a Russian nobleman, in spite of the English look of his name. Beethoven had known him at least two or three years earlier, for he had already dedicated to him the three string Trios Op. 9, published in July 1798, and inscribed to the countess the three piano Sonatas Op. 10, which came out in print the following September. It is clear that Beethoven had a high regard for the count and thought him worthy of the best of his creative efforts, for the string Trios were offered '*au premier Mécène de sa Muse*' as '*la meilleure de ses œuvres*.'

The B flat major Sonata, published by Hoffmeister & Kühnel of Leipzig in 1802—a couple of years after its composition—was another work of which Beethoven thought a great deal. He said it 'had washed itself' (*hat sich gewaschen*), which, as Sir Donald Tovey suggests, might be freely translated into 'takes the cake' or regarded as akin to Stevenson's proud announcement that *The Master of Ballantrae* was 'a howling cheese.'

Allegro con brio.—The two rapping figures with which the first movement opens look at first sight like a survival of the fanfares built on the tonic chord with which eighteenth-century music so frequently began: the kind of forcible digging in the ribs administered to people seated at dinner, reminding them that the table-music was about to begin, that conversation and the rattling of knives and forks had better be subdued:

Ex. 99

But this nudge is very Beethovenish indeed. The figure is made memorable at once by the insertion of that semiquaver ornament, which makes it into a distinctive and fertile thematic feature. It is characteristic, too, that the call to attention is singularly emphatic without being loud. One is so accustomed to its peremptoriness that whenever this Sonata is played one has to remind oneself carefully that the opening is marked *piano*. The first impulse is always to hit out with great energy. Generally speaking, it is always worth remembering that Beethoven can be astonishingly downright without noise, can bring his fist down in a velvet glove.

The motif is immediately used for that swinging ascent to the only melodic feature that belongs to the first-subject group:

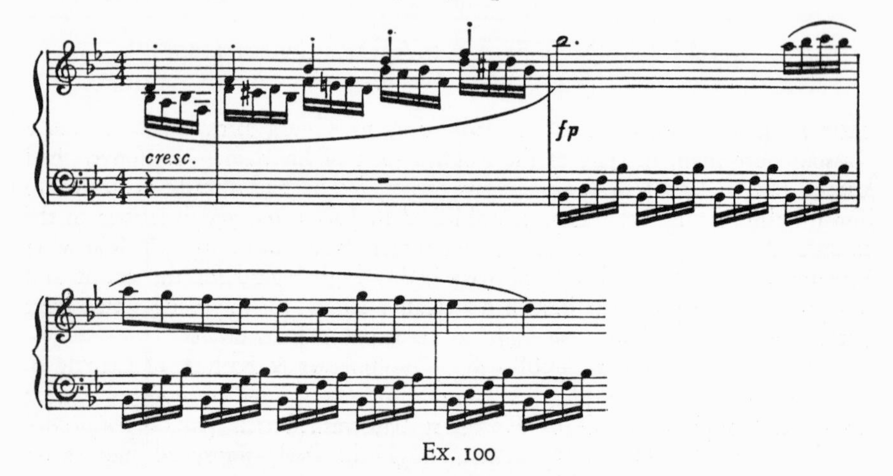

Ex. 100

The tone here swells impulsively, but at the crest of the rising phrase it is at once subdued and the melody enters softly. Only when it is heard a second time, an octave lower, does it increase in force. It plunges hard upon a chain of figures derived from Ex. 99, but now makes a tonic-and-dominant pattern. This veering towards the dominant naturally arouses expectations of an immediate approach to the second subject. But let us see with what infinite subtlety Beethoven delays this by a transition that shows as convincingly as any other passage in his music, and perhaps more clearly than most, his immensely keen sensitiveness to the significance of key manipulations. (Modern composers who choose atonal—keyless—music for their vehicle must be prepared with great compensations for their inability to produce any interplay of tonalities.)

A lengthy passage is well worth quoting to make Beethoven's procedure clear:

[*Continued*

Ex. 101

The first bar shown above turns decidedly from B flat major into F major, with E♮ establishing itself as the leading note of the latter key. Yet Beethoven, by carefully refraining from strengthening the F major implication by means of harmony, still leaves us with a lingering impression that his two-octave leap of Fs may possibly represent a dominant of B flat major. The entry in the bass of the motif from Ex. 99 would seem to dispel all doubt; we are surely in B flat major again. All the same, the chromatic inflections that follow in the third bar of Ex. 101, with an E♮ again, raise a suspicion that F major is after all not very far off. But still the composer goes on tantalizing us, for in the next bar he once again emphasizes E♭. However, just as we wonder what is at last to decide the issue between these two keys, he resolves to step entirely away from both of them for a moment, and then, surprisingly, to approach F major by quite another route. For in bars 5 and 6 he now modulates circuitously to C major, only to make us realize an instant later—by the introduction of a B♭—that this C is the dominant of F major, the key for his second subject. He has thus lingered on the threshold of his dominant tonality for some time, turned this way and that, and in the end reached his new subject by the back door, so to speak.

It is all very well explaining such things technically. What matters, though, is that this hinting at various keys and deferring a decision has, in the hands of a master who makes use of it at precisely the right moment, an effect of extraordinary dramatic tension. It is not too far-fetched to compare the incident just described to the uncertainty before a crisis in a drama. The state of mind into which the listener is put here may be said to be not unlike that of a spectator who watches Othello at a stage of dawning suspicion, not yet convinced of Desdemona's guilt, but no longer sure of her innocence. I am not, of course, hinting at any sort of programme in Beethoven's music, much less at an actual parallel between this Sonata and *Othello*; but taken merely as abstract artistic phenomena, the two cases may be regarded as comparable.

The last bar of the example above shows an effect of a purely pianistic order, worlds removed from the harpsichord style that was but a relic of the vanishing century by the time this Sonata was composed. The astonishing passage goes on for five bars, with the stabbing accents coming closer together in the last, and then the long-delayed second-subject group appears, in unmistakable F major, yet with a C major shading (B♮) retained to the last moment before its entry:

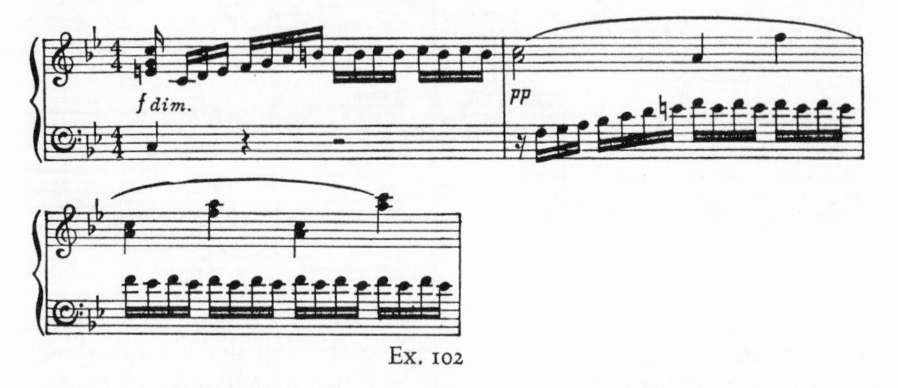

Ex. 102

Here two things are interesting: the way in which Beethoven uses the scale that links the second subject to the preceding transition as an accompanying feature to the subject itself, and his derivation of a vital thematic idea from nothing more than the common chord of F major. The latter procedure, of course, enhances the effect of the succeeding modulations, which take the shape of a counterpart to bars 4 to 6 of Ex. 101. They are set over continuously running semiquavers. But the music bends back to F major, for the second-subject group has yet to be completed in that key with another theme which is melodic and rhythmic, in contrast to what has immediately preceded, where harmony and texture were the chief attractions:

Ex. 103

(The right hand only is shown here; the left plays the same an octave lower.) A curious feeling of unsettlement is most artfully created just where the musical idea itself tends to be a little commonplace by the displacement of the accent from the first to the third beat. The effect is that of the insertion of a 2–4 bar into the 4–4 motion, and no doubt the passage would have been written thus by a modern composer (I note the right hand only and show the end of the cadence preceding Ex. 103):

Ex. 104

At the end of this incident another three half-bars would then have restored the balance:

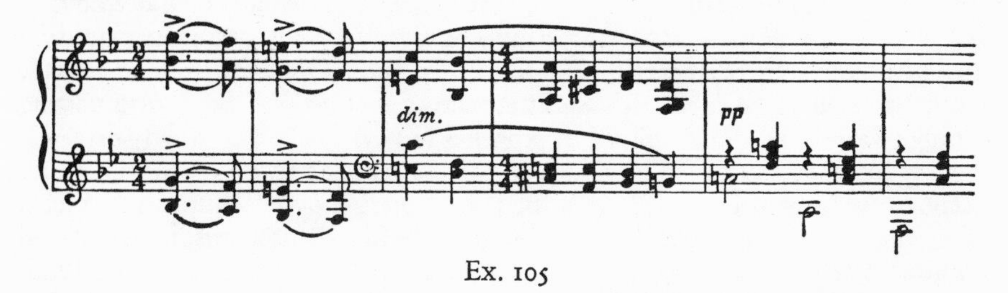

Ex. 105

This, at any rate, shows quite clearly what is intended by the rhythmic contraction, by that crowding together of the musical pulse aimed at by Beethoven, though it was not the custom of his time to draw the attention of the eye to such metrical subtleties. He wrote the whole movement down in common time, the effect to the ear being, needless to say, the same. The idea of which Ex. 103 is the opening is stated over again in a new rhythm broken up by syncopation, and the exposition is then concluded by another page of music that lays stress on pianistic brilliance (arpeggios and broken octaves). However, two new motifs appear towards the end—new, yet relevant to what has gone before:

Ex. 106

Ex. 107

It is difficult not to think that the last must have been in Wagner's mind when he wrote Wotan's wild evocation of Erda in *Siegfried*, for we see here, in a kind of black-and-white cartoon, as it were, what appears there in full theatrical display:

Ex. 108

The exposition closes with a cadence into which a reference to the semiquaver figure of Ex. 99 is ingeniously drawn. The whole is repeated.

It is with the last two themes (Exx. 106 and 107), episodic though they may have appeared at first, that the long working-out section is chiefly concerned, especially the Wagnerian ascent and descent. But the motto figure of Ex. 99 also plays a very important part, and the hearer should particularly note Beethoven's skilful way of gradually liquefying it into figures of accompaniment, played by the right hand over references to Ex. 107 in the left. Once the brilliant passage work has established itself, the interest becomes modulatory, the music passing through various keys and oblique approaches to keys over a bass slowly descending by chromatic steps. The figure of Ex. 99 remains in evidence so far, but becomes submerged by arpeggios at the point where Ex. 107 returns in the form of a muttering, smothered bass. This, too, gradually loses its identity until nothing is left but a rising scale leading to a pause on the dominant-seventh chord of B flat major. Thus the ear is at one and the same time led to expect the return of the tonic key and made to long for a definite thematic statement.

Both occur at once at the opening of the recapitulation, which could not have been brought about with a greater sense of the art of arousing expectation. Scarcely anything now happens that is not entirely in accordance with traditional sonata form, though the transition to the second subject, which now has to be in the tonic key, shows how infallibly Beethoven can apply a new touch of the chisel just at the place that most requires rehandling. For the rest, so normal a recapitulation, which differs from the exposition only in keeping more consistently to the main key, is merely like a fuller view of something already contemplated as a whole before the detailed examination of the working-out was undertaken, an examination thanks to which it is now more fully understood. The awareness of a greater surface of fundamental tonality (B flat major) is rather like a full front view of a piece of architecture, obtained at last after a first survey made from an angle. Indeed, the interest we take in the exposition and recapitulation of a classical sonata is much the same as that shown in some beautiful plastic object beheld from two different viewpoints.

Adagio con molt' espressione.—It has been observed (by Paul Bekker) that this slow movement points forward directly to the nocturnes of the romantic period, and it is true that Beethoven's emphasis on singing melody, which was none too congenial to the early piano and far from usual in its music, is one of those prophetic touches which show a great genius guessing future achievements and insisting on them before their time. If we take John Field as a middle link, we may without extravagance see a direct connection with Chopin in this *adagio.* Chopin would have dissolved the rigid accompaniment into more fluid, more congenially pianistic figurations, but it was Field who showed him how to do it, though he would himself, standing half-way between two worlds, still occasionally be content with accompaniments less exclusively suited to the keyboard. As for Beethoven, the left-hand chords with which this movement opens are merely music that happened to be set down for the piano; they are not music of necessity imagined in pianistic terms. Beethoven did not say: 'Here is a piano, let's write something for it'; he said: 'I must write this music: the piano will do very well for it.'

Here is the opening of the first subject—for the movement is in a quite regular sonata form:

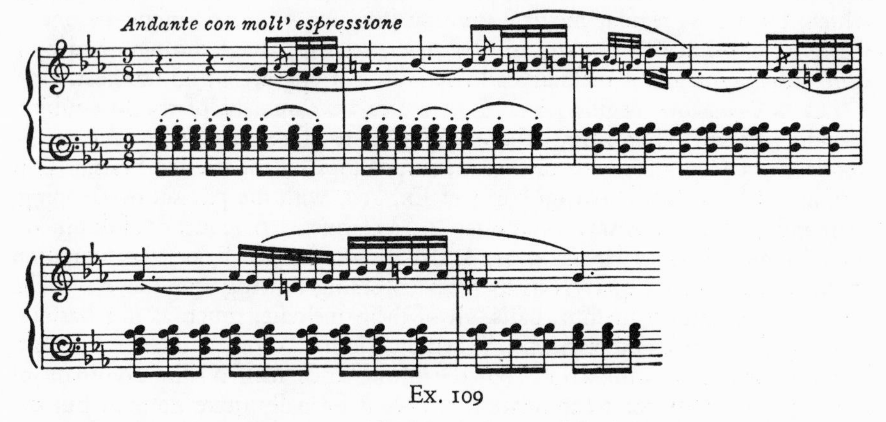

Ex. 109

Now this melody is, in spite of its ornamental richness, essentially a vocal tune, transformed into instrumental terms by an elaboration very similar to that which Chopin applied to his recollection of familiar vocal music, sometimes Polish folksongs and sometimes operatic arias, the most inspiring of which he found in Bellini. Field, too, transformed vocal types of melody into true keyboard music (one of his nocturnes [1] is in the shape not only of an operatic air, but of a whole operatic scena), and he might very well be imagined to have written the melody just quoted, if we happened to be ignorant of the fact that Beethoven did so. However, while Field *could* have set it over an accompaniment similiar to Beethoven's, it is not likely that he *would*. But play Beethoven's tune over some such accompaniment as this:

Ex. 110

and a Fieldish, indeed, almost a Chopinesque nocturne stands before you.

The first subject is exceptionally long for a continuous melodic formation. It covers nine bars of slow 9–8 time, not counting the repetition of the final cadence and two extra bars of peroration. A transitional subject in the same key follows.

[1] C major, No. 14 in Breitkopf & Härtel's edition.

leading over a purposely ambiguous modulation to B flat major for the second subject. This is rounded off first by an ornamental demi-semiquaver passage which, but for its regular metrical division into two 9–8 bars, might be one of Chopin's cadenza-like *fioriture*, and by an expressive passage distinguished by a rising bass figure and a melodic cadence with a strong accent off the beat.

The working-out begins here. It is a free development of the first-subject melodic phrases. Three times the opening figure of Ex. 109 is heard over the dominant of C minor, with discordant suspensions on the stressed beats. This is followed by a duet based on bar 4 of Ex. 109, with the phrases overlapping, as though played, let us say, by an oboe and a clarinet. A sequence of dominant sevenths modulates as far afield as A flat minor, in which key the figuration changes, the repeated quavers in the bass becoming flowing semiquavers. The music is now strictly in three parts, all of them melodic, much as if a bassoon had joined the oboe and clarinet. When the trio has become a quartet, a second bassoon coming in with a low B♭, the music finds itself on the dominant of E flat major, ready for recapitulation. This is formally quite normal, but the passage-work in the right hand is frequently elaborated, very much as it might be in a Chopin nocturne.

Menuetto.—This movement is particularly interesting in view of what has been said in the essay preceding the annotations to this Sonata. Small as it is, it shows Beethoven in the twofold act of looking back upon the music of the eighteenth century and predicting that of the nineteenth. Broadly speaking, the minuet itself is music of the past, the trio music of the future, though there is an episode in the middle of the former which may be said to stand for the present —the very urgent present Beethoven was so determined to face.

The bland opening strain is akin in character to the well-known minuet in the Septet, Op. 20, of which a pianistic version appears in the little Sonata Op. 49 No. 2. In none of the preceding ten sonatas had Beethoven written so conventional a dance movement as this appears to be for the first eight bars. He had, in fact, described only two movements as minuets at all, one in Op. 2 No. 1 and another in Op. 10 No. 3, neither of which was much of a minuet in anything but name. Both are typical early Beethovenian scherzos, not in the least like dance movements of the suite or divertimento sort, as is the minuet in the Septet, a work that is very much of a divertimento or serenade.

The episode that hints at a break with the past will be easily recognized by the undulating passage which swells like a wave and breaks into an emphatic cadence. The first strain is then charmingly varied—again in a kind of concerted wind-instrument style—and the minuet closes with a quiet afterthought.

The stormy trio in G minor, with its angry rumblings in the continuous semiquaver left-hand passages and the cutting accents off the beat in the right-hand chords, is like a gathering of revolutionary forces. In a musical sense, it certainly is subversive: a violent overthrow of the placid courtliness of the minuet.

Allegretto.—The finale is a last farewell to convention, with here and there a sign of straining at the leash. Its principal theme is suave and elegant; the episodes show some audacity and impatience. On the whole, though, formality wins, and the piece is cut to a regular rondo pattern. The theme is, again, very extended. The following quotation shows but half of it:

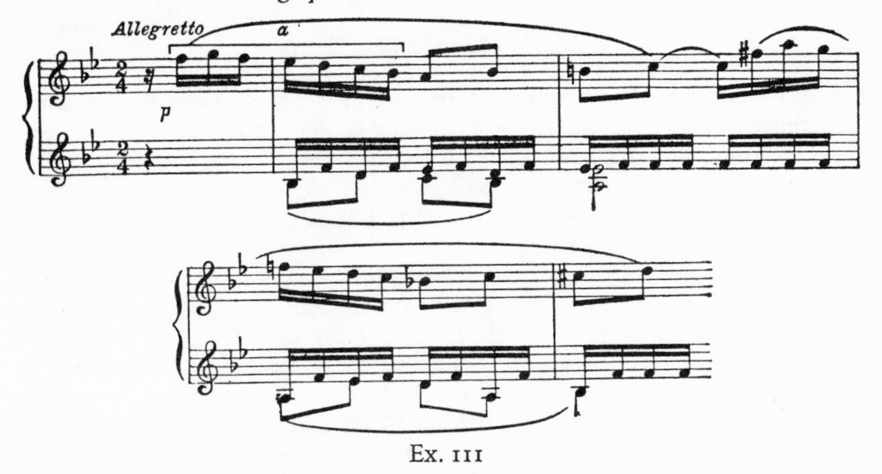

Ex. 111

It is repeated in octaves and has a long, ornamental final cadence. New material leads gradually to the first episode, the main features of which are demi-semiquaver arpeggios and modulations by whole-tone steps from G to D♭ in the bass. A bridge-passage is then constructed from the opening phrase (Ex. 111*a*) and makes for the first return of the subject by means of an unaccompanied right-hand passage which curiously anticipates a very similar incident in the third *Leonora* Overture—the famous and very difficult rush of strings in the coda. It is shown here as it appears in the Sonata:

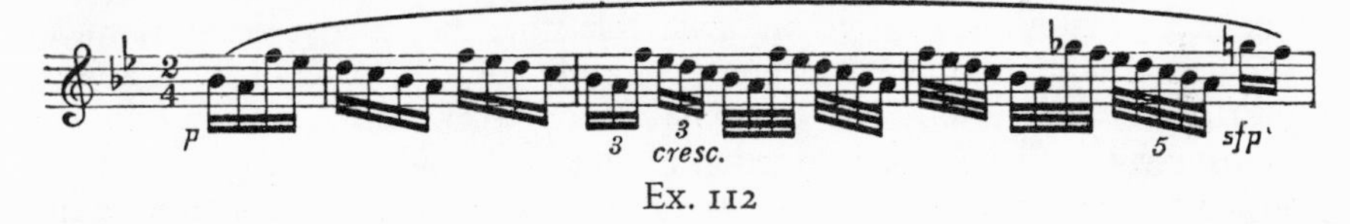

Ex. 112

Bar 1 of Ex. 111 follows on what has just been quoted, slightly modified by details of figuration. The next episode begins with an energetic, strongly rhythmic theme, continued with brilliant demi-semiquaver work, treats the rhythmic theme contrapuntally with a figure of different pattern, and returns by way of the demi-semiquavers and a charmingly modulated transition to the main theme once more. This now appears in the left hand at first, with a broken dominant pedal note in the right, but reverts later to something like its original presentation, though rather more lavishly decorated. The first episode returns in the tonic key, in other words as a second sonata subject. After one more restatement of the rondo theme, with new variations, there is a coda based mainly on the rhythmic theme of the second episode. The passing of the subject into the bass at the end was not so much of a novelty in Beethoven's time as might appear. The device is found in Mozart's piano sonatas.

INTERLUDE V

NEW WAYS AND MEANS

THE end of the eighteenth century, not too roughly speaking, marks the beginning of Beethoven's new approach to the pianoforte sonata, an approach he may best be seen to make with the *sonata quasi una fantasia*. The first two works so called are the two Sonatas Op. 27, composed in 1801. A new orientation, however, is to be noticed already in the A flat major Sonata, Op. 26, which may therefore be briefly studied here as a point of departure.

The use of a set of variations as a first movement was not an innovation. Mozart's A major Sonata (K. 331) of 1778 is a famous precedent. Nor is Op. 26 in the 'fantasia' form. Still, for Beethoven himself the variation movement was a novelty, and still more so was the use of a funeral march for a slow movement, not so much because it happened to take that shape, which is after all only the slow counterpart of old dance forms with contrasting trio sections, but because he expressly gave it the title of *Marcia funebre* and suggested a programme-musical connotation by adding the description *sulla morte d'un eroe*. Whether he had the death of some hero of his own in mind we do not know, although the story connected with its composition, to be told presently, seems to discountenance any such assumption; but his title indicates clearly enough that a new note of personal concern was beginning to creep into his music, for an artist of Beethoven's stamp does not deliberately hint at an emotional afterthought unless he really has one.

For Beethoven's eighteenth-century sonatas—a classification which happens to suit them here—the conventional forms and sequences of movements had sufficed. Three or four movements were his invariable rule, the scherzo being admitted or omitted at will and more than once, curiously enough, made to revert at least nominally to the minuet. In three-movement works slow pieces were not always present. The slow introduction of the *Sonate Pathétique*, Op. 13, was no innovation either, and although it would be easy to imagine that the daring device of letting it recur in the middle of the *allegro* was without precedent, it may in fact be found in a G minor Sonata by Clementi, Op. 34 No. 2, composed some ten years earlier.

We may, then, look upon Op. 26, Beethoven's first nineteenth-century piano sonata, as a boldly novel work, not yet of the 'fantasia' type, but pointing that way. It is to be described as new not so much in form as in the ways and means employed, both in technical and in expressive matters. This is shown most clearly by the variations, for all that Beethoven does not depart from the eighteenth-century practice of embroidering the theme without materially changing its structure, except in the remarkable fifteen bars of coda to be referred to in the analysis that follows. If the framework of the melody is here left much more plainly discernible by Beethoven than he leaves it in later sets of variations, such as those on a theme by Diabelli, Op. 120, those in the finale of the last piano sonata or those in the slow movement of the ninth Symphony, the pianistic foliage, so to speak, that overgrows this scaffolding has become noticeably richer and juicier than anything we know in eighteenth-century variations, where the drier harpsichord manner still shows its influence. This luxuriance of the pianistic lay-out is partly due to the developments undergone by the instrument round about the turn of the century, but also, and at least as much, to the growing imaginative power and the surer grasp of the keyboard Beethoven showed year by year, which developments were, of course, themselves conditioned to some extent by the improvements discovered by pianoforte makers. Only a composer who took delight in new instrumental resources and exulted in his masterful way of handling them could have written music so essentially pianistic as these variations, music which it is impossible to imagine transferred without loss of effect to any other instrumental medium, even that of the full orchestra.

The scherzo, though it distinctly foreshadows the mood of the *allegretto* in the 'Moonlight' Sonata, Op. 27 No. 2, is if anything less novel than the similar movement in the E major Sonata, Op. 14 No. 1, of 1799, and scarcely more so even than that in Op. 10 No. 2 of 1798. The final rondo, on the other hand, exploits an entirely new manner. It is the kind of piece in almost continual semiquaver motion (though not made into a *moto perpetuo* with pedantic deliberation) which we meet again, more mature but similar in character and mood, in the F major Sonata in two movements, Op. 54.

But the outstanding feature of the Op. 26 Sonata is unquestionably the funeral march, with its bold use of a key (A flat minor) at that time regarded as tolerable on the piano alone, on account of its tempered scale, and with enharmonic modulations that would be unacceptable if played in just intonation with the sharps and flats as Beethoven wrote them. (He transposed the march a tone and a half up when he orchestrated it for the occasion to be mentioned presently.) Even a commentator who usually scorns any kind of literary interpretation of music that can be self-sufficing draws attention to the programmatic nature of this movement by referring to the trio section as 'obviously representing salutes fired over the grave.' That Beethoven did not have a particular hero in mind to whom he wished to pay a personal homage seems to be proved by the fact that the composition of this march was suggested to him by an opera in which the death of one of the characters (Patroclus) is announced to the strains of a funeral march.

That opera was *Achilles* by Ferdinando Paer (1771–1839), which Beethoven heard in the composer's company in Vienna on 6th June 1801, if he attended the first performance, or very soon after that date. The story goes that he turned to Paer when the funeral march was being played and said in effect: 'How beautiful! how interesting! I shall have to compose that.' His freedom from jealousy being always as conspicuous as his lack of good manners, the tale may quite easily be believed. At any rate, his funeral march exists and the fact that he heard *Achilles* just before its composition is established. A study of that opera even shows that it exercised a certain amount of influence on him when he wrote *Fidelio*, though not as much as the operas of Cherubini, which he frankly admired to the point of emulation. In this connection one feature of

Achilles at least is very striking: a trumpet fanfare very closely resembling the signal of the approaching rescue in Beethoven's opera, which was produced in its first version four and a half years later. Paer's fanfare is, however, heard first close at hand and at a greater distance afterwards, and it makes a remarkable effect by being played in D the first time and in B flat the second, a device not unlike that employed by Verdi in the *Aida* march.

Achilles is on the whole a typical example of the aftermath of the Italian *opera seria* which Gluck at first cultivated and afterwards repudiated, and of which Mozart produced two specimens that have never been regarded as truly representative of his art: *Idomeneo* and *La clemenza di Tito*. The species may be said to have finally died with Spontini, unless one likes to regard Wagner's *Rienzi* as in a sense a descendant from it, for all that it owes at least as much to the French *grand opéra* of the Meyerbeer type. At its best *Achilles* comes near the dramatic pathos of *Idomeneo* in Mozart's less intimate moments, though as a whole it shares the frigidity of that master's later and less appealing *opera seria*. It is often beautifully and hardly ever extravagantly vocal, and much of the music has a kind of current of simple strength running through it that is by no means without nobility and impressiveness. What the opera lacks is humanity and characterization: all the personages in it sing precisely the same kind of music and no situation can essentially affect the composer's collected competence.

All the same, the work is still interesting, and since the funeral march, which is played when news is brought to Achilles that Patroclus has been slain by Hector, incited Beethoven to write a similar piece, if not indeed two—for the slow movement of the *Eroica* Symphony may be regarded as the outcome of the same impulse—the reader may like to see a few bars from Paer's march quoted here. It opens thus:

Ex. E

and it goes on in much the same vein throughout, for there is no contrasting trio section. The resemblance to Beethoven, it will be seen, is only quite superficial, though the following cadence containing the conventional 'pathetic' harmony of the period:

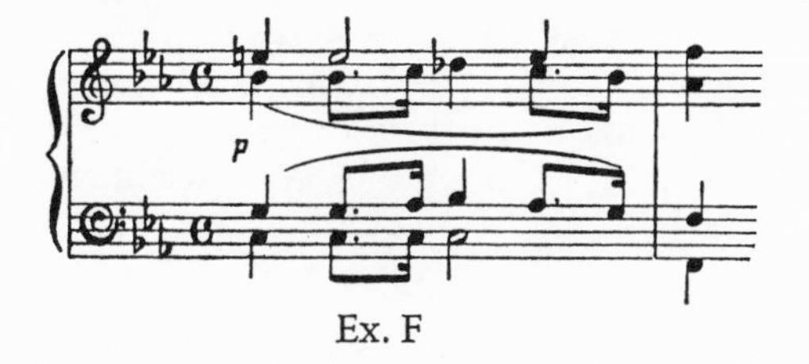

Ex. F

may well be regarded as the direct model for Beethoven's poignant incident shown on page 99 as Ex. 124.

Three years later, in the 'Waldstein' Sonata, Op. 53, Beethoven is seen to be making an advance in form similar to that we have just seen him make in the matter of ways and means. He is there actually discovered making his conquest of the two-movement sonata, a deliberately planned specimen of which he was to produce in the work in F major bearing the very next opus number. He originally contemplated three full-length movements for the 'Waldstein' Sonata, but cut out the slow movement and published it separately, as will be gathered later on from the notes on that work, putting in its place a short introduction to the finale. Thus did he prepare himself for that dual form which served him so admirably for four of the most characteristic of the later sonatas.

SONATA IN A FLAT MAJOR, Op. 26 (1801)
(B.S.S. RECORDS, VOL. IX)

THE work whose curious history and significant position in Beethoven's catalogue has just been discussed was published on 3rd March 1802, by Cappi of Vienna, with a dedication to Prince Carl von Lichnowsky. It is in a way, as we have seen, the most significant composition written by Beethoven in 1801, a year not very fruitful in great music for other media than the pianoforte, and although the two sonatas in fantasia form that followed it are at least as interesting, they obviously owe much of their new boldness and freedom to the experience gained with the work now under notice.

But if no other work composed in 1801 meant a greater advance in Beethoven's development than this Op. 26, it is interesting to recall here one written the preceding year, the first performance of which took place nearly a year before this Sonata was published. This was the Ballet, *Die Geschöpfe des Prometheus*, produced at the Burgtheater in Vienna on 28th March 1801. Its connection with the Sonata is obvious, if indirect: it contains the theme Beethoven used in 1804 for the finale of the *Eroica* Symphony, and the funeral march in that Symphony has often been regarded as the second outcome of Beethoven's playful threat to Paer to 'compose that,' the march in the Sonata being the first. At any rate, the slow movement in the Sonata may justifiably be regarded as a kind of sketch or exercise for the greater one in the Symphony.

The earlier funeral march was orchestrated by the composer in 1814 for use as incidental music in a drama by one Duncker, entitled *Leonora Prohaska*, which was never produced, the censor having banned it on account of its subversive glorification of political freedom. Not having a scheme of tonalities between different movements to consider, Beethoven transposed the march a tone and a half up, into B minor, in order to write in keys more convenient to orchestral instruments.

Andante con variazioni.—The five variations are built on an extended theme in three sections of which this is the first strain:

Ex. 113

It is repeated with a very slight elaboration and a full close in place of the half-close at the end. A middle section modulating by way of a descending sequence makes a contrast both of melody and of key—a turn of phrase of a kind that is easily memorable and therefore readily identifiable when it occurs again in varied form. The theme is rounded off by a return of the first section, stated only once this time and with the harmony of the full close laid out in a slightly different form.

Structurally the variations keep so close to the theme that it could hardly escape the least attentive of listeners even when the decorations grow as exuberant as in the second variation or when the harmony changes, as it does in the third. Variation I intersperses the melody with little arpeggios on the first beat and spreads it more widely over the keyboard.

The second variation looks as modern on paper as one of Schumann's *Variations symphoniques*, and indeed as far as the instrumental treatment goes it is ahead of anything that could have been effectively played on the earliest piano-fortes, not to mention the harpsichord or clavichord. The syncopated right-hand chords and octaves are very modern—relatively speaking—and the wide intervals in the following passages daring in the way they display the strain shown in the second half of Ex. 113 in disguise in the middle of the keyboard:

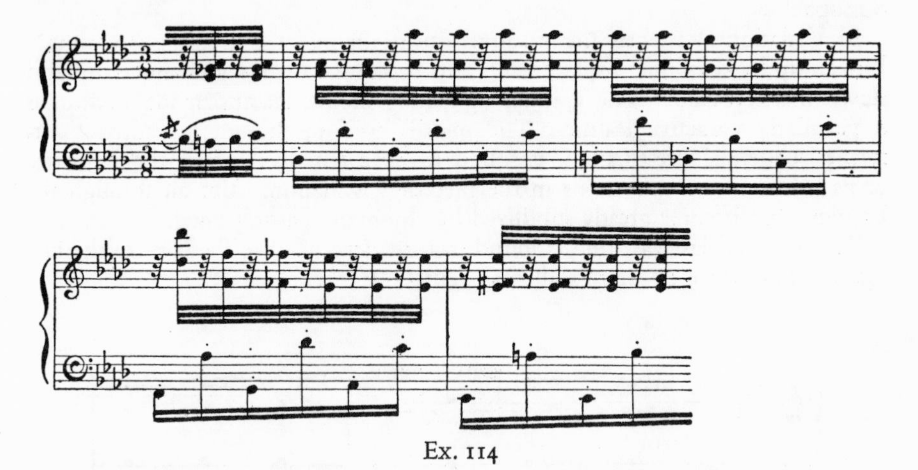

Ex. 114

A second glance at this quotation will show that the notes are repeated exactly as before, but for octave and time displacements, and this is in fact what happens throughout the present variation.

The third variation, in A flat minor, is very interesting. As it comes half-way through the movement, it is taken farthest away from the original form of the theme, thus giving the impression of a central peak we have been gradually climbing to gain a new view, and from which we are as gradually to descend again. It is in the middle section that the fresh outlook becomes especially fascinating. Whereas it stood thus in the first statement of the theme:

Ex. 115

with a downward sequence following, it is now given this new form:

Ex. 116

the sequence being transformed into a wider modulatory step that gives the music a wholly new turn. The variants of the chief strain of the melody, enclosing the passage just quoted, are syncopated in the right hand throughout.

In Variation IV, where the music returns to the major, everything is curiously broken up by rhythmic displacements and by constant capricious moves up and down the keyboard. The gradual tightening of the accompanying rhythm is a peculiarly attractive feature. The middle section, though it returns to its former sequential presentation, is found to have remained under the influence of its harmonic complications in the preceding variation. But all through the harmony has become greatly subtilized by chromatic passing notes.

The fifth and last variation is found to have descended to the level of the first again. Except for its more elaborate figuration:

Ex. 117

Ex. 118

it resumes the harmonic and rhythmic simplicity of the earlier statements of the theme. But when Beethoven is so deliberately intent on keeping our attention comparatively disengaged, we may be pretty certain that he has a surprise up his sleeve. Sure enough, the surprise comes just when he seems to have arrived at the end of his theme for the last time, and when apparently there is nothing more to be said. What he does say, in fact, and not at all *zum Überfluss* (by way of superfluity), like Schumann's 'Eusebius,' is something quite new and unexpected. He tacks a coda of fifteen bars on to the end of the last variation, just to clinch matters conclusively, since there is no reason why one ordinary straightforward variation should be final rather than another, and since this one, without any particular qualifications for it, happens to have been chosen to act as conclusion.

This is the theme of the coda:

Ex. 119

It is not nearly as independent as it appears at first. Apart from balancing the composer's whole design wonderfully by being itself in the form of a tiny variation (for the melody quoted above is immediately repeated in a more decorated form), it may be regarded as being directly derived from a telescoped version of the main theme (Ex. 113), as the following dissection of Ex. 119 will show:

Ex. 120

Molto allegro.—The scherzo opens, very curiously, not in its own key, A flat major, but in that of the dominant, E flat major, and even then the first chord (F minor) is one outside that key. We may thus safely assume that Beethoven meant to play one of his favourite games—that of momentarily confusing the ear as to harmonic issues. The pace being rapid, the witty point is made in a flash, and as the movement is explicitly called a scherzo, we need have no compunction in letting it amuse us.

At the fourth bar the right key establishes itself, and at the sixth it becomes clear:

Ex. 121

These two phrases are restated with variants, which is doubtless the reason why the first section remains unrepeated. The second, on the other hand, is given repeat signs, although it is three times as long even as written. But as it contains new variants of Ex. 121 after a statement of matter that is episodic rather than strictly thematic, the proportions are perfectly kept. Much of the new material, having begun by promising some striking features, turns out to be merely transitional. The main theme then returns in the left hand, with evenly running quaver passages above it. Afterwards the process is reversed, the theme being transferred to the top and the runs to the bass. This cannot be called a case of double counterpoint, however, the quaver passages not being reproduced with absolute fidelity after the exchange.

The trio section, in D flat major, is built wholly on trochaic figures in single bars (a minim followed by a crotchet), and its interest is harmonic rather than melodic. There is a beautiful final cadence set into relief by a *sforzando*. Each of the two short sections is repeated, and at the close there is a transitional passage referring to the scherzo theme (Ex. 121) and in fact forming a bridge for the return of the main section. The long repeat is not made this time.

Maestoso andante (*Marcia funebre sulla morte d' un eroe*).—The funeral march for Beethoven's unknown or purely imaginary hero begins as follows:

Ex. 122

A comparison with the first quotation from Paer's march shown as Ex. E on page 92 will at once reveal Beethoven's weightier and more significant manner, and his harmonic daring will strike the hearer a few bars later, when the following drastic turn occurs, surprisingly early in the movement:

Ex. 123

The final cadence shown at the beginning of the example above will be seen to stand in C flat major. To the ear alone the impression of what follows is simply a transition to C flat minor; but as that key would require seven flats and three double flats, Beethoven transforms it into B minor, which on the piano is the same thing, and he is in any case intent on finding somewhere in the course of the transition a short cut to the sharp side of the circle of keys. We discover in the course of a very few bars that he uses B minor as a stepping-stone to its nearest relative, D major, which is however very far from his original key. Arrived there, he at once turns towards the flat regions again, this time by way of a chord of the diminished seventh:

Ex. 124

This is the incident already referred to as being akin to Paer's conventional 'pathetic' cadence (Ex. F, page 93), and it will be seen once again how much more interesting Beethoven's device is. The first strain returns, exactly as in Ex. 122 at first, but with a change in the bass (note the shake) and a harmonic extension of the final cadence.

The trio, in A flat major, is quite short and so simple that it needs no illustration in music type. If we like to hear the 'salutes fired over the grave,' and rolling drums into the bargain, it will be quite easy to identify them—as easy as such things almost invariably are in music, once they have been pointed out by commentators. There are two sections of four bars, each of which is repeated.

The main section of the march returns exactly as before, but it is rounded off by a short coda this time. A curiously ambiguous tone prevails here, very far removed from any suggestion of mere official mourning, but hinting with great subtlety at the complex mixture of feelings attending a personal grief. The harmony clears serenely into an A flat major, but at the same time it is clouded by inflections of minor ninths, all of which may, if we like, convey to us an impression that although sorrow has become outwardly calm, it secretly stings the mourner all the more poignantly.

Perhaps such interpretations are far-fetched, but it is at any rate as legitimate to try to discover psychological subtleties in the art of Beethoven as to make it an excuse for the kind of picturesque illustration that has been attempted in the case of the trio section of this march. One thing is certain: although we know that Paer wrote funeral music to express the grief of Achilles over the death of Patroclus and have no information as to what personal emotions Beethoven may or may not express, a comparison of the two marches shows that the greater composer had a far richer store of imagination and poetry to draw upon, whether his inspiration was due to some particular 'situation' or sufficed of itself to engender great music. Beethoven was no doubt well aware of this, and that is what makes his remark about having to 'compose that' understandable and even excusable.

Allegro.—The finale is in rondo form—Beethoven's highly organized rondo form, which brings back the first episode like the second subject of a sonata-form movement. Apart from its formal construction, this movement is par-ticularly interesting by reason of its texture. Two principles are at work almost throughout: inversion and interchange. This can be shown at once by quoting the first dozen bars (which are continuous, although given here in three detached fragments). Here is the rondo subject:

Ex. 125

Next comes the inversion:

Ex. 126

where, it will be seen, the left-hand part is an exact reproduction of the opening of Ex. 125, except that it stands an octave lower, while the top part presents the same figures turned upside down and inside out. The interchange of parts that follows is easily seen if we compare the second half of Ex. 125 with this passage:

Ex. 127

Save for the fact that the tune first heard from the left hand now appears in octaves in the right, and that the harmony in the last bar is differently distributed, this is a case of strict double counterpoint. The music continues with another specimen of the same kind, complicated this time by the displacement of the two interchanging parts by means of a sequence:

Ex. 128

The music continues for a while with Ex. 128 and a fragment of Ex. 125; then comes the first episode, an undistinguished theme in itself, perhaps, but admirably suited to the composer's scheme because it enables him to refine still further upon his ingenious arrangement of parts. For here the principles of inversion and interchange are actually applied simultaneously:

Ex. 129

This episode, being treated as a second sonata subject, stands in the key of the dominant, E flat major. The main theme is then repeated exactly as before, the only difference being that the final E flat of the episode still lingers on in the bass when Ex. 125 returns, a point of great interest, a complete break between the episode and the return of the subject being thus avoided in the simplest possible way.

The second episode, consisting of two sections in C minor and G minor, strikingly new in character, need not be quoted. The next return of the theme is again unaltered, except for a new transition to the third episode at the end, necessitated by the fact that this takes the form of a restatement of the first (Ex. 129) as a second subject, and is therefore in the key of the tonic this time. A short coda, based on the opening figures of the main theme and gradually sinking down to *pianissimo*, brings the Sonata to a close.

SONATA IN E FLAT MAJOR, Op. 27 No. 1 (1801)
(B.S.S. RECORDS, VOL. II)

THE exact date of composition of this Sonata is uncertain, but it may with reasonable accuracy be placed in the year 1801, since it was published on 3rd March 1802. It is dedicated to the Princess Josephine Sophie von Liechtenstein, *née* von Fürstenberg, wife of General Field Marshal Prince von Liechtenstein. Beethoven first met her at Prince Lichnowsky's, and she became his pupil and one of his patrons. He must have been on as friendly terms with her as their respective positions would allow, for when his pupil Ries was conscripted in 1805 and found himself obliged to leave Vienna penniless, Beethoven wrote a letter to the princess asking her to assist the young musician.

The two Sonatas Op. 27, the second of which is the so-called 'Moonlight' Sonata, are the first works of Beethoven's to bear the significant title of *Sonata quasi una fantasia*. They show the composer emancipating himself from the classical sonata pattern and doing it as drastically as possible by substituting pieces in a freely chosen form for the traditional first movement that was always the most important part of a sonata, though not invariably in what we now call sonata form. In the first Sonata of Op. 27 Beethoven may be said to be looking back, in his opening movement, to the old suite form, in the second forward to that of the Schubertian impromptu or even the Mendelssohnian song without words.

Whence came this sudden decision, it may be asked, when Beethoven had already shown so surprising a mastery over a form which, without seeing any necessity to distort greatly, he never allowed to master him? The answer is that the change was not so very sudden after all. For one thing, the very ease with which he adjusted the strict form to his individual needs could not fail to lead him gradually to try its elasticity more and more daringly; for another, he made his preliminary advance by no means independently, but with the sanction of celebrated precedents.

The first definite break with the established first-movement form was, in fact, made by him in the Sonata preceding the present one, Op. 26, in A flat major; but that was not by any means an original departure on Beethoven's part. He uses the variation form for a first movement much as Mozart did before him. What he does contribute to the evolution of the sonata with absolute independence, however, is his way of transferring the most vital part of his musical discourse into the finale. Even this did not flash upon him suddenly: the last movement of the Op. 26 Sonata fails to compensate for the absence of a strict form in the first, for it is above all a brilliant virtuoso piece. But with Op. 27 No. 1 the second step is made towards a goal it would have been too much of a miraculous achievement to reach in a single stride even for so bold an artistic rebel. The finale of this Sonata, as we shall presently see, is at once the support and the chief aesthetic feature of its structure.

Andante—Allegro—Tempo primo.—The very choice of a slow pace for the opening movement is unusual, and even more so is the insertion of an entirely independent quick section in the middle. The *andante* is in the form, though not in the nature, of a dance, hardly more extended than an allemande or sarabande in a seventeenth-eighteenth-century suite, but with a slight thematic development unlike that of any music found in that species. The rhythmic pattern of the opening strain:

Ex. 130

will be found to permeate the whole, even the contrasting tune, the chief difference of which consists in the fact that it has an up-beat. Here are two of its characteristic forms:

Ex. 131

From the middle section based on these two fragments the main tune again detaches itself and is then repeated with two rhythmic alterations, the first transforming the two opening crotchets of the theme into four quavers, the second into eight semiquavers.

The *allegro* is an extremely simple dance tune in 6–8 time—a real dance this time, somewhat of the German country dance or *Ländler* type. One would expect to find this section among Beethoven's *Bagatelles* rather than in a sonata. Although it is in C major and thus closely connected with the main key by its relative minor—a sort of cousin once removed—it tends strongly towards E flat near the end and finishes in fact on an unresolved dominant seventh of that key.

This opens the way for the return of the *andante*, of which, however, only the main section is heard again, substantially as before, but with the right-hand and left-hand parts exchanged at each repetition of the two strains. The very short, tranquil coda is made only of chords over a tonic pedal. There is a pause on the final chord, but no actual break between this movement and the next.

Molto allegro e vivace.—In the C minor scherzo Beethoven seems to be deliberately restricting his music to a purely harmonic and rhythmic interest, for throughout the piece, including the trio, there is nothing that could be called a melody. The scherzo itself consists of a succession of groups of three crotchets, laid out in single notes (occasionally in octaves) for each hand and generally in contrary motion:

Ex. 132

It will be seen from this specimen, which shows the kind of figuration that persists throughout, that there is nothing more than two-part harmony at any point; but the motion is so rapid that for the ear the effect is that of listening to a series of complete chords. The notes pass as quickly as the shells and stones and bits of coloured glass in a kaleidoscope, and the result is that we do not perceive these fragments separately, but fused into a rich pattern. Needless to say, the effect of harmonic amplitude can be very easily heightened by means of the sustaining pedal; but it is questionable whether this ought to be used at all during this portion of the Sonata, for it modifies the peculiar artistic result of these illusory chords by substituting an actual harmonic fullness.

The trio section, in A flat major, again predominantly harmonic and rhythmic, nevertheless introduces some fragmentary, tentative melodic features. But to say that there was a tune would be going much too far: Beethoven keeps very consistently to his scheme of holding songfulness in reserve, for what purpose will appear as soon as the recapitulation of the scherzo is over. It is resumed at first exactly as it stood before, but at the repeat of the first portion the right-hand part is delayed for the value of a quaver by syncopation. It is played *legato* while the left hand anticipates it *staccato*. The second portion, instead of being repeated, is briefly supplemented by a coda that ends in C major. This, however, has not the effect of a lighting up of the prevalent minor tonality by a major tonic chord at the end, for the harmony immediately preceding indicates that this C major chord is to be felt as the dominant of F minor. It thus makes a connecting link with the next movement, which follows without a break and is in A flat, the relative major of F minor.

Adagio con espressione.—The tunelessness of the scherzo now explains itself. Beethoven at once opens his slow movement with one of those great emotional melodies to which an *adagio* was so apt to inspire him, and it is, of course, all the more telling for the melodic aridity that had been purposely maintained before. Here is the beginning of the tune:

Ex. 133

but it goes on for a dozen bars after that and is then resumed an octave higher with a different accompaniment and, as it were, in a more luminous setting. However, only half of it is thus restated, and suddenly a rapid upward run, culminating on two shakes, marks the end of this brief lyrical interlude. There is only a short cadenza by way of conclusion, and once again the music flows straight into the next movement.

Allegro vivace.—We have now reached the movement into which Beethoven chose, in the *quasi una fantasia* form, to throw the greatest intellectual weight. It is both the longest and the most highly wrought as regards thematic workmanship and form. The rondo form, always a rich field for exploration in Beethoven's eyes, appears here in an uncommon shape and with some interesting special features. The principal theme begins as follows:

Ex. 134

It is repeated an octave higher and comes to a full close in E flat major. There is a second strain, played in octaves by the right hand to a persistent semiquaver accompaniment for the left:

Ex. 135

This at first takes twice as much space as the first strain, which, however, returns in a new guise, with a small fragment of it scattered up and down the keyboard:

Ex. 136

The first episode, in B flat major, then begins with the following figure, which it continues for some time:

Ex. 137

One may here see a lingering influence of the harpsichord style of the preceding century. To play a single repeated left-hand note in the middle of a right-hand figuration was, of course, very much easier on the harpsichord with two keyboards. That, however, does not detract from its novelty as an effect on the early pianoforte, where, in fact, it was a daring enough thing to attempt precisely because it must have been thought of in Beethoven's day as essentially a two-keyboard device.

The second half of the episode makes use of entirely new material, beginning with striding arpeggios on the triad of B flat and continuing with a theme in octave figures for the right hand, the left being again busy with semiquavers.

The return of the principal theme is modified towards the end, where the second strain (Ex. 135) goes into the minor and thus leads to G flat major. Now Beethoven indulges unexpectedly in a development of his material that approximates to the working-out section of a sonata. After so much mere diversion and lyrical expansion in the first three movements, he evidently feels an imperative need to strengthen his edifice by some solid constructive feature. This may not be the only way of writing a fantasia, but it is for him one of the countless varieties of the only procedure of composing what is, after all, still a sonata. At any rate, it is *his* way, perfectly logical and, it follows, aesthetically satisfying.

The development begins with a quasi-fugal transformation of three notes of the main theme (Ex. 134*a*), with running figures in double counterpoint against it (i.e. sometimes above and sometimes below). This way of handling a brief motif of this sort already foreshadows the fugal treatment of the principal theme in the last Sonata, Op. 111, in C minor, dating from 1822. The three notes in question take this form:

Ex. 138

The added new figure marked *a* is then used in a variety of ways as the development proceeds. Next comes a new treatment of the first episode, the theme now taking the form shown in brackets under Ex. 137. This, gradually broken up as though losing its way, is at last cut off by an energetic shake in the bass that heralds the next return of the principal theme. It begins as before, but presently the second strain (Ex. 135) is transferred to the bass. The version shown in Ex. 136 again follows and leads as before, though in a different key, to a restatement of the first episode (Ex. 137). Here again we have a feature of the sonata form, for this idea now reveals itself as a second subject and is accordingly reintroduced in the orthodox manner in the principal key. But Beethoven, by no means content to let tradition sway him, has a surprise in store yet. The whole of the first episode having turned up again as a regular second sonata subject, he suddenly makes his music come to a standstill on a dominant-seventh chord and then brings back the broad melody of the slow movement (Ex. 133), this time in E flat major and with minute but significant changes. (Note the demisemiquaver run which enhances the emotional climax at the third bar.) This brief quotation, like the movement from which it is taken, ends with a free cadential passage, similar to the first, yet altered with astonishing subtlety. It leads into a final *presto* of twenty bars based mainly on the first two notes of figure 134*a*.

SONATA IN C SHARP MINOR, Op. 27 No. 2 (1801)

(B.S.S. RECORDS, VOL. IV)

THE two Sonatas Op. 27 were published in 1802, and it is more than probable that both were written in 1801, to which year Beethoven's famous letter to the 'Immortal Beloved' is also conjectured to belong. The dedication of the present Sonata to the young Countess Giulietta Guicciardi is one of the reasons why it was for a long time taken for granted that this letter was addressed to her, sentimental commentators insisting on seeing in it a musical counterpart to the love letter. That view, however, is now no longer favoured, though it has never been definitely decided who the woman may have been to whom Beethoven addressed this passionate message, which may or may not belong to the year in question. That he was at one time in love with Giulietta is certain, but it is almost as sure that she was never the object of such devouring care as the letter discloses.

Among other indications to that effect is the curious story of the dedication of the C sharp minor Sonata to Giulietta. It is pleasantly romantic to think that he addressed this work, which is so popular a favourite, to the 'Immortal Beloved.' Unfortunately he did not himself very particularly care for this Sonata, and he did not mind saying so on one occasion. What is more, we have it from Giulietta herself that he at first intended to inscribe the Rondo in G major, Op. 51 No. 2, to her, but, having to dedicate something to the Princess Lichnowsky, changed his mind and assigned to Giulietta the C sharp minor Sonata instead. Not only would it thus appear that he preferred the rather slight Rondo to the Sonata, and perhaps the Princess Lichnowsky to the Countess Guicciardi; it is certain that the idea of finding romantic dreams of a beloved woman in the first movement of the Sonata is all moonshine—the only 'moon-light,' in fact, that may legitimately be sought in connection with the work.

As for the title of 'Moonlight' Sonata, it was by no means the invention of Beethoven, who would at once have seen that it could not possibly fit the bright scherzo and the passionate finale. Its perpetrator was the critic Rellstab, who at once exposed its ridiculous subjectiveness by informing the world that the Sonata made him think of moonlight on the Lake of Lucerne. Why it might not just as well be the Lake of Geneva or the Lago Maggiore or Windermere only Rellstab could have explained. No doubt it was simply because he had not happened to visit these. However, this designation is too palpably superficial for music-lovers to be warned nowadays not to use it; as a distinguishing nick-name it may continue to serve a purpose, so long as it is not taken seriously.

As a new departure in sonata form the work is one of extreme interest. The big sonata movement, instead of coming at the beginning, is placed at the end and the slow movement comes first. It is a peculiar slow movement, too, not unlike some of the non-polyphonic preludes in Bach's *Well-tempered Clavier*. At the same time it was, for its period, distinctly modern. As already pointed out (page 102), it looks forward in some respects to the impromptus of Schubert and to the songs without words of Mendelssohn. Like the former, it is in the nature of a free improvisation, without a great deal of detail, and unconventional from the sonata-form point of view; like the latter, it sets songful phrases of a distinctly vocal character over figures of accompaniment that keep to the same pattern throughout. One might add that this movement also anticipates the type of Chopin's nocturne in some ways, though the direct approach to that was made by the line of specialist pianist-composers through John Field and by way of the operatic aria through Bellini.

Adagio sostenuto.—The first movement of the C sharp minor Sonata is so familiar that it would be absurd to quote any of it in music type; nor is it neces-sary to refer to any features of a structure that is at once so simple and so perfectly rounded as to persuade the hearer that for once Beethoven wished to appeal to the ear and to the emotions alone, giving the mind a rest. His own mind, to be sure, was alert enough when he set down this music; but he clearly did not wish it to engage the listener in speculations about construction. His principal melodic element is a persistent rhythmic figure and there is quite evidently a plan to include a middle section that should make a contrast in figuration without breaking the mood. This is of set purpose kept melodically rather featureless. The more tuneful portion is then recapitulated with modifications and at the close, by way of a coda, the figures of the middle section are drawn upon again, with the prevalent rhythm set against them in the bass.

Allegretto.—Here for once those who do not look at the printed page are at a slight advantage. They are in no danger of being startled by an apparently violent change of tonality at the sight of the key signatures of the first two movements—four sharps for the *adagio,* five flats for the *allegretto.* To the ear there is nothing abrupt in the change, for it represents in reality nothing more than a passing from minor to major by the enharmonic side-track. This scherzo-like second movement is in effect in C sharp major, Beethoven writing it enharmonically in D flat major merely for the player's convenience. It is easier to read a piece with five flats than with seven sharps—that is all.

Anything less like moonlight than this piece could hardly be imagined. It is sunny music, the clear and blithe melody of bright daylight. The whole of the first section has a large melodic sweep that is exhilarating, and what makes it curious that it should produce this effect is the fact that it is made up entirely of short two-bar figures. This sectional treatment is at first accentuated by the device of making the phrases alternately tied and detached:

Ex. 139

Afterwards this process is abandoned, perhaps because it is no longer required; the hearer has been made sufficiently aware of this periodicity by a slight initial exaggeration to keep it in his consciousness as the prevalent rhythmic pulse of the piece.

In the trio a similar procedure is to be noticed. In the first part strong accents off the beat are marked by the composer:

Ex. 140

while in the second they are omitted, though the rhythmic scheme remains the same. It is surely not too fanciful to imagine that Beethoven knew that they would be felt without being actually played, once the ear had caught the intention. The art of musical innuendo need not be put past him.

It is hardly necessary to say that there is a repeat of the first part of this scherzo-like movement.

Presto agitato.—We have now arrived at the true sonata movement—the most important section, into which Beethoven throws all his ardour and constructive skill, going out of his way to crown it all with a very spacious coda that contains moreover the concerto-like feature of a cadenza. Clearly brilliance as well as eloquence and action is the intention here; moonshine and the Lake of Lucerne have vanished wholly out of sight, and so, no doubt, has the Countess Guicciardi, whom such towering passion must have terrified, if she could have understood it. As she evidently had a hankering after the G major Rondo and considered herself treated second-best with this Sonata, we may take it for granted that she did nothing of the sort. On artistic grounds it is surely the Princess Lichnowsky who ought to have been offended; but then, again, she might have felt this movement to be too indecorous an offering for one of her rank. The probability is that few of Beethoven's contemporaries grasped such music as this, stuck fast as they still were in eighteenth-century conventions. The wonder is that the Viennese aristocrats of the time were enlightened enough to tolerate his musical revolts and his incredibly boorish behaviour for the sake of his genius.

In the finale of the C sharp minor Sonata all pretence at courtly formality of demeanour, at which the composer still aimed to some extent in that of Op. 22, is ruthlessly abandoned, though mastery of musical form is maintained as firmly as ever. The music plunges at once wildly into the first subject, which is not a tune, but merely a reckless sweeping of the keyboard with frenzied arpeggios, punctuated by an explosive accent at the end of each:

Ex. 141

The effect of the accents is the greater because the rest is kept in a suppressed tone until the next feature presents itself, a long passage poised on the dominant and ending with a pause on a bare G sharp. The initial process is then repeated with varied harmony, modulating into G sharp minor, in which key the second subject presents itself. Here at last the music is given a melodic feature:

Ex. 142

This is followed by some remarkable scale passages with crashing accents and breathless syncopations in the accompaniment, and another extensive theme, also in G sharp minor and thus belonging to the second-subject group, succeeds to this. It is characterized by repeated notes and little broken phrases:

Ex. 143

The exposition closes with an allusion to Ex. 142, still in the same key. It is repeated. When it has been heard again, the music is carried over into the working-out by a conversion of Ex. 141 into C sharp major. It then modulates to F sharp minor for an almost immediate return of the second subject (Ex. 142), the melody of which soon passes into the left hand and is developed at some length. The material that serves as a bridge to the recapitulation is new.

The working-out has been very concise, no doubt because some development of the thematic matter is still in store for the extended coda, which follows after a perfectly normal recapitulation. It begins with a contraction of the arpeggios of Ex. 141 into a different, more convulsive rhythmic grouping and then re-introduces the second subject, first in the left hand and afterwards in the right. Next comes the cadenza, beginning with arpeggios kept strictly in time and later, after a shake, introducing a freely ornamental figure that falls rapidly into the bass, which is arrested by two bars of *adagio*, containing merely a cadence of bare bass octaves. The coda is rounded off by a reference to the afterthought to the second subject already heard at the end of the exposition and recapitulation.

SONATA IN D MAJOR, Op. 28 (1801)
(B.S.S. RECORDS, VOL. III)

THIS work was written in 1801 and published, by the Bureau des Arts et d'Industrie in Vienna, on 14th August 1802. It is dedicated to Joseph, Edler von Sonnenfels. The period is a rather uneventful one, productively if not biographically. Outwardly, at any rate, Beethoven's life ran on without any great disturbance, though it was only the following year that the so-called Heiligenstadt Testament, that suicidal document, was wrung from him by adversities which at least momentarily seemed to him no longer bearable. The major calamity, so far as we can tell, was his approaching deafness.

It is true that the famous letter to the 'Immortal Beloved,' dated 6th and 7th July, very probably belongs to the year 1801; but that, to whomsoever it may have been addressed, is so unrestrained an outpouring that the feelings which prompted it had very little effect on the music Beethoven wrote at this time, which is on the whole remarkably placid. Even the funeral march in the A flat major Sonata, Op. 26, was probably not an expression of personal grief, and the most emotional work of the period, the 'Moonlight' Sonata, was thought by the composer himself to be much overrated by the public.

The four piano sonatas that fall into 1801 were much the most significant music of that year. Next in importance are the two violin sonatas, Opp. 23 and 24. Otherwise these twelve months were lean enough. The Ballet of *The Creatures of Prometheus*, though it contains delightful music of a rather formal kind, was, as Haydn somewhat acidly remarked, not a *Creation* by a long way, nor was the string Quintet in C major Op. 29 of great importance, much less the cello Variations on a theme from *The Magic Flute* and the twelve Country Dances for two violins and bass, which complete the output for the year.

But although 1801 may be regarded as a breathing-space between the first and second Symphonies and after the first six string Quartets, it is interesting to note how significant the piano sonatas are in comparison with the rest. Not that they carry any especial autobiographical message. We have seen that even the 'Moonlight' Sonata did not mean to Beethoven all that it has meant to sentimental pianists ever since his day. Apart from the fact that the 'Immortal Beloved' may have been Therese von Brunswick or even Magdalene Willmann, if not indeed any other woman, just as well as Giulietta Guicciardi—for Beethoven was a man in love with love rather than attached to any one person—it would have been surprising if the fervent emotions expressed in the famous letter had been poured into his music as well. It is feelings that do not find any other outlet which, in a man of genius, become distilled into art. So long as they are vented through some external channel, even if it be only a perfervid letter, the artist is free to work with serenity. Had Wagner been able to run away with Mathilde Wesendonck without any let or hindrance, his music would most probably never have expressed the whole unhappy restlessness of *Tristan* so poignantly.

There are certainly no heated passions displaying themselves in the four piano sonatas Beethoven wrote in 1801, except in the finale of the 'Moonlight' Sonata, and Op. 28 is the calmest of them all. Hence, no doubt, the title of 'Pastoral Sonata' given to it later by the Hamburg publisher Cranz, which, though it is doubtful whether Beethoven would have countenanced it, is at least less inappropriate than many other sobriquets of the kind. The movement it fits best is the last.

It is in form rather than in subjective expression that Beethoven advanced at this time. The first two works he called by the name of *Sonata quasi una fantasia*, Op. 27, are greater departures in the matter of shape than in that of content. Beethoven found a new mould first, while the new thought that was destined to fill it did not at once pour itself out very freely. Perfect adjustment of the new outlook to the new manner of presentation was to come later. It is rare enough for both to manifest themselves in one and the same composer, as they did in the maturer Beethoven; to have appeared together at a single moment in the career of one of them would have been too much of a miracle even for so great a creator.

The present Sonata, it must be confessed, is in no sense an advance upon Op. 27. It contains a good deal that is fanciful and imaginative, but nothing that is particularly prophetic, and it reverts to the classical form—a regular sonata movement, a piece in a moderate tempo based on the song form, a scherzo and a final rondo. It may be noted that Beethoven here for the last time uses this normal four-movement form in a piano sonata. Three movements predominate thereafter and as he goes on there is a tendency towards two, a compression compensated for by greater enlargement within each piece. Where there are still four movements by way of exception, some other departure from the conventional plan is to be found. Thus Op. 31 No. 3 has both a scherzo and a minuet between two movements in sonata form; Op. 101 has a march-like movement instead of a scherzo and an *adagio* that is not complete in itself, but leads straight into the finale; and if that be regarded as a fourth movement, then we must also look upon the *largo* introduction to the finale of Op. 106 as a fifth one, or if we do not, but say that here are four movements, with a scherzo and an *adagio*, even then we must recognize, among other irregularities, that the finale is, quite contrary to tradition, a fugue. In Op. 110, as we shall see later, the slow movement and finale (also a fugue) are inseparably fused.

Allegro.—The principal strain of the first subject is at once introduced:

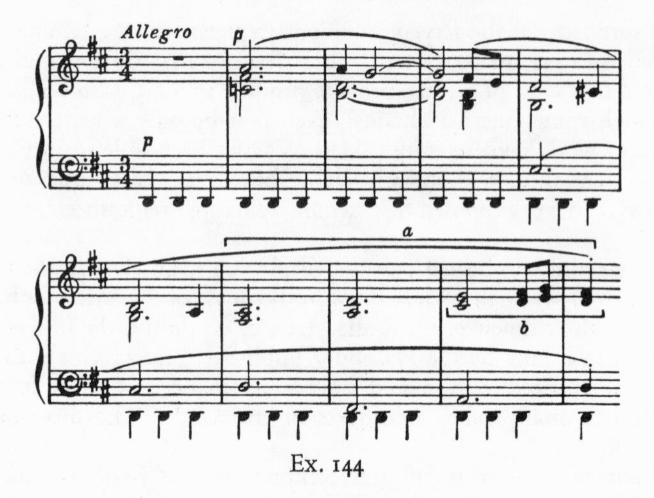

Ex. 144

The pedal bass, rising an octave, as does the theme itself, continues for another fifteen bars when it forms itself into a cadence and then tries to become fixed again. It is not until the third time that the cadence finally dislodges it and leads to a subsidiary idea:

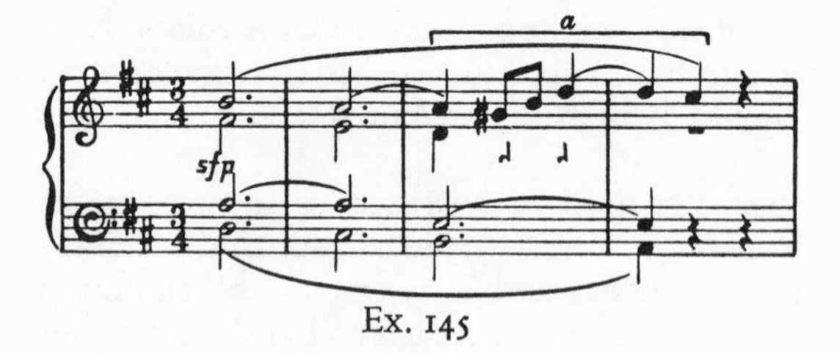

Ex. 145

This is repeated a fifth higher, and then restated, both in its original position and in its transposition, with a flowing quaver decoration. The quaver figures, extended into a downward scale, lead to the second-subject group, which opens thus:

Ex. 146

The key of A major, to which this leads, and which is that properly assigned to the second subject, never settles down for any length of time during the extended melodic periods of this important section of the movement, which are of this type:

Ex. 147

At two points they are intersected by brilliant runs.

There is an additional clause before we reach the end of the exposition:

Ex. 148

The working-out is astonishingly economical in the use of material: every bar of it is derived from what has gone before. Yet an entirely new light is shed upon the music by that combination of mechanical ingenuity with imagination which is one of the secrets of Beethoven's greatness. At first the opening theme (Ex. 144) appears in G major, the bass having risen to G from the F sharp which naturally followed upon the closing bar of the exposition. It is restated this time, not simply an octave higher, but with a new quaver figuration which in itself is akin to the elaboration of Ex. 145 heard previously. Then comes a passage built on figure 144*a*, appearing over and under scale passages and at the same time serving as a modulatory bridge. After four statements this clause is shorn of its first two bars and further extended use is made of the motif that remains (Ex. 144*b*). Presently this is contracted in such a way that the closing note of one statement coincides with the opening one of the next, an impression of growing urgency being thus gained, and lastly the thematic allusions dissolve into mere syncopated chords that come quietly to rest on a pause. From this a new statement of Ex. 148 gently detaches itself, but its phrase marked *a* is now exchanged for that similarly marked in Ex. 145, the composer thus establishing a relationship between these two phrases that had not so far been obvious. The music becomes more hesitant and Ex. 145*a* presents itself, slowly and questioningly, in the shape of a dominant seventh of D major. From this, by way of answer, the music drops quite naturally into the recapitulation. This proceeds normally until we have again reached Ex. 148, this time in the key of the tonic. This gives rise to a coda based at first on an extension of this theme, followed afterwards by a last statement of Ex. 144, and concluded by a chain of cadential figures based on Ex. 144*b*.

Andante.—The slow movement (not very slow) may be said, though with some qualifications, to be in the form of a *da capo* aria. It is at any rate formed on the plan of A: B: A, the chief irregularity being a coda that may be represented by the formula C(A+B), being a new idea shaped out of the elements of both principal sections of the movement itself.

The music begins as follows, in D minor:

Ex. 149

The clause that immediately succeeds the fragment quoted is a corresponding phrase beginning in F major and ending in A minor. The whole section is repeated and then comes a new strain in the dominant of D minor, followed by a modified restatement of Ex. 149. That is, so to speak, the main section of the aria.

The key changes to D major for the middle section, which is entirely independent of what has gone before. Here is the opening:

Ex. 150

which shows the kind of patterns the music maintains almost throughout. There are two sections, each of which is repeated.

The opening portion of the movement is resumed, at first exactly as before; but instead of being merely indicated, the repeats are now fully written out, for Beethoven, in order to introduce variety, sets them out in demi-semiquaver figuration. It may be objected that the comparison with the form of the *da capo* aria breaks down here, since the old composers who handled it merely indicated the repeat and did not write it out with varied ornamentation. This, however, is to reckon without the *continuo* player, who, always free to fill in the figured bass as he chose, so long as he kept to the harmonic directions, must in the case of *da capo* arias have frequently, if not generally, introduced new patterns of accompaniment at the recurrence of the first section. Indeed, one may very well hold the view that it was this factor which made this form of song, often regarded as so tedious nowadays, not only tolerable, but actually extremely interesting to its contemporaries.

In the coda Beethoven at first gives us a bare outline of Ex. 149 in two different harmonic versions, each time arrested on a pause; then he alludes three times to Ex. 150 with a dramatic tension that culminates in the chord of the dominant minor ninth, and he concludes with a broken cadence that resolves itself into a chord of D minor from a discordant mixture of dominant and tonic.

Allegro vivace.—The whole of the scherzo—apart from the trio section—is built on or derived from the two figures which are at once presented at the opening:

Ex. 151

The notes descending in four octaves are especially important. They recur again and again, sometimes unharmonized, sometimes in chords, cartwheeling humorously down into the bass; but when the left hand sets them against a kind of waltz accompaniment in the right they turn upwards on the last note, thus effecting short-cut modulations.

The trio is entirely different, a short four-bar tune in B minor alternately turning back into that key and away into D major. It is heard eight times over: variety, apart from the two different turns of the cadence, is left entirely to the accompaniment to provide, which it does with the readiest resourcefulness. The scherzo proper is, of course, repeated.

Allegro, ma non troppo.—The final rondo has a principal subject which will at once show that this must have been the movement which led Cranz to call the Sonata a 'pastoral' work:

Ex. 152

It has continuing figures of this type:

Ex. 153

A series of arpeggios, which deliberately withholds any thematic interest for a moment, leads to the first episode, also of a distinctly bucolic nature and, as will be seen at the end of the quotation hereunder, varied in much the same way as the strain of Ex. 153:

Ex. 154

Brilliant broken octave passages lead to the first restatement of the main theme (Ex. 152), now slightly modified by a new embroidery. To this succeeds another long episode, or rather an episodic group of three distinct incidents, which make for variety at once of tune and of key. The connecting octaves are then used again, but in a reversed form and followed by descending scales which had not previously appeared. These are arrested on the dominant and bring back the theme a second time, with the embroidery amplified a little. The arpeggios are then used to lead to a return of the first episode (Ex. 154), now in the principal key, and again the broken octaves follow, leading to G major this time.

The coda opens in that key, with the bass of the main theme, deprived of its melody, but with syncopated chords added:

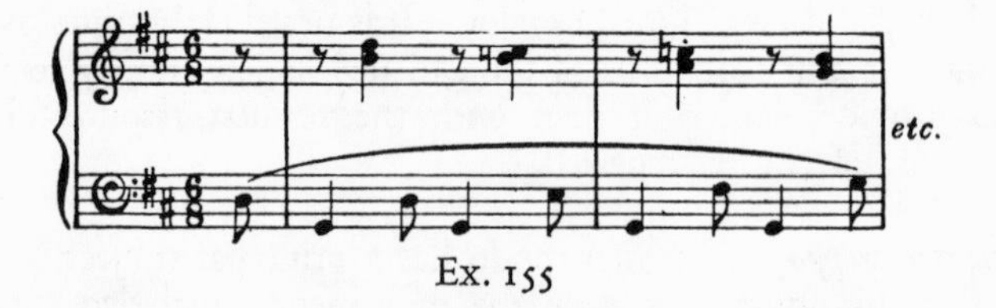

Ex. 155

A delightful harmonic transition takes us back, still with the same rhythmic beat, to the dominant of D major, in which the bass persists for some time while the treble at first strains back towards G major. The dominant-seventh chord is consolidated at last by a rising arpeggio, four times repeated with diminishing emphasis, to which succeeds, *più allegro quasi presto*, a short and dazzling peroration, still making use of the bass of Ex. 152 and breaking up its melody into rapid semiquaver figures which to the eye obliterate its outline but still let the ear remain conscious of it. No art but music is capable of thus making things appear the same and yet not the same, and Beethoven is among the musicians who best understand the secret of such subtle transformations.

INTERLUDE VI

ON THE PLAYING OF BEETHOVEN

THE great problem that confronts all performers, indeed the circumstance that accounts more than any other for the rarity of great reproductive artists, is the fact that while countless bad interpretations of a work of art are possible, only a comparatively limited number of good ones are acceptable. Some artists, of course, go to the length of asserting that only one single interpretation of each work is interesting—their own. But that is preposterous and shows deplorable limitations, not in the work, but in the player, who makes up for narrowness of sympathy and imagination by an arrogant conceit that may relieve him of the discomforts of an artistic conscience, but is apt to make him impressive only to the least desirable section of his audience.

Most of us know from experience that there are a hundred ways of performing *Hamlet* badly or perversely; but no one, except possibly an actor whose self-esteem exceeds discretion to an almost fabulous extent, would be so absurd as to pretend that there is only one way of doing the title-part of that work—not to mention others—convincingly. And we may say much the same of Beethoven's sonatas, for it is an almost mathematically exact truth that the greater the works of art confronting the interpreter, the wider becomes the range of possible great performances. Still, that range does remain definitely limited, if only we could say exactly where the limitations begin, whereas to the risks of bad performance there is no end.

It follows that it must always be much easier, but also far less useful, to say how Beethoven should not be played than to suggest what can be done to render him justice, and unfortunately it cannot be taken for granted that any bad habit which has been condemned will automatically become a valuable artistic precept by being turned into its opposite. If I tell a child that it is a sin to steal a sack of coal from a Tyneside merchant, this does not mean that it is therefore a virtue to carry coals to Newcastle. One may thus say, for instance, that no phrase of Beethoven's should ever be played in a slovenly way; but it is not enough simply to play every phrase carefully. There are various ways of careful playing, and some of them may be nearly as bad as slovenliness at its worst.

Perhaps one may go so far in safety as to say that carefulness should only be technical—the kind of mechanical assurance that can be taught and learnt—and that it should never cramp a spiritual adventurousness. The more certain the pianist is of having every detail of a work technically in hand, the more ready will he be to yield to momentary promptings of his imagination during the performance. These promptings, again, must however be subject to a kind of moral control that never lets him violate a code of general conduct he has established for himself beforehand. Within the exigencies of this code he is free, and the more free the greater the care he has taken to think out the laws to which he intends to submit.

Two sonatas that happen to be known by descriptive titles may serve as illustrations of the point. It would be ridiculous to sit down to their study with the intention of seeing how every phrase of the *Pathétique* can be made pathetic and every incident of the *Appassionata* impassioned. That is the way to reduce the 'Moonlight' Sonata to mere moonshine. But the player may, so to speak, set the stops marked 'Pathos' or 'Passion' before he settles down to work on either of these two sonatas. It is not a matter of forcing himself to feel certain things. If he is obliged to do that, he is no artist and may as well give up all attempts at interpretation from the beginning. It is a matter of letting a mental process induce an emotional reaction, not with cold deliberation, but certainly with a distinct predominance of mind over feeling. Once the mind is made up definitely, feeling will respond quite spontaneously, but without running away with the player and leaving him helplessly floundering in a morass of uncontrolled emotionalism. Nothing could be worse than that, not even the most mechanical of performances. The pianist who hands Beethoven to his public cut and dried, without daring for a moment to let the music sway him by its own power, is as lifeless as the actor who simply follows the producer's instructions like an automaton; but to sit down to a great sonata trusting to the feelings of the moment is like going on the stage to play Hamlet with no clear notion of what one is going to do at any moment, but with the optimistic amateur's conviction that 'it will be all right on the night.' A performance approached in this frame of mind is never all right on any night.

Thinking before feeling is what it comes to; that is the first principle. Then, during actual performance, emotion may be safely given the lead. Having been controlled by the mind during preparation, it will be in no danger of mocking the composer by letting the interpreter interpose his own personality too obtrusively. But the performance will not be mechanically like any of the artist's trial playings, nor will it be quite the same again when it is repeated in public.

Yet the notes will have been the same each time. One has a right to expect that, though if something must be slightly amiss, one would rather have a wrong note now and again than a wry phrase or a dry phrase. Accurate pianists are as plentiful as word-perfect actors, and among them are as many dull musicians as there are mediocre stage-players among the latter. It is what lies behind the words or the notes we listen for. But what is that? And how does the interpreter bring it out? Formidable questions to which no technical answer is enough, yet which can be answered only technically, if at all. And, since we have discovered that there are infinitely more wrong than right ways of playing Beethoven, it is easier to say what the pianist who tackles the sonatas should avoid than what he should do.

The most useful precept, generally speaking, is perhaps to begin by approaching Beethoven's instrument in the right way. They say nowadays that the piano is a percussion instrument. This is as obviously true, in a technical sense, as it is ridiculous to draw the inference that all music must be played as though it had been written for the dulcimer or the xylophone. It all depends on how the composer regards his medium. If Stravinsky chooses to write for the piano as an instrument of percussion, by all means let his music be hammered upon it like nails into a coffin. But Beethoven, in spite of the fact that he affected the German name of *Hammerclavier* for a time, did not think of it in that way. For him the piano was a substitute for the orchestra. This is not by any means to suggest that his writing in the sonatas is unpianistic. On the contrary: keyboard writing is often the better the more orchestral it sounds. Liszt's piano music, always most congenially written for the instrument, is richly orchestral in its effect, and so often is Schumann's—in whose case we see in fact the curious phenomenon of a substitute that sounds a great deal better than the real thing. Schumann's symphonies are very poorly scored for orchestra and very much more satisfying in sound in their arrangement as piano duets.

Beethoven's piano sonatas are often not particularly good piano music as such; they are great music requiring a medium of expression manageable by a single performer, because that expression is meant to be intimate and flexible. But that medium is to some extent a makeshift. The music seems to call now for this string or wind instrument, now for that, and the player's business is to suggest these instruments by every device of touch and every power of imaginative mimicry at his disposal. This is no reproach to the piano; no greater tribute could in fact be paid to it than that of demonstrating how far it can surpass itself, how much more than the mere aggressive instrument of percussion it can be. The reader need only glance through the sonatas to find innumerable examples of quasi-orchestral writing, or let us say of admirable keyboard writing that is somehow improved by orchestral treatment. Or if he will look at this book rather than at the music, he need go no farther than the first three musical examples quoted from the F sharp major Sonata, Op. 78 (Exx. 212, 213, and 214, pages 173–4). The right-hand *legato* phrase shown in Ex. 212 cannot be imagined as anything but violin music in its ideal as distinct from its material reproduction, and the glorified Alberti bass, quite undistinguished if rapped out in a percussive way with each note exactly like the others, is incomparably beautiful if treated in a fluid, freely flowing manner. Again, the three chords shown as Ex. 213*c* can only be played with all their potential poetry if they are imagined as scored for clarinets, horns and bassoons, and, as I suggest later, the top notes of the semiquaver figures in Ex. 214 can be regarded as an implied flute phrase (see Ex. 215). One could go on for a long time citing such instances of a latent orchestra in Beethoven's piano music.

What other hints could be useful? Phrasing, phrasing and again phrasing: that is perhaps the most important. It is astonishing how few pianists, even professional pianists, know that good phrasing not only heightens the plasticity and significance of the music as it comes, but saves making all kinds of exaggerated points as a composition progresses. Something has to be done to herald the return of a rondo subject, let us say. Well, instead of doing it by means of an obvious *rallentando*, it can be less blatantly yet just as eloquently done by means of a little extra emphasis on significant delivery. One cannot explain this on paper and it makes a difference if shown on the piano only to players imaginative enough to do similar things for themselves in any case, though perhaps they will do them differently. For it is a matter of musical response that comes from within and cannot be instilled.

The more obvious tricks, however, will sometimes be avoided if due warning is given. The *rubato* is not safe in the hands of uncertain performers of Beethoven, because it is not natural to him, as it is to Chopin. Playing in time—let it even be said in strict time—is the norm. Sensitive players will know where to depart from it; the others will be helpless in any case. A good working rule, though, is to make the foundation of that norm of strict time as brisk as the music will bear, not as slow as the hearer may be imagined to stand it. Elasticity is the life of music, and an elastic will stretch, but cannot be pushed together. In other words, and words applied to Beethoven, the pace of any movement of his, slow or fast, can often be slightly spread out with advantage, whereas it can scarcely ever be tightened and hurried with anything but an untidy, scatter-brained effect.

'Effect' is a dangerous word, anyway. No effects should ever be consciously devised, and few aimed at on the spur of the moment. The music is already immensely telling: to try to make it more dramatic, more spectacular, is only to risk falling into bathos and tawdriness. Let the player beware of taking upon himself more than interpretation in the proper sense of the term. One secret of interpreting a great composer adequately is to eschew supererogation. Although performers are safe from the Beethovenian fury that befell the hapless Nägeli, they should shrink from emulating the enterprise that publisher showed in adding to his music what he did not intend or ascribing ideas to him that could never have entered his head. The story of Nägeli's interpolation into the G major Sonata, Op. 31 No. 1, may be read farther on. He thought, doubtless, that he was adding both rhyme and reason to the coda of the first movement (rhyme by balancing the phrases, reason by answering the dominant with the tonic). But the 'effect' was rather as though, if I may return to *Hamlet* once more, a publisher had made the following emendation at the end of the first act:

> *Hamlet* (*Beethoven*) :
> The time is out of joint: O cursed spite,
> That ever I was born to set it right!
> Nay, come, let 's go together.
> *Horatio* (*Nägeli*) : What a night!

No pianist could be guilty of inserting such an appalling commonplace, or at any rate he could not attempt to set it down for posterity; but he can do mis-chief enough if he is wanting in fidelity to Beethoven's text. Not that he need be pedantic about it. Where it is clear from a parallel passage that the com-poser was obliged to alter the lay-out of a higher transposition merely on account of the shortness of the old keyboard, there is no reason why it should not be adjusted to the wider range of the modern piano, just as it would surely be excusable to omit Shakespeare's 'Nay, come, let 's go together,' since he would no doubt have closed the act with the rhyming couplet had the theatre of his time made use of a curtain and had he thus not been obliged to give his characters an excuse to go off the stage. But to add anything, even as little as a note to a chord or an extra pause, merely because it appears rhyme or reason to the player, is inadmissible. It cannot possibly mean that the performer knows better than Beethoven; it can only show that he has no notion of what Beethoven was about.

SONATA IN G MAJOR, Op. 31 No. 1 (1802)
(B.S.S. RECORDS, VOL. XI)

THE first two Sonatas of Op. 31 were composed in 1802, and they were published in 1803 without the E flat major Sonata which now completes the group. They appeared in the *Répertoire des Clavecinistes* published by Nägeli of Zürich, and afterwards in an 'édition très correcte,' issued by Simrock of Bonn as Op. 31. But Cappi of Vienna also brought them out as *Deux Sonates pour le Clavecin ou Pianoforte*, under the opus number 29, which was still retained when the complete set appeared in 1805. However, 31 now remains the definitive number, and Op. 29 is the string Quintet in C major. A noteworthy circumstance is that this set of Sonatas bears no dedication.

The terms 'clavecin' and 'clavecinistes' are very curious. Only the G major, a somewhat reactionary work for its time, can possibly be imagined as being played on the harpsichord, and it is quite beyond belief that Beethoven could have sanctioned the performance of such thoroughly pianistic music as the D minor and E flat major on the older instrument. Only two explanations seem admissible. One is that a publisher took it upon himself, not for the first or the last time in history, to mislead his public in order to increase his sales. Considering that many households at the beginning of the nineteenth century must still have possessed only a harpsichord and no pianoforte, for all that the earlier instrument was by that time quite obsolete where modern music was concerned, it must have been tempting for a publisher to make his customers believe that the keyboard music he issued could be played on either. The only other possible reason for Cappi's description appears to be that the French terminology for the keyboard instruments was but vaguely understood by the Viennese, who may well have taken *clavecin* to stand for any stringed keyboard instrument. They may have loosely associated the term with the instrument which Beethoven later, in an attempt at inventing a German name for it, called the *Hammerclavier*, and Cappi may simply have intended to offer two alternative names for one and the same instrument.

The *très correcte* on Simrock's title-page implied, of course, that Nägeli's edition had been very faulty, and indeed, apart from various misprints, there were four bars in the first movement which had been added by the enterprising publisher, who was a not undistinguished composer in his day. Beethoven first detected the impertinent interpolation when Ries played the Sonata to him from a copy in the *Répertoire des Clavecinistes*, which Nägeli had begun to issue in 1803. Here is the monstrosity in black and white. It appears in the coda of the first movement:

Ex. 156

The reader need only compare this with the authentic version to see at once how commonplace this tonic-and-dominant sea-saw is compared with Beethoven's deliberate avoidance of the tonic answer the first time, which is in fact his whole point.

The only one of Nägeli's compositions that is still known to some extent, at any rate in his native Switzerland, is the song *Freut euch des Lebens,* quite familiar at one time in England under the title of *Life let us cherish.* It was famous enough, indeed, for Joseph Woelfl to use it as a theme for variations in the finale of his Sonata *Non plus ultra,* a work that claimed to be the most difficult piece of keyboard music any pianist could possibly be expected to play, until Dussek challenged this view by writing a Sonata he regarded as more difficult still and called *Plus ultra.*[1] Here is Nägeli's tune as it appears in Woelfl's finale. It is worth quoting because it shows the same extreme naïveté in the use of alternating tonic and dominant harmony that prompted the 'correction' of Beethoven's work and because it goes some way towards explaining why the ambitious publisher thought that his contributor ought to be taught a lesson in musical symmetry:

Ex. 157

[1] Better known as *Le Retour à Paris,* Op. 70.

Allegro vivace.—The first subject begins without any introduction by setting down the following group of short motifs, all of which are important ingredients of the musical development:

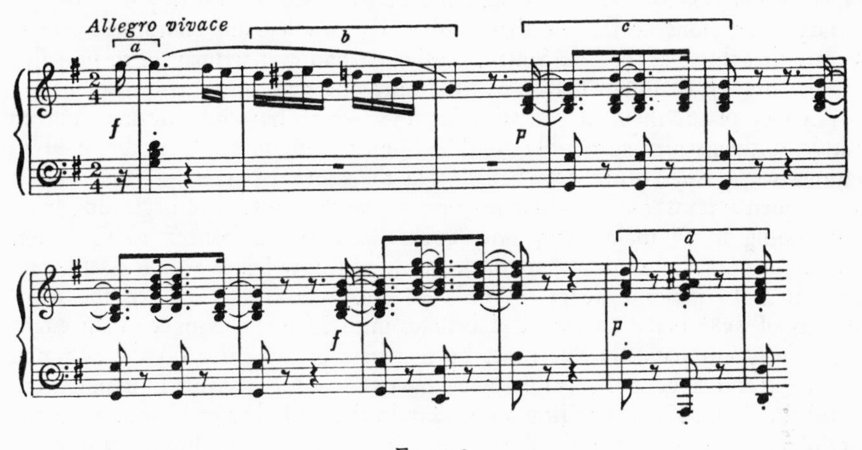

Ex. 158

The characteristic stutter, which makes the music hesitate between an attack before and on the beat, remains much in evidence throughout the movement. It is a new device which, once discovered, the composer exploits for all it is worth—or perhaps for a little more. But then this is a Sonata that seems to have been specially written for the sake of such exploitations, and as these are concerned mainly with keyboard technics, one is conscious of a momentary setback in purely musical inventiveness on Beethoven's part. Of all the thirty Sonatas (that is to say, the complete collection if one regards the two small and early works of Op. 49 as sonatinas) this is undoubtedly the least favoured by musicians and by the public at large. There is no harm in saying that, since in every race one horse must necessarily be the last, though it is true that this comparison is not altogether a happy one, the loss of a race being an indisputable fact, whereas the designation of one work of art in a whole group as the weakest remains to a large extent dependent upon personal taste. Here, however, the question of taste enters into the argument less than in most similar cases, perhaps; at any rate, there is a pretty general critical agreement that the G major Sonata of Op. 31 is the least representative of Beethoven's genius in the whole of that class, while nobody could for a moment dispute the assertion that it is decidedly not on a level with its two companion-works, in D minor and E flat major.

However, one cannot have everything all the time, even from a great master. Here, for once, we have Beethoven in the unaccustomed part of a technical experimenter so taken up with purely theoretical and mechanical considerations that he is not particularly interested in the music as such; he comes near being one of those people—with whom our own century is only too familiar—who are so satisfied with the solution of certain problems that they quite forget to weigh the merits of the resulting music. This, of course, is an exaggeration amounting to something like a distortion of Beethoven's aims even in this experimental Sonata; but one would not be surprised to hear any day that the literary champions of this or that deliberately problematic composer were to declare that this was the best Sonata Beethoven had ever written, or to hear that dabbler himself maintain that it was the only one with any merit at all.

The very plastic thematic scraps of Ex. 158, which have little intrinsic interest but lend themselves admirably to development, are presently to be used in various ways, each being detachable from the other. But at first they appear in a sequence transposed a whole tone down, so that instead of beginning in G and ending in D major, they now appear progressing from F to C major. Almost at once, however, we are back in G, and now figure 158*d* is heard three times in a G major cadence on different chord inversions. Then the semiquavers of 158*b* make an extended bridge, until D major is once again established, very emphatically this time, by five bars of arpeggios on the common chord. Yet in spite of this emphasis we have the feeling that this D major chord is still the dominant demanding an answer in the tonic key of G, not an actual modulation into the key of the dominant. This is a truly Beethovenian subtlety. We are expected to wonder whether the music is to go to the second subject, in its orthodox dominant relationship, already at so early a stage. Then comes the most unexpected answer to our question. The dominant has proved elusive, and the opening of Ex. 158 is heard again. But now 158*c* and 158*d* between them make up a new scheme of modulation, which leads us a very long way off—to B major—and it is in this remote key that the second subject appears, in defiance of all the rules:

Ex. 159

This is repeated by the left hand in B minor, and the figure 159*a* is to some extent developed to carry the music on to a concluding melodic phrase which maintains the B major-minor colouring. The following, rhythmically derived from Ex. 158*a* and 158*d*, makes a link to the repeat of the exposition:

Ex. 160

After the repeat the working-out section begins with a series of modulatory statements of Ex. 158*c*. The music has veered to B flat major, in which key the runs of Ex. 158*b* are made much of and rise sequentially to C minor and D minor. This is so near D major that Beethoven is able to slip back quite naturally into the arpeggios previously heard in that key. But if it was merely felt then that D major was still the dominant of G major, this time we are quite explicitly and unequivocally apprised of the fact, for after the first four bars of plain D major arpeggios come another four into which Beethoven inserts a C♮, which, of course, dispels any sort of notion that we are in D major and quite firmly establishes the dominant seventh of G:

On this dominant further play is made with matter derived from figures 158*a* and 158*c*, and a harmonic distortion towards a diminished seventh is effected incidentally to the introduction of an E♭ as the dominant minor ninth:

The music hesitates and seems to fade away; but it suddenly plunges into Ex. 158 for the recapitulation. The first-subject group is considerably curtailed here. Beethoven has already made a very significant use of the arpeggio idea in the working-out, and to restate it here in its original form would have meant an anticlimax. Thus he simply omits it and leads us straight to the second subject, this time by a modulation to E major. And now we grasp the point of the previous appearance of this subject in B major. Beethoven enjoys letting us know how much farther he saw ahead than we did when he puzzled us with this apparently erratic excursion into so remote a key. It will be remembered that the second subject (Ex. 159) turned into the minor. It does so again, in the same left-hand presentation as before. But of course this is now in the key of E, the direct relative minor of G major, which thus re-establishes itself itself with the utmost ease. The second subject is repeated in this tonic major and the music proceeds exactly as at the end of the exposition, but for the displacements of tonality demanded by the new key-orientation of the music.

A page of coda follows. We are once more back at the opening of Ex. 158; but now the runs based on 158*b* are joined on immediately and lead to the arpeggios, stated in plain D major again. The coda ends with passages built on 158*a*, including a single allusion to the rhythm of 158*d*, which will be seen in the musical quotation No. 156, from which the reader must, of course, mentally omit Nägeli's four redundant bars.

Adagio grazioso.—This Italian direction is unusual and, from Beethoven, surprising. His slow movements as a rule aim at profundity, not at graciousness or elegance; but here, for once, we have a deliberate intention to be playful and a result that comes as near shallowness as any slow movement in the whole series of Beethoven's piano sonatas can. There is a great deal in it that is merely decorative or of purely dynamic interest, rather as though the composer had wished to contradict his publisher, who announced the Op. 31 Sonatas as being 'pour clavecin ou pianoforte' by showing that this could not possibly be anything but pianoforte music and would sound unconvincing on the harpsichord, though unquestionably the more old-fashioned households still used that instrument at the opening of the nineteenth century. Those minutely indicated *crescendo*, *sf* and *fp* marks show a conscious use of the new resources of the pianoforte.

The movement opens with an expansive but not very eloquent theme of which this is the beginning:

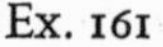
Ex. 161

The last complete bar quoted may be taken as another example of the 'finger-print' mentioned on page 29. It occurs at the juncture of the phrase where one would expect it, though the phrase itself is less significant than most others that bear this personal impress. The reader should compare the figures of accompaniment with those used by Woelfl in Ex. 157. In both cases they are based on a conventional form of keyboard-writing; but it is instructive to observe that whereas the small composer uses the convention without thinking twice about it and with the flattest and dullest effect, the great master is careful to make something relatively original and individual even of so commonplace a device.

The theme is repeated with its first part in the bass and with its sequel altered so as to bring us to a new idea—the most expressive in the movement. It has beautiful drooping cadences which lead to an interpolation where 'time is broke and no proportion kept'—an ornamental flourish bringing back the chief theme, which is now slightly more elaborate and shows that one of the guiding principles here is that of variation.

The music darkens to C minor, and this leads to A flat major by way of a new theme:

Ex. 162

The repeated staccato chords with right-hand and left-hand scales above and below them and biting accents at each change of harmony are pure pianoforte music and must have been as ineffective on the *clavecin* as they are telling on the newer instrument. Next, as the chords change more frequently, the accompanying figures of Ex. 162 (transferred to the treble and turned upside down) are used thematically, and cadential passages with strongly chromatic inflections lead back to the chief theme. The semiquavers continue as an accompaniment to it and the right hand indulges in freer ornamentation towards the end.

The second theme is now heard in syncopation and the cadenza following it breaks the time with a much longer ornamental interpolation. The main theme is brought back for the last time in its complete form, still more elaborately treated, and next its shakes are turned into a new transition leading to the coda, in which the opening bar of Ex. 161 is once more alluded to in the bass, with a new melody answering it in the middle register, like an expressive cello solo. The pulse of the music then falters and a timid upward flutter ends the movement.

Allegretto.—We have here a rondo so organized as to approach sonata form. The development is closely wrought, almost dramatic, but the musical material is urbane, as witness the principal subject:

Ex. 163

It holds much promise of development, though not more than a second strain that follows:

Ex. 164

The figure 164*a* is particularly important. After some general development it comes to the fore as the harbinger of the first episode, which appears thus, in the dominant, like a second sonata subject:

Ex. 165

The triplet motion prevails all through the return to the chief theme, and in fact remains as an accompaniment when that theme recurs, until Ex. 164 is restated over a bass in broken octave quavers.

The second episode is particularly interesting because instead of containing new material, as in a normal rondo, it is more in the nature of a sonata working-out section. Ex. 163 is first heard in the bass with a triplet accompaniment above it, derived from Ex. 165; next it is presented in a series of canons; and it makes for the second return of the rondo subject by way of repeated statements intersected by a new cadential phrase that spaces this section out to a size commensurate with its thematic importance. When the chief theme does turn up again, it has a new and essentially pianistic accompaniment of this type:

Ex. 166

We are farther than ever from the harpsichord.

A regular recapitulation, with the first episode in the key of the tonic, is now on the way and merges over the transitional material heard before into an extended coda which sums up the chief subject with a masterly superiority that can afford to take a humorous view of itself and of the subject-matter with which it deals. The first half of Ex. 164 turns itself into a kind of mock-fugal episode, like a stretto on a dominant pedal. Then a new phrase to which it has given rise makes a tentative approach towards the main theme, which it eventually reaches by tiptoeing from C up to C♯. After the first half of Ex. 163 there is a portentous pause, and the second half is given out in a much slower tempo, feelingly and yet with a touch of amused parody. This process is repeated, and the *adagio* drags itself out longer the second time, with the theme broken up and a softly rising bass turning into a shake that remains as a pedal above which the turn of figure 164*a* comes in *presto*. This fast motion is retained to the end and so, almost throughout, is the thematic scrap 164*a*, out of which a remarkably original and conclusive page of music is made.

SONATA IN D MINOR, Op. 31 No. 2 (1802)
(B.S.S. RECORDS, VOL. VIII)

THE only D minor sonata Beethoven ever wrote has a formal scheme of extreme originality. No wonder that commentators, trying to account for the unusual way in which it develops, have jumped gratefully at Schindler's revelation of Beethoven's advice to 'read Shakespeare's *Tempest*.' To what lengths such dangerous encouragement can carry even serious scholars will be gathered from my seventh 'Interlude'; but it may be as well to quote one who shows admirable common sense in the matter, since the reader had better be reminded that, while Beethoven's own words should not be entirely disregarded, they can only too easily be over-interpreted. The following sentences, which may be considered as a final sentence, come from Sir Donald Tovey, who is never far from one's consciousness when it comes to analysing Beethoven:

> With all the tragic power of its first movement the D minor Sonata is, like Prospero, almost as far beyond tragedy as it is beyond mere foul weather. It will do you no harm to think of Miranda at bars 31–8 of the slow movement [see Ex. 172 below] ; but people who want to identify Ariel and Caliban and the castaways, good and villainous, may as well confine their attention to the exploits of the Scarlet Pimpernel when the *Eroica* or the C minor Symphony is being played.

Largo–Allegro.—When a classical sonata begins *largo*, we expect adherence to the precedent of a slow introduction. So here, unless we happen to know this work, a postulate that is, of course, irrelevant to analysis, which must take it for granted that all it reveals is news, if it is to be of any use at all. But after a single bar and three-quarters we find that we are already in one of Beethoven's most agitated quick movements, though not one of his fastest:

Ex. 167

All the same, the introductory slow matter is there; only it has been broken into small fragments and distributed over the first movement in the most enterprising way imaginable. After the six bars just quoted, the slow initial gesture is repeated in the key of C major, and the *allegro* subject follows in a more extended version, with basses rising by semitones to the dominant of D minor, which is hugged for eight bars and then gives way to an important new feature of the first-subject group, or rather new with the exception of the figure marked *a*, which is of course the *largo* phrase:

[*Continued*

Ex. 168

Of its two clauses, bass and treble, the first is the one to be more consistently developed. It is heard, in fact, in a chain of seven rising sequences. The next idea is, for a second subject, rather closely allied to the first (Ex. 167); yet, the dominant key (A minor) having been reached by this time, there is no doubt that this does belong to the second-subject group, the next feature of which, however, is more striking:

Ex. 169

Having soared up through three octaves, this presently appears in the bass with new, syncopated figures above it. The exposition is concluded with two new thematic shapes alternating in double counterpoint between the pianist's hands.

The exposition is repeated. Then, by a new transition of the utmost simplicity, the music merges into the working-out section, where the slow opening figure of Ex. 167 is heard three times, not only in different keys, but in different chord positions which yield harmonies of strongly contrasting colour and lead from D major to F sharp major.

A depression to F sharp minor brings with it the return of the *allegro* motion, and the working-out now concerns itself with Ex. 168, the figure *b* again disappearing after two statements and *a* taking command. When its bass note has risen by degrees from F ♯ to D, Beethoven settles down to a long-drawn and thematically featureless stretch of music firmly poised on the dominant of D minor, with which expectation of the approaching recapitulation is cunningly aroused and kept in suspense. That suspense is still to be dramatically heightened. A flowing bass melody in bare octaves, rather like the cadence in an operatic aria, leads to the return of the opening *largo* (Ex. 167), which is now surprisingly followed by a few bars of unaccompanied recitative, as expressive as any vocal phrase, and tempting, one must suppose, to annotators who feel like ransacking *The Tempest* for some suitable quotation to fit to the music and are prepared to overlook the awkward fact that any one who searches assiduously enough may find only too many.

The *allegro*, followed by a bar of *adagio*, returns as before, and so does the C major repetition of the opening phrase. Another sentence in recitative, although unaccompanied like the first, implies F minor harmony by its last note, which is the mediant of that key. This A ♭ is changed to G ♯ at the resumption of the *allegro*, which now does a very surprising thing. It cuts out all further reference to the first-subject group and proceeds straight to the second, which remains firmly in D minor. The recapitulation thereafter proceeds normally and is rounded off by a short coda that does not draw on any important thematic material, but merely on the quaver figure of the concluding double-counterpoint idea.

Adagio.—Beethoven chooses sonata form for this slow movement; but another fully developed sonata movement would have meant not only tautology but much too great an expanse in the middle of a work that is going to be rounded off with a very swift finale. We are therefore given here an exposition and recapitulation only, without any working-out section; and to compensate for the absence of thematic development, there is going to be a great deal of thematic elaboration by means of ornament. Note, for example, how the principal theme is embroidered at once at a second statement that follows immediately upon the first:

Ex. 170

Ex. 171

The principal subject is concluded where little rapid triplet figures, as of kettle-drums, are heard alone in the bass, and there is a lengthy transition in which this figure, top and bottom alternately, plays a conspicuous part. The second subject is the tune which may, we have been told, without harm be regarded as representative of Miranda, if, one should perhaps add, the hearer is really convinced that it is suitable, which as likely as not he will fail to be:

Ex. 172

It is repeated with slight but subtle modifications and gives way to another transition, in which the drum figure turns up again. The main theme then recurs, at first in a form akin to Ex. 171, but with somewhat lightened texture, and then with a rich ornamentation of demi-semiquaver figures which display themselves by turns above and below it.

The transition to the second subject, with the drum triplets, reappears in a different disposition which should be compared with the earlier version by the reader who is curious to take an instructive peep into Beethoven's workshop. The second subject (Ex. 172) returns in the tonic (B flat major), but otherwise unaltered, and then the second transition, changed in the same way and somewhat extended by new modulations, makes a bridge to the coda, which is at first based on the chief theme and then, surprisingly, but quite naturally, introduces an entirely new melodic passage at the last moment.

Allegretto.—The finale is a practically unbroken *moto perpetuo* of semiquavers, beginning as follows:

Ex. 173

The D minor flow, after turning into the dominant, reverts to the tonic through a Neapolitan inflection of E flat (minor sixth above the subdominant G). When this has happened twice the figure *a* of the first subject (Ex. 173) passes into the bass and the music turns, by way of C major, into A minor for the second subject, which by a cross-rhythm creates the momentary illusion that the 3–8 motion has been replaced by 2–8:

[*Continued*

Ex. 174

A new concluding theme brings the exposition to a close in the key of the dominant (A minor), with a figure which again divides the bar into 2–8 groups:

Ex. 175

But Beethoven is careful here to mark accents on each first beat: he has already safeguarded himself against the danger of rhythmic monotony by relieving the continuous semiquaverage by an incident of metrical ambiguity and is now content with a similar device in a much milder form. Four connecting bars lead to the repeat of the exposition which includes the connecting passage at the end. This, by a diminished-seventh turn of a harmony, opens the working-out section, sustained wholly by the rhythmic life of Ex. 173 and, although spun out for a very long time, full of an interest that is mainly modulatory, but depends also upon such variety as change of position, inversion and density can impart to the unchanging figuration.

By way of an extended run of unaccompanied right-hand semiquavers the recapitulation is at last approached. It proceeds normally, though, of course, with the necessary change of key for the second subject's appearance in the tonic and the new transitional procedure which this involves. When Ex. 175 has been played again, this time in D minor, the connecting passage already heard at the end of the exposition paves the way for a long coda based on material that has by now become familiar. The whole concluding section is, in fact, an extension of the first-subject group, made structurally important by its persistent emphasis of the key of D minor.

SONATA IN E FLAT MAJOR, Op. 31 No. 3 (1802)
(B.S.S. RECORDS, VOL. VI)

ALTHOUGH the composition of the three Sonatas Op. 31 dates from 1802, the present work did not appear until three years later. It was published without opus number in the *Répertoire des Clavecinistes*, by Nägeli of Zürich, in which Nos. 1 and 2, G major and D minor, had already been issued in 1803.

With the exception of Op. 106 this is the last of the piano sonatas to contain more than three movements and quite the last to include a formal minuet. That movement, indeed, points back to the eighteenth century. On the other hand there is a scherzo which makes a daring departure from the usual 3–4 time and is in other ways the most unconventional section of this on the whole fairly sedate work. The greatest enterprise shown in it by Beethoven is seen not so much in his musical idiom, always excepting the scherzo, as in his curious array of four almost violently contrasted sections. What makes this contrast still more remarkable is that not one of the four movements goes at a slow pace.

Allegro.—The opening of the first movement is magical:

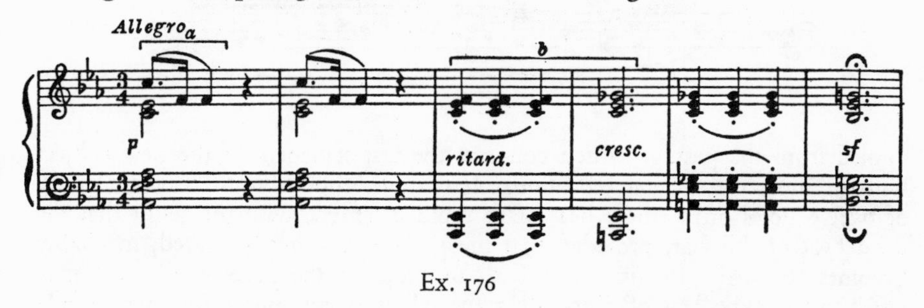

Ex. 176

'a wonderful soft call to attention—as if the Evening Star tapped on the casement,' to quote Marion Scott again. Note how Beethoven, usually so fond of constructing symphony and sonata themes from the common chord, here begins in an ambiguous harmony, which clearly reveals itself as poised on the subdominant of E flat major only when the chords have glided chromatically into the dominant. The *sforzando* and pause shown in the last bar of Ex. 176 go out of their way to emphasize that dominant, as though to make up for the initial indecision. On the other hand the tonic is hinted at only fleetingly, thus:

Ex. 177

The rising triplet scale again leads to the subdominant position, with the falling motif 176*a* descending by octaves. After a second appearance of the cadence shown in Ex. 177 a tonic pedal asserts itself, without however establishing the actual tonic harmony (E flat major triad) much more firmly. The whole first-subject group, in fact, fights curiously shy of it. The entire exposition, it might be said, is not so much *in* E flat major as *round about* E flat major, which is not to imply that Beethoven is undecided about the use of keys, but on the contrary that his grasp of the distribution of tonality allows him to play with them in exceedingly subtle and varied ways.

A transition produces interesting developments of Ex. 176, beginning with figure *a* in the minor and then cutting it out in order to modulate through figure *b* to B flat major for the second subject. This is a treble melody with a long, lyrical flow interrupted by little stuttering figures. It is set over broken chords in the left hand which revert frankly to the eighteenth-century 'Alberti bass.'

An interesting point arises in the following bar:

Ex. 178

quoted from the passage which connects the first statement of the new subject with its more ornamental repetition. It is quite impossible to play the group of twelve notes on a single beat of so rapid a tempo, with the result that the third beat of this bar, provided that the passage is correctly played, inevitably becomes retarded. Pianists who wish to keep up the pace at all costs may resort to the expedient of distributing the whole twenty-one notes more evenly over the bar, in which case it becomes just possible to fill it at the prescribed pace. But it is obvious that Beethoven could himself have so distributed them had he wished to do so, and therefore equally obvious that he meant the twelve demi-semiquavers to take up the third beat only. And if this cannot be done without retarding that beat, it follows that he wanted it retarded. In other words, he forces the player to make a particular rhetorical point without seeing the necessity of insisting upon it by any specific direction, since it is bound to produce itself automatically if the performer plays what is written. If there is anything wrong about Beethoven's notation, it is merely that, like other great composers, he was innocent enough to take it for granted that all pianists play what they see before them on paper.

The exposition closes with an ingenious expansion of the cadence that concludes the second subject, a longish ornamental passage with an extended shake in the right hand and a short new melody so constructed as to melt easily into the opening figure of the first-subject group (Ex. 176*a*). Thus the exposition is repeated without any apparent break in the musical continuity. In the same way the composer approaches the working-out section, which begins with the first two bars of Ex. 176. The section which now follows, unlike the corresponding one in the Sonata Op. 10 No. 2, is literally a working-out. Every scrap of it is derived from the material that has gone before, mainly from the first-subject group, but also from the auxiliary material used to round off the exposition. A glance at a copy of the Sonata will show how each of the three different thematic elements of the following couple of bars, drawn out of the context merely by way of an isolated instance, are based on earlier features:

Ex. 179

After a normal recapitulation there is a coda, short but laden with significance. The chief strains of the first subject (Exx. 176 and 177) make up the bulk of it, but one of the subsidiary motifs of the group, alternating in the player's two hands, supplies the concluding bars.

Allegretto vivace.—Nobody would have dreamt of calling this movement a scherzo if Beethoven had not explicitly done so. Such labels in music stick to particular forms, irrespective of mood; a scherzo is expected to be in triple time and to have a contrasting trio. As this piece is in 2–4 time and in sonata form, it could not have mattered to pundits that it has all the characteristics of a typically Beethovenian scherzo except the formal ones: they would not have dared to give it the composer's own title, and we ought therefore to be glad that he, perhaps foreseeing their difficulty, did so himself.

The principal subject might be an amiable rondo theme, if it were not for those cross-accents off the second beat which give the impression of 'crossness' in another sense. The strongly rhythmic rappings in octave unison which follow soon after are positively sinister. The whole dynamic scheme of the scherzo should be carefully noticed, for it is that rather than the melodic formation of the themes which gives it such a restless character. Harmony, however, also has a good deal to do with it. The sudden outburst of F major, like the crack of a whip, where the transition to the second subject begins, as well as the dominant minor ninths which delay its appearance, are quite in keeping with the irascible mood in which this piece seems to have been written. The second subject itself, in E flat major, tries to be more amiable, but is too jumpy and too short quite to achieve such a contrast.

The working-out manipulates the main theme in new keys (F major, C major) and also makes use of the minor-ninth preparation. Towards the end it goes off into little flickering, non-thematic figures, like angry flashes of distant summer lightning, and by way of descending *staccato* scales approaches the recapitulation, which shows the usual redistribution of keys. There is a very brief coda, ingeniously made from a perfectly natural continuation of the second subject and humorously clinched by bare dominant and tonic octaves.

Moderato e grazioso.—We have now come to the minuet which reverts to Beethoven's early style in its main melodic outlines and harmonic cut, though there are some novel features, notably in the trio and coda. The minuet itself has two strains of eight bars, each repeated, with the endings so modified as to interlock with the repeat at first and to make a full close, delayed by an *appoggiatura,* the second time. In the second half the dominant minor ninth makes itself heard again, but melodically this time. It assumes an important harmonic function, however, in the trio section, which consists of very short phrases and single chords. Diminished sevenths make another harmonic inflection in the first part, the minor ninths arising in the second, where the chords become for three bars grouped into a 2–4 cross-rhythm against the prevailing 3–4. It is perhaps worth mentioning that this trio was used by Saint-Saëns as a theme for a set of variations for two pianos. The minuet is repeated, but the final *appoggiatura* is replaced by a simple triad falling on the first beat. The tiny coda is governed by the minor-ninth complex of the second half of the minuet, but it now affects the tonic, not the dominant.

Presto con fuoco.—It is owing to the finale that this Sonata is sometimes called *La Chasse* or *Jagd-Sonate*; but fortunately this fancy name, which is at least as inappropriate to the work as a whole as 'Moonlight' or 'Pastoral' are to others, has not spread disastrously far. But however unsuited it may have been, there was no escaping it. Was there not 6–8 time? Was there not a theme like a hunting signal? And was not the favourite horn key of E flat major employed? All this coming together was too much for the conventionalists, who could scarcely be expected to come across even one of these features without thinking of the only sport that had so long provided a fashionable musical theme.

But let us abandon the chase and keep to music. The finale, which is again in sonata form, is a study in continuous rhythmic patterns, two of which are almost unceasingly used. The first, heard at the opening, is a figure of accompaniment:

Ex. 180

the second is the 'horn' theme, if we like to call it so, made of broken sextolets in a saltarello rhythm:

Ex. 181

Bekker calls the movement 'a kind of German tarantella,' which is at any rate descriptive if ethnologically far-fetched, and he too is unable to resist speaking of Ex. 181 as 'a simple hunting song.' With this material and a third theme, the first-subject group scurries along. The accompaniment continues the even triplet motion when the chief strain of the second-subject group appears, which will be recognized by the much-repeated note of its opening. The rhythm of Ex. 181, which is also that of the third strain, reasserts itself in the rising and falling theme with which the exposition ends, with a pause on a dominant-seventh chord.

After the repeat the passage leading to that chord is restated in another key, thus bringing the music abruptly to G flat major. In that key Ex. 181 returns, and it is developed in the course of the working-out section with a new, forcible theme in descending octaves, again accompanied by triplets. Other interesting new applications of the thematic material follow, and the turn into the recapitulation is effected in a most unexpected and fascinating way. Only a broken triplet is left, many times repeated and gradually dying away. Then suddenly Ex. 180 bursts out again emphatically. The music is by no means recapitulated without further changes, though the modified themes appear in their proper places. The coda begins by scrapping all melodic features and leaving only accompanying figures akin to those shown in Ex. 180. But it is the short melodic snatch quoted there which is the chief character to bring down the curtain, and Beethoven shows an inexhaustible fertility and imagination in the handling of it.

SONATA IN G MINOR AND MAJOR, Op. 49 No. 1 (?1796)
(B.S.S. RECORDS, VOL. III)

THE date of the two little Sonatas, labelled Op. 49 but not belonging to the time this number would seem to indicate, is uncertain. There is a vast confusion about the opus numbers round about that period. *The Creatures of Prometheus,* for instance, which we have seen to be contemporaneous with the Sonata Op. 28 (1801), is marked Op. 43, while the song, *Adelaide,* dating most probably from 1795, is Op. 46. The Sonatas Op. 49 were brought out on 19th January 1805, by the establishment that had published Op. 28, but the date of composition is evidently considerably earlier. Grove says 'not later than 1802,' which is putting it very cautiously indeed, while Paul Bekker assigns the work to 1796, which from internal evidence seems much more plausible, though he will not commit himself so far as to set it down in that year without a question mark.

It was Beethoven's brother Caspar who sent the Op. 49 to the Bureau des Arts et d'Industrie for publication, and he did so without the composer's sanction. This meant trouble for him and annoyance for his famous brother, but, as Sir Donald Tovey suggests, good fortune for posterity, 'as we might otherwise have been deprived of the two most beautiful sonatinas within the range of small hands and young players.' This is by no means the first time that these two small works have been called sonatinas: they have often been published under that title, and the fact is that it fits them perfectly. They are easy music in a compressed sonata form. As a curiosity it may be noted that Beethoven in both cases restricted himself to two movements, an economy he did not practise again until he reached the sonatas of a later period, beginning with Op. 54.

Andante.—The structure of the first movement is extraordinarily simple—sonata form reduced to its elements. The exposition contains merely first- and second-subject groups, with scarcely any elaboration or extraneous incidents. The first subject is, of course, in the reigning key of G minor:

Ex. 182

while the second appears in the relative major (B flat):

Ex. 183

(The group of four semiquavers on the up-beat shows what is actually played at this point, the quaver F is the implied thematic feature, which is seen to establish itself an octave higher.) The exposition closes in B flat major and is repeated.

The working-out begins with a very simple but none the less ingenious use of Ex. 183, modulating to E flat major, in which key some episodic material appears. But it is Ex. 183 which continues to dominate, although a definite connection with it is to be felt rather than traced in a bridge-passage leading to the recapitulation.

This begins exactly like the exposition, except that the opening note after the up-beat is now D instead of B ♭, this being the logical response to the leading C ♯ that precedes it by way of a link. Even in so early a work Beethoven knew how to refine the organization of a movement by smoothing the corners round which the music turns from one division into the next. No less masterly is his new transition to the second-subject group, which has now to remain in the tonic key. He cunningly draws attention to this point of interest by not only varying the modulation, but also the pianistic texture: the theme is transferred to the left hand and new figuration appears in the right. An almost dramatic cadence that traverses a chord of the diminished seventh opens a brief coda in which Ex. 183 appears with gentle insistence in the bass, as though reluctant to be dismissed. But the right-hand figures dissolve themselves into a mere accompaniment, under which a low G pedal becomes fixed, and this very softly turns the music into an unexpected close in G major.

Allegro.—The finale is a rondo in the key which has been cleverly prepared by the close of the first movement. Having restricted himself to two movements, Beethoven obtains variety by casting the second in the tonic major; but, as we shall see in a moment, he is careful not to make the change too drastic. The chief subject is this:

Ex. 184

As soon as it has been fully stated, the composer remembers that this work was after all begun as a Sonata in G minor, and he restores the balance by returning to that key for an episode that is approached by the following connecting passage:

Ex. 185

The reason why this is quoted rather than the episode itself is that it is the germ-cell from which not only the G minor incident springs, but also the following, in B flat major, which is later perceived to be in the nature of a second subject:

Ex. 186

A modulating passage, still making use of the figures *a* shown in Exx. 185 and 186, leads to a modified restatement of Ex. 186; then, by way of Ex. 185, back to the first episode, and so to the return of the chief theme (Ex. 184). There are some slight changes, including a more conspicuous use of the figure 184*a* (canon and contrary motion), and then Ex. 186 recurs in G major, thus revealing itself as a true second subject, restated, according to classical usage, in the fundamental key. Instead of going once again to the first episode, Beethoven dismisses it and lets Ex. 184 follow on immediately. Again the phrase 184*a* appears in a different form, whereupon, after a pause on a dominant seventh, a short coda closes the movement with free allusions to the basic material.

SONATA IN G MAJOR, Op. 49 No. 2 (? 1796)
(B.S.S. RECORDS, VOL. V)

SCHOLARS are generally agreed that the minuet movement in the second of the Op. 49 Sonatas is earlier than the minuet, based on the same melody, in the Septet, Op. 20, which was published in 1802. As Grove gives the date of composition for the Septet as 'before 2nd April 1800,' it is not easy to see why he should put 1802 as the latest possible date for the Sonatas. But a very similar theme occurs also in the slow movement of the Trio for clarinet, cello and piano, Op. 11, written in 1797, and if Bekker is right in considering that this too is later than Op. 49, one may also accept his date for the Sonatas (1796) as fairly safe. What is certain is that they are by no means more mature in style and manner than the first three piano Sonatas, Op. 2, published that year and known to have been composed in 1795. That Sir Donald Tovey even goes so far as to regard Op. 49 as anterior to Op. 2 is shown by a sentence in his *Companion to Beethoven's Pianoforte Sonatas*, where he speaks of the rondo of No. 1 as being 'in a peculiar form, only once partially adopted by Beethoven later on in the slow movement of Op. 2 No. 3.'

Allegro, ma non troppo.—It would seem at first sight that sonata form could not be demonstrated more clearly than by the present example. All redundancies and inessentials are dispensed with and only the bare elements of the traditional pattern retained in what is in reality a sonatina. Yet it must be said that the demonstration would result rather in a piece of evidence proving that Beethoven uses sonata form just as freely as the exigencies of the moment dictate. He works logically according to rules only so long as their modification does not seem expedient to him. If it does, he will not hesitate to bend or even break them. Here, for example, nothing could be more orthodox than his exposition and working-out, for even if the latter is very brief, it is not unusually so once we have accepted this work as a sonatina. But he does not scruple to extend his recapitulation in a startlingly drastic way, having once chosen to bring about the culmination of his third act, so to speak, by the particular order in which he wishes his characters to reappear.

Here are his four chief actors, as it were. The first subject:

Ex. 187

Its companion:

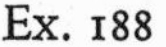

Ex. 188

The second subject:

Ex. 189

The companion of the second subject:

Ex. 190

They will be seen entering in that order, accompanied by some minor figures added for the sake of conversational flow and picturesqueness. Ex. 188 has the last word in the opening act—the exposition—which closes in D major.

The second act (working-out) is episodic and extremely short, a mere interlude with only a fleeting appearance of the second subject (Ex. 189), and that in a costume which almost completely disguises it. In fourteen bars all is over, and the third act (recapitulation) is reached without a break, by a descending scale that overlaps into the opening of Ex. 187. This (the first subject) duly returns, but instead of being followed by its own attendant (Ex. 188), this is very surprisingly displaced by that of the second subject (Ex. 190), now in a C major mood. However, 188 follows as soon as the key has changed to

G major, in which the second subject (Ex. 189) comes in last of all. But now the regular course of the first act is followed to the end, though one had expected that Ex. 188 would be allowed no further say. It does enter again, also in G major, which is now maintained to the end, though with some deceptive inflections tending towards C major. It is obvious now that the irregular intrusion of 188 was not intended to deprive it of its proper place later on, but to compensate for the surprising lack of events in the second act. It was simply an incident of development which by rights should have taken place in the working-out, but was delayed until the recapitulation was in full swing. It is thus that genius adjusts accepted forms to the inspiration of the moment without spoiling their symmetry. On the contrary, Beethoven here achieves a remarkable feat of formal balance by taking something away from his thickening of the plot in order to add it to his *dénouement.*

Tempo di Menuetto.—This movement is so simple that to elucidate it would be to insist on the obvious, much as that famous sentence did in a certain Spanish conversation book: 'Look, our postilion has been struck by lightning.' Moreover, there is not even any lightning here: the music is exceedingly mild, and its beautiful shape is as clear to the ear as it could possibly be made to the understanding by analysis.

Instead of that, it will therefore be preferable to supply a brief comparison with the similar movement in the Septet, a work scored for clarinet, bassoon, horn, violin, viola, cello and double bass. It is in E flat major, a convenient key for wind instruments. The likeness of the two movements in question is confined to the first strain, which I propose to quote in full from the Septet, but to leave the reader to compare with the sonata movement by ear or with the aid of a printed copy:

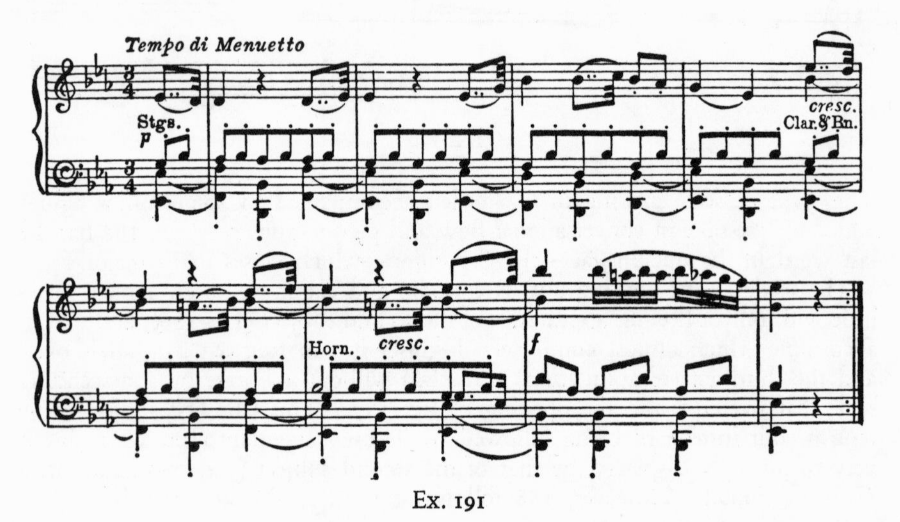

Ex. 191

It will be seen—to begin with a small difference—that the melody in the Septet version is made more incisive by double dots. Beethoven, it seems, wanted to make sure of a snappy rhythm where more lyrical instruments than the comparatively dry piano were to interpret this precise little movement. On the other hand he simplifies it formally there by mearly marking a note-for-note repeat of this first strain, whereas in the piano version the restatements are not only treated differently, but intersected by an auxiliary idea of four bars.

After that the music takes an entirely different turn in the two pieces. In the Septet the texture is finer, the part-writing more sophisticated; in the Sonata, on the other hand, the section that comes between the first and second complete statement of the principal theme is very much more extensive (27 bars as against 12). It seems to be a sort of multiplication of the four-bar incident already mentioned, everything being proportionately enlarged. To continue the analogy, the Septet movement may be said to be built up only by addition.

The fact is that in the Sonata the material is dealt with as in a rondo, not a minuet proper, as it is in the Septet. There we have a well-developed trio, which incidentally gives brilliant opportunities to clarinet and horn, whereas a section in the sub-dominant (C) major, which appears in the Sonata as though it were in the nature of a trio, proves to be simply a second rondo episode. For, unlike the Septet version, the keyboard piece does not revert to the first section by a *da capo* repeat: the opening strain is written out again in full, with the addition of a coda. This was not the classic way of dealing with the simple dance forms inherited from the suite. It is true that Beethoven was often given to a minuet-scherzo type that did restate the first section exactly as played and was rounded off by a freshly devised coda (e.g. Sonata Op. 10 No. 2, where, after the trio, we find the indication *scherzo da capo e poi la coda*); but where the feature of a coda is found together with a section that can be regarded as at most a rudimentary trio, as in this Sonata, one must really decide for the rondo form, even if that too, with only two episodes of very unequal size, must be looked upon as elementary.

SONATA IN C MAJOR, Op. 53 (1804)
(B.S.S. RECORDS, VOL. IX)

WE have seen that the Op. 26 Sonata is linked, by its funeral march and by way of the Paer anecdote, to the *Eroica* Symphony. More superficially, the present Sonata, dedicated to Count Waldstein and published by the Bureau des Arts et d'Industrie of Vienna in May 1805, also has some connection with the third Symphony, if only because it was composed in the same year—1804. This juxtaposition is not altogether arbitrary, however, for although the two works are entirely different in content and mood, they show us how Beethoven advanced in the art of composition on a larger scale than he had ever attempted before by handling two different species simultaneously. True, the difference between the Sonata Op. 53 and the three Sonatas Op. 31 is much less marked than that between the second and third Symphonies, although the distance of time is about the same (two years). But it must be remembered that the original plan of Op. 53 included, for a slow movement, the work afterwards published separately as the *Andante favori* in F major. This meant so vast a scheme, indeed, that Beethoven wisely removed that long piece and substituted for it the short 'introduction' which is little more than a bridge between the extensive first movement and finale, though a bridge so admirably constructed that it makes all the difference between two great separate pieces in C major in sonata and rondo form respectively and a single connected work on an enormous scale.

The dedicatee, Count Ferdinand von Waldstein, was eight years older than Beethoven and thus about forty-two when the Sonata was inscribed to him. But he had been acquainted with Beethoven already at Bonn, where the composer, still in his teens, was introduced to him about 1788, probably by his aristocratic friends, the Breuning family. As an intimate of the elector's he was a useful acquaintance, but he attracted the defiantly democratic Beethoven, who was not likely to be influenced by such considerations, by his genuine love of music, a love by no means unaccompanied by talent. Waldstein gave Beethoven a new pianoforte, and on it the two young men played duets together. The young nobleman seems to have contrived to obtain for his friend certain gratuities from the electoral court which he would doubtless have indignantly refused had they had been openly offered as alms. Whether Beethoven guessed this or not, it is certain that he was willing to write the music for a *Ritterballett,* produced by a number of aristocrats on Carnival Sunday in 1791, the composition of which was announced as being by Waldstein. On 29th October 1792 the young count wrote a farewell message in the autograph album of Beethoven, who was about to leave for Vienna. It may have been he who introduced his friend to Prince Lichnowsky, to whom the Op. 26 Sonata is dedicated. A set of Variations for piano duet on a theme by Waldstein dates from 1792.

The year 1804, incidentally, brought with it an event which seems to have urged Beethoven to act once more upon his humorous threat to Paer—and even more seriously this time. That composer's opera, *Eleonore, ossia l' amore conjugale,* based on Gaveaux's *Léonore, ou l'amour conjugal* of 1798, appeared in 1804, and by the spring of next year Beethoven had begun the composition of his *Leonore, oder die eheliche Liebe,* alias *Fidelio.* It seems that he 'had to compose that' too.

Allegro con brio.—The stormy, thundery opening movement at once broaches its first subject, of which the four initial bars contain all the chief elements:

Ex. 192

except this cadence figure, which is to assume considerable significance later on:

Ex. 193

The repeated quavers (Ex. 192*a*) are heard again at the fifth bar, now a sequential step lower down—in B flat major. The music, however, turns almost immediately to C minor, in which key the first statement of the theme ends as shown above (Ex. 193). It returns an octave higher, broken up into semiquavers, and it is characteristic of the whole key-scheme of this movement, which is like a fitful play of lights and shadows, that C major is established again, as though the C minor cadence had been set down expressly to enhance the brightness of that key. Still more astonishing, the sequence now goes upwards instead of down, the second statement being in D minor instead of B flat major. This, of course, leads the music easily into quite new regions of tonality. What happens, in fact, is an unheard-of thing: a transitional passage, the opening of which is obviously suggested by Ex. 192*c*, seems to prepare the way to E minor, but actually prepares it to E major, a very remote key indeed in which to present the second subject in a sonata of Beethoven's mid-career. However, this is what we encounter here, and the subject not only shows a striking contrast in key, but an even stronger one in character. It offers a moment of heavenly repose in an otherwise restless and agitated movement:

Ex. 194

A scale of triplets gives rise to a restatement of this theme in an exquisite new version, in which it is wrapped up in triplet figuration. This in turn engenders the following apparently unimportant idea which, however, is to play a more conspicuous part later on:

[*Continued*

Ex. 195

What follows is a very extended cadential section approaching the end of an exposition of abnormally large size, a section full of opportunities to display the brilliant figure work and explosive dynamic changes made possible by the pianoforte in Beethoven's time. A conclusive phrase is at last reached and takes this extended form the second time:

Ex. 196

Arrived at C major, it leads straight back to Ex. 192 and thus without any break to the restatement of the whole exposition.

All that has been heard so far having been played a second time, the problem arises how to let the music merge into the working-out section as naturally as it had previously led to the repetition of the expository section. Beethoven solves it in the simplest way: he lets the concluding figure (Ex. 196) undergo yet another modulation this time, and so brings back Ex. 192 in F major instead of C major.

That is enough to set him off on a quest after new interpretations of his material. He now detaches the figures *b* and *c* from Ex. 192, states them in new keys and gradually contracts them rhythmically, with an effect of extraordinary tension and excitement. A page later he discloses the real purpose of the apparently incidental notion quoted above as Ex. 195, which now forms a significant feature of the working-out, serving at the same time as a modulatory bridge for a return of C major. We are held up for some considerable time, however, in G major, as in a kind of traffic black half-way across the bridge. There are rumblings of thunder and flashes of lightning, and thematically speaking we cannot see that we are anywhere in particular; but Beethoven saves the situation with characteristic decision and resourcefulness. Without letting us see where exactly the change takes place, he converts what is at first unmistakably G major into the dominant of C major; or, to continue to speak pictorially (though with apologies), we are clearly on the bridge of G major at one moment, then in G as the dominant of C, as though on a bridge-head where nobody knows precisely what is part of the structure and what *terra firma*, until we suddenly find ourselves back with a rush (scales in contrary motion) in the main key and the main subject (Ex. 192).

The recapitulation is far from normal, for as soon as we have approached that C minor cadence figure (Ex. 193) which clinched the first statement of the theme at the beginning, we find that the music is wrenched out of its original course in the most surprising way. For now the final note of Ex. 193 is not G, but

A ♭. Which, if one may put it so frivolously, not merely blocks the traffic, but upsets the apple-cart. To what purpose? Beethoven intends to get back to his second statement of the theme, in C major, with the broken semiquaver figuration and with the rising sequence to D minor; yet he holds up his progress in this unexampled manner and has to set his key right again in a roundabout way before he can proceed. If the 'Waldstein' Sonata were an improvisation and not a work written down with every step it takes evidently thought out with the utmost care, one would say that the performer had hit on A ♭ instead of G by accident and then made up his mind quickly to a modulatory detour in order to come back to the required key again. As it is, all one can say is that if improvisation led to such fascinating expedients, it would have its decided advantages over deliberate composition, for nothing could have been more felicitous than this unexpected stroke in the middle of a recapitulation apparently planned to proceed normally, at any rate up to the second subject. It is not impossible, by the way, that Beethoven did light upon this notion in the course of improvisation, for although we cannot tell how many of his ideas came to him in that way, we do know that he was famous for his art of extemporization, and this passage certainly sounds like one of those accidental inspirations come by in that way.

The most surprising point before this curious incident was, it will be remembered, the appearance of the second subject in the major key of the mediant instead of in the dominant. Beethoven now makes still more of this by a compromise of the most extraordinary ingenuity. What is to happen now? Is the second subject to appear in its own dominant, which would be a relation to its original position not too out of the common, or is it to ignore its first appearance and return in the main key of the sonata, in the orthodox way? The transition now is certainly on the dominant of the second subject's own dominant (E), and we are thus led to A major.

The second subject does appear in that key, thus keeping firmly to its original resolve to put itself into an unconventional position. But to modulate on from this in the earlier way would be to throw the rest of the recapitulation out of its proper keys; so, having made this acknowledgment to its descent, the second subject decides to fall in with the classical sonata scheme after all and to make the rest of its appearance in C major, to which it modulates very easily through its own minor key, which is the relative minor of C. Nothing could have resolved itself more smoothly, and we almost forget how embarrassingly difficult Beethoven's formal problems had looked once or twice in the course of this movement. But then it is the height of mastery to make formidable obstacles appear not only easy to overcome, but beautiful and original in themselves.

Ex. 195 also reappears in C major, followed by the long brilliant episode rounded off by Ex. 196. This, in a new series of keys, ushers in a very extended coda of a curiously dual nature, half development and half cadenza. It is probably this feature in particular which has induced so many critics to call the 'Waldstein' Sonata a typical middle-period work of Beethoven's, for it certainly points both back and forward. An interrupted cadence brings Ex. 192*a* back in D flat major, and then 192 *b* and *c* follow in a contracted form similar to that in the working-out section and modulate back to C major. Next Ex. 192 appears in the left hand with new syncopations and scales in the right above it. 192*c* soon afterwards forms itself into rising sequences, with the scales still continuing over it, and this is followed by what becomes almost a conventional cadenza, leading, surprisingly enough, to a last appearance of the second subject (Ex. 194). Three times it makes a hesitant attempt to continue, but gives way to Ex. 192 *a* and *b*, which appear for the last time, the latter tightened into an abrupt little figure. Scales in contrary motion and four loud detached chords conclude the movement.

Molto adagio.—The *Introduzione*, as Beethoven deliberately calls this substitute for the large independent movement (the *Andante favori*) originally planned for this Sonata, is only twenty-eight bars long, though very slow in pace. Unlike its discarded forerunner, it could lead no independent existence, being devoid of a final full close.

Thematically it is of set purpose kept rather featureless but for a lovely melodic episode half a dozen bars long, the opening of which is suggested by the first bar of the movement, which is this:

Ex. 197

The melody begins as follows:

Ex. 198

After a very gentle and slow cadence the music reverts to the material that begins with Ex. 197, the chief interest of which lies in its very drastic modulations. It has now a new figure in the accompaniment, which presently becomes continuous and allows the music to trickle quietly away above it. The last three bars almost stand still and are nearly inaudible. In the end a high G remains suspended all alone.

Allegretto moderato.—The subject of the rondo is given out at once by the left hand, which crosses over a gently murmuring accompaniment in the right:

Ex. 199

A kind of rarefied mountain air at once makes itself felt, very different from the thunderous atmosphere and the fitful gleams of sunlight in the first movement, and although there are, of course, more strenuous passages in this rondo, a feeling of remoteness from human strife prevails throughout. Nothing could be more wonderful than the contrast between two exceptionally long sonata movements which resemble each other only in their proportions and their significance, unless it be the mystery of the page of music which connects them in the place of the comparatively ordinary variations of the *Andante* which Beethoven decided to publish separately.

Some fascinating inflections of changing major and minor, wrapped in a harmonic haze by the pedal, follow soon after Ex. 199, which is then repeated in octaves over a more widespread accompaniment. After a repetition of the major-minor idea, which is also differently laid out, the main theme is heard once more, this time *fortissimo* over a shake and a thrusting upward run in the bass followed by a gentler descent.

The first episode, a vigorous formation of rapid triplets, begins in C major, but soon moves into A minor, where it remains all the time. In the same key still an allusion to the main theme (Ex. 199) follows, echoed in F major and shifting to a dominant position on G for the return of the subject in the principal key. It is presented exactly as before and leads to a second episode, a new energetic theme in C minor, which modulates more enterprisingly than the first episode, but not very far afield. The octave theme and the triplet accompaniment alternate between the two hands. The end of this episode is marked by five Cs given out in bare octaves with diminishing force.

What now follows is a vast transition of the utmost beauty and interest. It begins with new enunciations of the main theme, more fully harmonized than before, in A flat major, F minor and D flat major. The music then modulates away from D flat in a syncopated passage of twelve bars that is perfectly non-thematic, yet must be counted among the most arrestingly beautiful things in the whole of the 'Waldstein' Sonata. Next comes a longish series of arpeggios, below which nothing more is outlined than the bare rhythm of the two opening bars of Ex. 199. This rhythm continues even when the figuration changes, and is in fact repeated with a persistence that has an almost hypnotic effect. At any rate it keeps the hearer in a state of extraordinary suspense, particularly when it begins to hover for a long time round the principal key by hanging on its dominant. When at last the subject gratifies us with a sudden return, we find that it has been shortened by the omission of the first thirty bars.

Beethoven now seems to be bringing back the first episode; what he actually does, however, is to begin a coda on an enormous scale which it happens to suit him to approach through the theme of that episode. He soon abandons this theme, however, and retains only its triplet motion, with which he carries on a long passage that is purely harmonic and paves the way for a cadential presentation of the rhythm with which we are by this time so familiar that it almost amounts to an obsession.

The tempo then changes to *prestissimo*, or at any rate the time-signature does, for actually the pace is very little, if at all, faster. What Beethoven does here is to double the note-values from semiquavers to quavers and at the same time to halve the speed. All the same, an impression of redoubled quickness is gained, at the outset at any rate, because the principal theme is actually heard twice as fast as before. It is repeated in a more elaborate version, and this leads to independent passages of great brilliance and beauty, into which it continues to be thrust here and there. Then, while arpeggios in triplets spread themselves over the keyboard, it is once again reduced to its bare rhythm. Soon afterwards, however, when a high shake on the dominant has established itself, it is heard higher still, ringing out softly but with a kind of serene assurance at about its original pace. Though it gradually sinks down again, it is finally made to merge, in its quickened form, into a jubilant peroration which asserts the key of C major—Browning's 'C major of this life,' if that was ever heard anywhere in music—with such emphasis that even the passing dominant harmony clings to the tonic in the bass.

INTERLUDE VII

LURID LIGHT ON BEETHOVEN

READERS of this book ought to be the very people to take an interest in a consideration of a new kind of Beethoven criticism which, fascinating as it is, can only be regarded as so wrong-headed as to require the strongest possible refutation. For the fantastic conclusions with which it teems are drawn by a writer who has earned a great and deserved reputation all over the musical world for many an earlier labour in musical research, which makes them all the more dangerous. Indeed the author's name alone carries such weight in musical circles that it needs some detailed examination of this recent example of his work to show how insidious is the kind of criticism which I feel urged to expose here.

When a German musical scholar of the great distinction of Arnold Schering issues a first volume of a work entitled *Beethoven in neuer Deutung*,[1] one is naturally anxious to learn what this new interpretation will amount to and very much disposed to consider it with respectful attention. When a glance at the contents further reveals Dr. Schering's discovery that no fewer than five string Quartets and eight piano Sonatas of Beethoven's are based on plays by Shakespeare and another Sonata on Schiller's *Jungfrau von Orleans*, one is naturally all agog to know how it is that not a single critic of the past hundred years and more has tumbled to any evidence supporting it. For surely, one argues, if Dr Schering can suddenly confront us with such masses of material throwing new light on the fourteen works he discusses, proofs must be scattered in abundance throughout the vast literature devoted to Beethoven, ready for any one's picking, but somehow persistently overlooked by specialists.

One thus turns eagerly to Dr Schering's own pages for chapter and verse. But what does one find? He adduces one or two shreds of evidence which, with a little goodwill, one may find reliable, and the rest of his proofs he ingeniously manufactures for himself. His is not a case of 'seeing is believing': he believes first and then proceeds to see. As was to be expected, he makes what he can of Beethoven's well-known reply to Schindler, who had asked him for a clue to the Sonatas in D minor, Op. 31 No. 2, and F minor, Op. 57 (the *Appassionata*). 'Read Shakespeare's *Tempest*,' said the composer. But unfortunately even here Dr Schering lays himself open to a grave objection, for although he does assign *The Tempest* as a programme to the D minor Sonata, his key to the *Appassionata* is not that play, but *Macbeth*. Schindler's evidence has thus been so warped by counsel for the defence as to become practically valueless.

[1] (Kahnt, Leipzig, 1934.) This series has not so far been continued; but since this essay was written a similar work, *Beethoven und die Dichtung*, by the same author, has appeared (Junker & Dünnhaupt, Berlin, 1936), for a detailed review of which, by Alfred Einstein, see *Music and Letters*, Vol. XVIII, No. 2, April 1937.

Now in the matter of *Macbeth*, having constituted myself counsel for the prosecution, I will cite a witness of my own: the actor Heinrich Anschütz. He tells us in his memoirs that he asked Beethoven whether he would not consider illustrating *Macbeth* musically, and that the composer, very much struck with the idea, replied: 'I have already thought about it.' This was some time in or after 1822; the *Appassionata* was published in 1807. Is it conceivable that, had he really embodied *Macbeth* in the Sonata, he could have said anything to Anschütz but 'I have already done it'?

If that is not enough, I may add with regard to Op. 57 that Dr Schering regards the calm, constrained melody of the slow movement as, of all things, music suggested by the witches' scene at the beginning of the fourth act. The reader who likes to pursue the matter further should turn to Shakespeare and to Beethoven's Op. 57. He will be no less puzzled by the task of imagining that any one of the least musical sensibility should pretend to find any correspondence between words and music than amused at being told that Dr Schering actually sets some words of the German translations under the theme of Beethoven's slow movement, words which, be it noted, fit the music metrically as badly as they do emotionally.

It is true that we are offered the testimony of Ries, Czerny and Schindler, which, as everybody has known for a long time, shows us clearly enough that Beethoven did have what Dr Schering calls 'suppressed programmes' in mind; but he takes it entirely upon himself to assert that these 'programmes' were not images created by Beethoven for himself, but literary models taken from the works of Homer, Shakespeare, Tasso, Cervantes, Goethe, Schiller, and whatever else he may yet have up his sleeve.

He is, it appears, still in search for clues to other works, and it is surprising that he has not yet discovered any for the two piano Sonatas Op. 14, which Beethoven himself said represented a struggle between two opposing principles, an argument between two persons. But perhaps he is here embarrassed by too great a wealth of choice, for almost any play could be accommodated, given only a fraction of Dr Schering's predisposition and ingenuity. I would suggest *Julius Caesar* or *Antony and Cleopatra*, neither of which, oddly enough, he has as yet fitted to any Sonata or Quartet, though I cannot do so without the warning that it might prove quite as easy to demonstrate that the Beethovenian struggle illustrated Ibsen or the Beethovenian argument Bernard Shaw.

To do Dr Schering justice, he does not imagine that everybody will agree with him; but he is himself so convinced of the fitness of his programmes that one cannot help examining his claims in detail, with the unfortunate result of discovering that they rest on the flimsiest foundations. This is not to deny the possibility of Beethoven's basing his music on literary instead of on personal experiences: what must be contested is the assertion that these literary programmes are to be discovered with certainty, either by Dr Schering's methods or by any one else's.

He is fond, as I have already shown, of setting actual words from Shakespeare or whomsoever under certain musical phrases. The string Quartet in E flat major, Op. 74, for example, he regards as being inspired by *Romeo and Juliet*. He drags a passage out of the slow movement which (at bar 45) for him exactly fits Romeo's words: 'I must be gone and live, or stay and die.' But, in the first place, Beethoven phrases the same figure exactly alike three times, whereas the syllabic distribution of the underlying words entirely destroys this symmetry. Secondly, Dr Schering chooses the Eschenburg translation, which may in some cases suit his purpose better than that of Schlegel, and he is careful to tell us, on Schindler's authority (and what an authority!) that Beethoven had no use whatever for the latter. He seems to have overlooked the fact that in a letter to Therese von Malfatti, in or about 1807, the composer says: 'Have you read Goethe's *Wilhelm Meister* and the Schlegel translation of Shakespeare?' and offers to lend her these two works. A small point, perhaps, but indicative of the danger of letting a desire to offer the world new enlightment play havoc with scholarship. The sophistries by which the final variations of this Quartet, about which there is not a vestige of tragedy, are forced to accord with the final scene of *Romeo and Juliet* must be read in full to be, I will not say believed, but duly appraised.

Still more astounding is the jamming together of a monologue of Joan of Arc with the slow movement in the *Hammerclavier* Sonata, Op. 106. Beethoven's phrasing is here quite fantastically modified to make the words consort somehow with the music—and even then with often more than doubtful accentuation. Moreover, where the two really will not go together either by threat or persuasion, a few notes here and there are simply left without any words and regarded as an instrumental interlude. The truth is that anything from a speech from Euripides to one by Mussolini could be matched with this particular movement in Beethoven, or any other, by these Procrustean methods.

The D minor Sonata, Op. 31 No. 2, is of course among those honoured by Dr Schering's attentions because it is the work in connection with which Beethoven himself mentioned Shakespeare's *Tempest* to Schindler. Our ingenious exponent, needless to say, makes the most of this, blandly overlooking the logical conclusion that he cannot at the same time disregard the fact that Beethoven also referred to the same play in the matter of the alleged *Macbeth* Sonata—the *Appassionata*.

However, here *The Tempest* is at any rate indicated. But we find that its interpretation is just as arbitrary as anything else in Dr Schering's book. That the storm at sea evidently plays no part in the music is explained plausibly enough by the observation that in the play itself it has not the least influence upon the action, once it has performed its function of throwing the characters together on the desert island. The remark that Beethoven was not interested in elemental phenomena, but only in human character, may pass too, although an uncomfortable question might be asked about the thunderstorm in the 'Pastoral' Symphony. Still, here Dr Schering lays a trap for himself, for how is it that the composer, so interested in character, forgot, as we are expressly told, to take the least notice of the most important person in the play—Prospero? Yet that was the case, it seems. 'At all times he turned only to those incidents,' we are informed, 'which are in themselves comprehensible, i.e. simple and incisive. He disregarded whole acts, and subsidiary personages existed for him only where they suggest some musical correlation by striking characterization.' In other words, one cannot help concluding, Beethoven very considerately chose only such features as suit Dr Schering's interpretative fancy. On the other hand, 'he keeps faithfully to the poem'—so faithfully as to omit whole acts and the figure of Prospero! One is left gasping. Truly, anything whatsoever may be proved by such reasoning.

Anything, in fact, is proved, to be sure. We are asked to believe that the first movement represents Ferdinand, just enticed by Ariel to 'come unto these yellow sands,' listening with emotion to the song, 'Full fathom five thy father lies.' A theme of Beethoven's happens to fit the German words, at any rate so far as the first line (see Ex. 168*b*, page 132): 'Fünf Faden tief liegt Vater dein.' But, mark well, this is not the Eschenburg translation, which alters Shake-speare's metre into 'Tief fünf Klafter liegt dein Vater,' and behold! it has for once suited the accommodating Beethoven to go to Schlegel's version after all, which also goes conveniently with one of the recitative phrases that are so characteristic of this movement:

> The ditty does remember my drown'd father.
> This is no mortal business, nor no sound
> That the earth owes.

Anything, then, absolutely anything, will prove just whatever Dr Schering happens to wish to prove at any given moment. The smallest detail is taken from the context if it will do—a spasm of Ferdinand's heart, a sob breaking from him—and the most important matters are omitted if they will not. The sequence of events is radically altered, not because the music will otherwise fail to fit, but because Dr Schering decides, when he likes, that needless to say Beethoven would not 'slavishly submit' to the poet, but was determined to choose only what would go into the framework of a sonata. That in this case a thousand other incidents would go just as well as those selected on Beethoven's behalf does not appear to perturb his self-constituted interpreter in the least.

The slow movement, it seems, is a love duet (yes, duet!) between Ferdinand and Miranda; the finale leaves us alone with Ariel as depicted by himself in the song, 'Where the bee sucks,' there being no chance to introduce any of the other characters. A copper engraving, which formed the title-page of the twelfth volume of the Eschenburg translation, we are instructed (it is Eschen-burg again), depicts Prospero sending Ariel forth on a mission. Beethoven saw this and, it appears, took the suggestion of the 'gently soaring figuration' of this movement from the butterfly wings of the airy servant. And if that is incom-patible with the rapid and passionate motion of the music, why then, we have but to remember that Ariel also appears to thunder and lightning in the shape of a harpy. Nor does Dr Schering forget the well-known anecdote, recounted by Czerny ('credulously and without intending any harm') of the rider galloping past Beethoven's window, who is supposed to have inspired the music; but he dismisses it in a footnote with the calm assumption that Czerny is an unreliable witness. How, indeed, could he be otherwise, since unlike Schindler he does not happen to support the advocate?

The F major Sonata Op. 54, an analysis of which follows this 'Interlude,' apparently illustrates *Much Ado about Nothing*, or such fragments of it as will fit. We are asked to take it as a fact that the clue is this famous passage from Act II, Scene i:

> For, hear me, Hero: wooing, wedding, and repenting, is as a Scotch jig, a measure, and a cinque pace: the first suit is hot and hasty, like a Scotch jig, and full as fantastical; the wedding, mannerly-modest, as a measure, full of state and ancientry; and then comes repentance, and with his bad legs, falls into a cinque pace faster and faster, till he sink into his grave.

Eschenburg, unable to reproduce the pun at the end, let a polonaise take the place of the 'cinque pace,' as being more generally known to German readers, and for the same reason replaced the 'measure' by a minuet, which he thought well described by Shakespeare's 'mannerly-modest' and 'state and ancientry.' Thus Beethoven's *in tempo d' un menuetto* gives Dr Schering as much of a hint as he wants, and he is off once more into wild speculation. Not only is the minuet-like music Shakespeare's 'measure,' but the wilder triplet theme (see Ex. 201, page 160) is the 'Scotch jig,' hot and hasty, and he also visualizes the scene of the masked ball in the second act, with the different couples appearing: Hero and Don Pedro, Ursula and Antonio to the 'measure,' Margaret and Balthasar to the 'jig.' And how fortunate that all themes appear in twofold combinations!

Only Beatrice and Benedick are left out. They come into their own, however, in the second movement, which is supposed to illustrate their animated, malicious verbal sparring, their ironic repartee. But Dr Schering here does not deign to go into details. The analogy is so evident to him that 'it does not require another word of elucidation.' To which one has not another word of comment to offer, for where no proof is forthcoming it is impossible to disprove anything.

All the same, I wish I could go on dealing here with Dr Schering's books, which contain matter for endless dispute, and showing how he will not let Beethoven take fire until the middle of a play because the first half does not chance to suit his argument, how he selects scenes capriciously according to his peculiar requirements, and above all how he violates not only words but moods. One can only wonder, by the time one comes to the last piano Sonata, Op. 111, for which *Henry VIII* has to do service, that the theme with four variations and coda of the second movement are not made to stand for that much-married monarch's six wives.

SONATA IN F MAJOR, Op. 54 (1804)
(B.S.S. RECORDS, VOL. VIII)

BETWEEN two large sonatas of the year 1804, both of which are distinguished by sobriquets ('Waldstein' and *Appassionata*), stands this smaller nameless work, to which nothing and nobody shall tempt us to give any title, least of all that of *Much Ado about Nothing*. It was published in Vienna, by the Bureau des Arts et d'Industrie, in April 1806, and bears no dedication.

It has long been a commonplace of criticism to regard it as a transitional work, indicating the advent of the two-movement form to which Beethoven later became partial, and its exceptional form actually led many commentators into thinking of it as an experiment of no great positive value, as though so unique a composition had necessarily to be regarded as merely preparatory for something else, and that for no better reason than that it is on a small scale. (And is it, anyhow?) The rash conclusion was even arrived at that it was, for Beethoven, comparatively flippant, because of its humorous tone and the idea that a first movement *in tempo d'un menuetto* could no more be taken seriously than any other piece in dance form, though it is not a conventional minuet at all, but merely happens to go at that pace.

In tempo d' un menuetto.—There is no musical form and no classical precedent to which this first movement can be made to conform. It has been called a minuet with a modulating trio, part of which recurs between the varied repetitions of the minuet strain; but as trios never behave like that and minuet themes do not recur with variations in any normal dance movement of this sort, it is not more fantastic to think of this piece as representing a very special treatment of sonata form, which is after all much more elastic than a dance form that remained conventional even after it had produced the new offshoot of the scherzo. And as Beethoven, when all is said, did call this work a sonata, why not think of it thus?

We will call this the first subject:

Ex. 200

It continues rather than develops (for it is always stopping on full closes) for a while and has two more extended cadences slightly sophisticated by chromatic harmony. Then comes what we may take as the second subject:

Ex. 201

for although as such it shows its lack of classical breeding by not being definitely in the key of the dominant, it at least never holds for long to any other centre of tonality. It is developed at much greater length than Ex. 200, until at last it begins to spin round a figure of three semitones, rather tentatively, all over the key-board. This eventually becomes fixed in the bass and after two bars alters its note-sequence as though making a humorous compromise with the first subject, for which it seems anxious to pave the way in the original key. Ex. 200, thus re-established, dresses up in its first variation, after which Ex. 201 makes a much briefer reappearance, ending on the dominant seventh of F major, broken into two triplet groups followed by a pause on the chord, the first time *fortissimo*, the second *piano*.

Ex. 200 comes back again, treated still more elaborately this time and ending with a cadenza in which all metrical distinctions are blotted out. A coda follows with the first theme planted firmly on a low pedal F and still varied, though no further developed. On the contrary, it is simplified and gradually dissolved into a merely harmonic, non-melodic close. But the harmony is extremely interesting and, for its time, daring. Note the dissonant clusters in the following cadence:

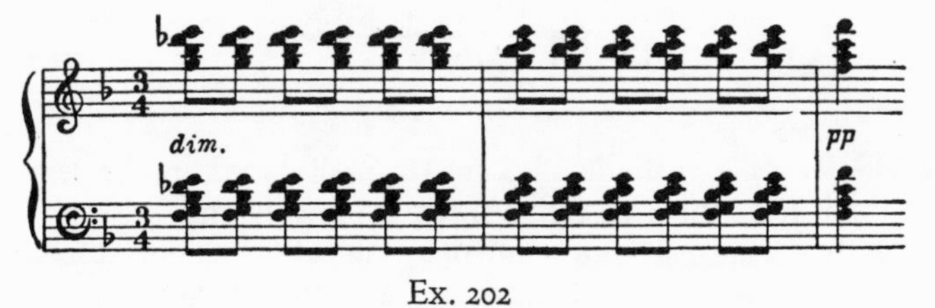

Ex. 202

The tonic pedal (F), it will be observed, is retained throughout.

Allegretto.—Here we have another *moto perpetuo* of continuous semiquavers, a fascinating movement made of the kind of music one would hum to oneself in a train going at a steady pace—but a train that would have to take one into some land of fantastic beauty to awaken such music. What is even more re-markable than the unbroken flow of even notes is the fact that practically through-out the music is written strictly in two single parts, with the result that such harmony as is produced is transparent and constantly shifting in the most alluring way.

There are two main thematic features: this rising figure with a kind of Scotch snap at the end:

Ex. 203

and this falling one:

Ex. 204

When both have been exposed and repeated, their development begins in a key as far removed as A major; but Ex. 204, which has an incorrigible tendency to modulate, almost at once takes the music into other tonal regions. After chromatically descending minims, heard strongly accentuated in the bass, a new rhythmic figure comes to complicate the music with its syncopations:

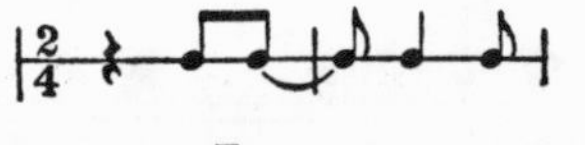

Ex. 205

Shortly afterwards a melodic idea makes itself heard in the left hand, but tentatively, for it introduces its initial figure repeatedly and brokenly, as though somebody with a stammer endeavoured to contribute to the discourse. Over a phrase derived from this theme the music modulates through the whole 'cycle of fifths,' an occurrence that is unique in the whole of Beethoven's work, as Sir Donald Tovey points out, except for the two Preludes in all the major keys, published as Op. 39.

At last the music lands back in F major, and there is a kind of recapitulation, though the texture is differently laid out, Ex. 203 appearing over a pedal F. A new allusion to the left-hand melodic feature gives rise to chords that make their appearance for the space of ten bars and almost for the only time in the whole movement.

A long repeat turns back to the beginning of the development where, as we have already seen, Ex. 203 appears for a moment in A major. When we have once more arrived at the chord passage of ten bars—during which, by the way, the semiquaver motion does not stop—there is a regular full close into F major instead of an interrupted cadence tumbling into A major. A short coda, stirred into *più allegro* and containing references to the chief thematic features (Exx. 203, 204 and 205) brings this remarkable, fantastically humorous and curiously shaped but formally quite satisfactory movement to an end.

SONATA IN F MINOR, Op. 57 (1804–6)
(B.S.S. RECORDS, VOL. V)

THE date of composition of this work is uncertain, but it is fairly safe to say that it was not completed until 1806, although sketches must have existed as early as 1804, since they appear together with those for the 'Waldstein' Sonata in that year. Op. 57 was published in February 1807 by the Bureau des Arts et d'Industrie in Vienna and dedicated to Count Franz von Brunswick, the brother of the Countesses Therese von Brunswick and Josephine von Deym, with both of whom Beethoven fell in love about that time, all but simultaneously and very much according to the dual, not to say many-sided, nature of his infinite longing for feminine companionship.

As far as one can see, and dare probe the matter, the impression is that Josephine made a predominantly physical and Therese an almost entirely spiritual appeal to him. Perhaps he was so torn between two different but equally strong affections that he could come to no conclusion as to a decided preference for one of the two: the fascinating, rather frivolous young widow and the inscrutable, placid and perhaps secretly very passionate maiden sister. What is even more likely is that he could never come to terms with himself, never screw himself up to the point of asking any woman to marry him—and we know that Therese at least would have accepted him. No doubt he felt, deep down, that for one absorbed in music to the point of utter indifference to the world, indeed often to the normal decencies of life, a final choice had inevitably to be made between art and a wife. Beethoven never knew the meaning of compromise. There could be room enough in his life only for one of the two things he most cared for: music and love. And, being the most purposeful of composers and the most vacillating of lovers, he decided in favour of his art.

But perhaps, too, the fact that the two Brunswick sisters captivated him at almost, if not actually, the same time, made him suspicious of himself, as well it might. How was he to trust to his own heart, a heart so much at the mercy of nature on the one hand and ideals on the other? It may well be that he found the choice between senses and sentiments to be as hard to make as that between music and marriage, and that he quailed before that also.

All this may seem hardly relevant to a discussion of the F minor Sonata, except chronologically; but I think the work reflects something of that duality of his inclinations which must have plagued him more than ever at the very time of its composition. It was the Hamburg publisher Cranz, once again, who nicknamed the Sonata, as he had done before with Op. 28; but Beethoven, thinking only of the first and last movements, might well have called it a *sonata appassionata* himself. It is more than doubtful, on the other hand, whether he would have felt that description to be appropriate to the slow movement, which breathes a profound peace—a peace oppressed by sorrow too deep for wild utterance. Is it possible that when he wrote these meditative variations on a quietly brooding theme, he was not filled with thoughts of Therese? And who shall say that the passionate swirlings that surround this tranquil pool are not expressive of the feelings roused by Josephine, if only, by this time, feelings of revolt against her domination? It seems almost unimaginable that thoughts of a dedication of so personally expressive a Sonata to one of the sisters should not have come to Beethoven. But a dedication to which of the two? It ought to have been to both, no doubt; but Beethoven, whose instinct was sound though his manners were atrocious, would have felt this to be tactless. I cannot help thinking that the brother was asked to accept the tribute of the Sonata as the representative of both sisters.

Assai allegro.—The music plunges at once into a sort of subdued turbulence with the principal strain of the first-subject group (marked *a* below):

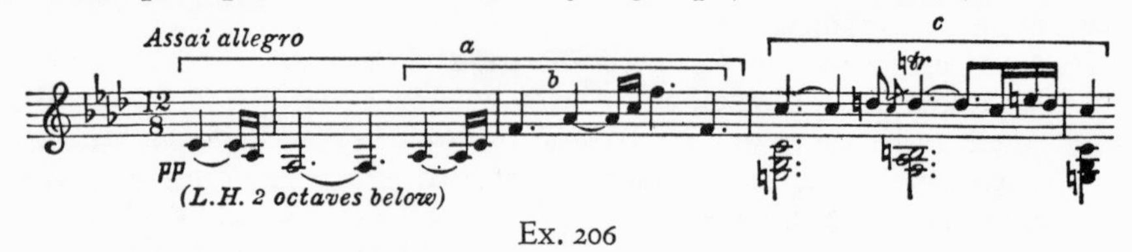

Ex. 206

The phrase 206*c* is very soon found to become detached from its companion and associated temporarily with figures akin to the well-known 'fate' motif in Beethoven's fifth Symphony:

Ex. 207

an important thematic feature of the Sonata, as will be found presently. After a pause hammering chords rising upwards in syncopation separate the figures 206*b* and 206*c*, and then an anxiously fluttering, pleading theme is heard over repeated notes in the left hand. This gradually dies away, as though stifled, and then the first idea of the second-subject group asserts itself in A flat major:

Ex. 208

In spite of its quietness and its major tonality, it brings scarcely any respite. No doubt the impression of its sullen quality is largely due to the fact that it is derived from the gloomy first subject—a very unusual procedure by the way, the traditional practice having always been to keep first and second subjects in contrast to each other. After a series of whole-bar shakes and an unaccompanied descending passage—a kind of measured cadenza—a new second-subject idea asserts itself in A flat minor, careering wildly along in semiquavers. Below it the following figure rears itself up frantically in the bass:

Ex. 209

The diminished-seventh formation and the allusion to the 'fate' motif (Ex. 207) at the end of the phrase conspire to make it intensely dramatic. But now the music calms down towards the end of the exposition.

That end is not clearly marked. For the first time in any first movement in regular sonata form does Beethoven rush straight past the signpost between exposition and working-out section, hitherto always marked by a repeat indication, and it is singularly appropriate that the new departure should have been made in this headlong Sonata. The working-out draws upon all the material already shown in music type, except Ex. 209, and also upon the fluttering theme which has not been quoted but will be easily recognized in the score or in performance. This section begins with a false start made by the descending phrase with which Ex. 206 opens, followed by another that takes it into E major. The great fantasia which Beethoven now elaborates from his material need not be described in detail; once the themes have been retained by the memory—and who does not know them?—there is no escaping the mastery with which they are made to press onward as if urged by an inescapable tragedy.

A curious point occurs where, as the recapitulation is approached, the musical features become lost in diminished-seventh arpeggios. 'The passion is beyond articulate utterance,' says Sir Donald Tovey, and one feels that to be as near the truth as any commentary may get. But presently the 'fate' theme (Ex. 207) becomes clamorous, the more impressively so because it emerges at first in the form of four similar notes and only makes its descending step at the fourth statement, thus delaying the appearance of the dominant of F minor and then approaching it hesitatingly with an astonishingly dramatic effect.

The bass remains fixed on that dominant C, even when the first subject has re-entered in F minor, It then rises a semitone, thus continuing to provide an accompaniment to the music which had at the outset been heard in bare octave unison. About the rest of the recapitulation nothing need be said; but the immense coda calls for a few words of description. It makes use at first of Ex. 206*a*, the rhythmic pattern of which it quickly contracts with an effect of passionate haste. Then Ex. 208 appears, foreshortened by a drastic modulation. After that all thematic features are once more submerged, and for a longer time. There is only breathless, galloping rhythm. The keyboard is swept with arpeggios as an Aeolian harp under a hurricane. But suddenly they drop into a whisper and the 'fate' theme is heard muttering its last pronouncement, more and more slowly and softly, until it stands still on a pause. A moment later, though, its rhythm breaks out forcibly and a precipitate peroration begins with a modified version of Ex. 208. Then the theme disappears in a strenuous passage of convulsively distorted rhythm, as though all control were lost, and the movement ends with all its force suddenly spent, the figures 206*a* rising feebly to the top of the keyboard, only to drop resignedly to the bottom. A 'dying fall' if ever there was one in music.

Andante con moto.—The slow movement, having but a single theme, requires no illustration in music type. The lovely, reposeful, yet strangely constrained melody is stated at once without any introduction. It has two periods of eight bars each, both of which are repeated. Four variations follow, the first two with the repeats marked as for the theme, the third with the repetitions themselves varied each time, and the last without any repeats at all, which makes it only half as long as the others.

The first variation does little more to the theme than break it up in syncopation between the two hands. The second variation disintegrates the right-hand melody into flowing semiquavers, which, however, do very little to disguise it, and gives a more even shape to the bass. It is, so to speak, the inner core of the theme's quietness, peaceful as the touch of a beloved hand. There is rather more agitation about the third variation, with its melodic cross-accents and its rapid demi-semiquaver accompaniments. The varied treatment of the repeat should be noticed, with the second statements given to the left hand each time. The final variation reverts almost to the original form of the theme, but places much of it in higher registers, so that its whole tone becomes clarified. There is no final tonic chord: an interrupted cadence lets a diminished seventh intrude with a disquieting effect, first softly, then with startling energy.

Allegro, ma non troppo.—The long finale, in sonata form, has the character of a *moto perpetuo*, with its almost uninterruptedly running semiquavers. Only Beethoven, not being the man to work to preconceived notions and then coercing his inspiration if it will not conform to plan, does not scruple to break this regular motion in the middle of the movement. What is more, he does so with an effect which the mere manipulator of a 'good idea,' conceived before invention has got into its stride, could never hope to achieve.

Having thus chained two movements together and kept the haunting melody of the variations still lingering in his mind, Beethoven prepares the way for a new thematic idea gradually by an introduction that at first keeps the music poised on a subdominant (which is implied rather than heard) and then, one step nearer his goal, on the dominant of F minor, in which key the first subject, foreshadowed for some time, enters thus:

[*Continued*

Ex. 210

The snapping rhythm in the bass should be noticed, as it very soon becomes an important feature—a kind of obsession that haunts all the music of the first-subject group. The second-subject group, in C minor, begins as follows:

Ex. 211

A peroration to the exposition is based on Ex. 210. There is no formal ending to it; the music is made to merge into the working-out section by means of a diminished-seventh arpeggio that sweeps up three octaves and down five.

Before I deal with one or two features of the working-out and recapitulation, something may be said regarding the very unusual fact that these two sections are both repeated at full length, and I cannot do better than let Sir Donald Tovey say it. Here is a quotation from his *Companion to Beethoven's Pianoforte Sonatas*, which I have had occasion to mention before and to which I cannot forbear paying a grateful tribute in passing. This is what Tovey says:

> Now, whatever may be said against it, this is not conventional. No other sonata movement has ever repeated its second half when it did not repeat its first. Beethoven has two purposes vividly in mind here. First, he values the interrupted close and the effect of the sub-dominant that will follow; secondly, he wishes to delay the appearance of an entirely new theme in his coda. This second point is really important. But it is not an absolute necessity. And Beethoven has unquestionably overlooked the difficulty ordinary mortals must feel in enjoying such a crisis . . . (lasting 43 bars) . . . twice in one performance!
>
> It is at least significant that the two points here mentioned do certainly concern the moments at the double bar, viz., the impact of the first explosion and the surprise of the new theme after the repeat is over. Beethoven may easily have considered such present moments to the neglect of the total effect.

At the fourth bar of the working-out an imitation in canon will be noticed. Shortly afterwards an entirely new theme with agitated syncopations is heard, and when this has been dealt with, Ex. 210 again appears in a different sort of imitation. Then comes the incident where the semiquaver motion is arrested by pauses and afterwards retarded by quaver triplets, then even quavers and finally minims. Thus the recapitulation is approached.

The coda, marked *presto*, has a wholly new theme of two emphatic chords followed by rapid quaver staccato passages. It is as if all restraint were lost and any random thought were snatched in a frantic effort to drown the wild fancies that have been rushing in on us in this finale. But they come back again faster than ever and crowding more closely together, for it is Ex. 210 which the final pages gathers furiously into a hurricane of dramatic force.

INTERLUDE VIII

THE THREE STYLES

IN 1852 was published, at St Petersburg, a book written in French and entitled *Beethoven et ses trois styles.* The author was one Wilhelm von Lenz (1808–83), a Livonian and a councillor in the Russian capital. He was an ardent Beethovenian and wrote, a little later, another work on his favourite master in no less than six volumes.

Lenz was not the first to decide that Beethoven's music could be divided into three periods, each showing a distinctive style. It was Fétis who had made this supposed discovery, which has often been disputed since. Liszt, for instance, said that there were not three styles, but two, and he might just as well have put it at twenty instead. It is all a question of what features of Beethoven's music are singled out for analysis, and if only enough of them were considered it would not be impossible to see a different style in each work. One thing is clear: Beethoven's evolution did not proceed by a series of jolts, but by a continual growth in mental stature and technical address, and particularly by a gradual fusion of the two into identity of means and ends.

All the same, there is no reason why we should not, quite arbitrarily, mark three stages in this development for convenience of study, so long as we remember that such divisions have no more significance than

> . . . Mercator's North Poles and Equators,
> Tropics, Zones, and Meridian Lines.

They help us to explore a fascinating territory in the realm of music; but we must admit, with Lewis Carroll's crew, that

> They are merely conventional signs.

Lenz's divisions are just as disputable as any one else's might be; but we may accept them as landmarks with the proper reservation that they may sometimes stake off the frontier between two distinguishable territories without making any valid distinction between their features. A certain transitional work may be, considered from the point of view of its form, for instance, as natural a borderline between two musical zones as a mountain range or a river is between two geographical ones. At the same time, it may mark out no difference whatever in some other particular. In the matter of expression, for example, these artificial formal boundaries may at times be seen not to have affected Beethoven's idiom any more than the changing territorial ones of Alsace-Lorraine have affected the languages spoken in that region. Form and subject-matter do not always progress simultaneously in Beethoven's music; in fact, as they are seen to be perfectly reconciled only towards the end of his career, their disparity is something of a feature of his early music. Here is one clue to the three periods: in the first these two elements strive separately towards expression; in the second they create vast structures in their effort to amalgamate (*Eroica* Symphony, 'Emperor' Concerto); in the third they unite in the building of unconventional musical shapes, each different from the other and each as perfect in its way as the wits of genius can make them, still on a large scale sometimes (ninth Symphony, Sonata Op. 106), but often compressed into the smallest frame that may enclose an abundance of expression without being shattered by it (last piano Sonata, last string Quartet).

So far as the piano sonatas are concerned, Lenz makes his divisions thus: First period—up to and including Op. 14 (10 works); second period—Op. 22 to Op. 90 (17 works); third period—Op. 101 to Op. 111 (5 works). In order to see how arbitrary his method is, we have only to study the work immediately in front of his second border-line. There is surely a much greater departure towards a new style between the two Sonatas Op. 81*a* and Op. 90 than between the latter and Op. 101. The Op. 81*a* (*Les Adieux, l'Absence et le Retour*) would appear to most students to be obviously the last sonata of the second period, while Op. 90 they can hardly fail to regard as belonging most decidedly to the third.

The mistake Lenz made is revealed by a glance at the whole catalogue of Beethoven's works, in which he was anxious to draw a Carrollian 'meridian line' after the string Quartet in F minor, Op. 95, which one must agree with him is of the second period. Accepting the opus numbers as they stand, he did not consider the fact that Op. 90 was written nearly four years later than Op. 95, and he thus let the E minor Sonata pass as a second-period work. This is the more curious because elsewhere he was by no means so ready to take the extremely deceptive evidence of Beethoven's opus numbers, which show the chronology not of composition, but of publication, and not even that always reliably. In marking off the first and second styles between the first Symphony, Op. 21, and the Sonata Op. 22, he is careful to assign the second Symphony also to the first period, although it is two years later than Op. 22 and bears the opus number 36. Later on, too, in beginning the third period at Op. 100 (elsewhere he does so after Op. 95, so that a few works, including the very important Trio, Op. 97, appear to be falling between two styles, if not between two stools), he expressly makes an exception of fourteen works in the hundreds which he thinks are decidedly in the second manner. We are, then, well justified in regarding his demarcations as 'merely conventional signs' and removing that placed by him after so decidedly a third-period work as Op. 90 elsewhere. That is the only correction we need apply to him for the purpose of classifying the piano sonatas: his first division, between Opp. 21 and 22, or, more relevantly to the subject of our study, between Opp. 14 and 22, must clearly be allowed to stand.

It is impossible in a short essay to give an exhaustive answer to the questions of what all this dividing amounts to, what the three Beethoven styles are and in what ways, and how many ways, they manifest themselves. Another book might easily be devoted to them, and not inconceivably a better one than that by Lenz. All the same, that earnest and enthusiastic writer may well be consulted for his views, whether we agree with them or not, before a few points are raised independently—a minute fraction only of the many that might arise if the study of Beethoven's creative procedures could be carried to greater lengths here.

On the first style Lenz has little of value to say beyond that it is derivative; but in discussing the second period he still reflects now and again on the earlier one by making comparisons. Thus he says, for instance, that Beethoven there comes to despise gardens and prefers parks or the silence of forests; houses become castles—and more vaguenesses of the sort. However, we come down to something more than hints on being told, among other things, that 2–4 time signatures now come frequently into first movements; that repeats no longer occur in an *andante*; that formal minuets disappear (but what about that in the eighth Symphony?); that an *allegretto* movement, if not a scherzo, is often substituted for the minuet; that the scherzo no longer has a trio explicitly so called, and that it can now be in 2–4 time, as in the Sonata Op. 31 No. 3; that finales tend to grow larger; that an *adagio* is sometimes enormously long, but often omitted or turned into an introduction to the next movement. More generally, that the sonata form grows less rigid, but not so loose (!) as it becomes in the third period.

For some reason or other Lenz approves of Beethoven's making but the rarest use of the extreme keys for his works in the second style, as though, more than a century after Bach, he could not yet reconcile himself to tuning by equal temperament. It is amusing to find that for the sake of this fad of his he decides to regard the beautiful Sonata in F sharp major, Op. 78, one of Beethoven's own favourites, with its horrid six sharps, as '*d'un moindre intérêt*.'

The third style evidently baffles the good Lenz, as it has, be it said, baffled more enlightened people. It is not very helpful to talk of the music found in the last piano sonatas and string quartets as in 'a style of majestic revelation.' One wants to be told what it is that is being revealed, but on this Lenz is bound to remain discreetly silent. However, he is more suggestive, if only a little less vague, when he goes on as follows (I translate from the original):

> Utter deafness cut him off from external impressions at that time; he no longer reproduced mankind and the world such as they are, but as he would have liked them to be or supposed they were. . . . Beethoven's third manner is without the spontaneity of the first two, but it has, and will ever have, the interest of showing genius at grips with reality. While he bases himself on the conditions of our sphere of impressions, Beethoven surpasses it and continues it beyond the limits it sets us.

Lenz then goes on to say that Beethoven's last period is more experimental and at the same time more scholastic. (No doubt the growing tendency to write fugally makes him say the latter.) There are more extreme keys and far more frequent and violent modulations.

Some of this is clear and sensible enough, but Lenz mixes sound observation with too much random talk that appears to be profound only so long as one does not inquire too closely into its meaning. What, for instance, can he possibly mean by saying that towards the end of his career Beethoven used a far greater number of notes because he wanted more of those things which life was bent on denying him?

However, for all his looseness, Lenz is not wrong-headed. He clearly has more than an inkling of Beethoven's intentions, which cannot be said of Fétis, who was quite incapable of appraising that third period invented by himself.

> Repetitions of the same ideas [he says] were pushed to excess; the development of a subject sometimes went to the length of divagation; melodic notions became less defined as they became more dreamy; harmony grew ever harsher and from day to day showed a failing of aural memory; in short, Beethoven claimed to find new forms not so much under pressure of sudden inspiration as in order to conform to the conditions of some preconceived scheme.

Fétis, although he is so manifestly floundering, may help us precisely because he has gone so utterly astray. Some of his assertions we have only to turn into their opposite in order to find some clue to Beethoven's third manner that may prove really illuminating. Could anything be less evident in the master's last works, each of which differs from the next in shape as much as they all resemble each other in logical continuity, than any sort of formal preconception? No, Beethoven did not *claim* to find new forms. We may even doubt whether he intended them at the outset. It was, on the contrary, precisely the high pressure of inspiration, intensified perhaps by his isolation from actual aural experience, which constantly led him to discover new formal vehicles more or less instinctively, possibly almost unawares. His was an inspiration so practised by that time, so trained and disciplined—and, one might add, so undistracted by the intrusion of tonal suggestions from outside—that in the end it forced his genius to reach an indissoluble fusion of musical notions with their practical realization. I say practical, not practicable. That is another matter. Beethoven's late works are not really playable, and some of them never quite convey in performance all that they contain. But should a superhuman imagination go fettered because of human debilities? It is good for us to go on struggling with it, and if we fail, the loss must not be counted Beethoven's.

Some of the differences of style in Beethoven's work will not fail to occur to the reader who has the patience to peruse the annotations in this book; but a few of a more general nature may perhaps be indicated here in addition to what has already been taught us, positively or negatively, by Fétis and Lenz.

In his early work Beethoven accepts the current conventions and works willingly to the models of his predecessors. The example of Carl Philipp Emanuel Bach, Haydn and Clementi, to name only the outstanding figures, is more congenial to him than that of Mozart, with whom he has scarcely any temperamental affinity. To say that his early music is Mozartian is merely to follow the first signpost that shows itself without inquiring whither it points. The traditional sonata form is at first simply filled by Beethoven without any drastic attempts at modification. Ideas are presented for their own sake and the accepted mould accommodates them because they are as unenterprising as itself, though by no means impersonal. Stereotyped figures of accompaniment abound and melodies of a regular periodicity predominate vastly.

During the second period Beethoven becomes more and more explicit in his directions to the player, not only in the matter of tempo at the head of each movement, but in that of mood, often indicated in the course of the music. The texture of the keyboard writing grows much more varied, and conventional figuration is displaced by a lay-out that is in every case better suited to the idea it presents. Altogether, musical invention and contrivance tend to become one; the latter, in fact, is now itself part of invention instead of being, as before, a ready-made vehicle. So with form as a whole. It can still be perfectly regular in such a Sonata as Op. 28, except for the growing tendency to expand the coda, but in the *sonata quasi una fantasia* type it assumes great independence. Melodic formations in irregular periods are now more frequent.

The quickest way to characterize the third period, perhaps, is to say that the indication *quasi una fantasia* has now disappeared, not because Beethoven has given up letting his fancy roam as it will, but on the contrary because it must now be taken for granted that he will always give it free rein. His ideas now burst through conventional patterns; formality for its own sake no longer has any meaning for him, but his immense strength of will and imagination enable him to compel new forms to accord perfectly with expression. His deafness itself, though materially a hindrance, has become spiritually his strength. He is rewarded for a heroic, Promethean defiance of his fate by creative achievements such as will continue to satisfy the choicest musical minds.

SONATA IN F SHARP MAJOR, Op. 78 (1809)
(B.S.S. RECORDS, VOL. I)

BEETHOVEN had a special affection for this Sonata and quite decidedly expressed his preference of it to the so-called 'Moonlight' Sonata, in C sharp minor. Each of the two works is dedicated to a beloved woman, the earlier one to the Countess Giulietta Guicciardi, the later to the Countess Therese von Brunswick. We should be merely wise after the event if we attributed the greater profundity of the present work to a deeper love for Therese than Beethoven had ever felt for Giulietta, the dedication to whom of the earlier of these two sonatas was in any case an afterthought; but it is tempting to see some correspondence at least between a favourite work and its inscription to a favoured woman. It is certain that the Sonata Op. 78 is emotionally as well as musically riper than the 'Moonlight,' which, perhaps like Beethoven's affection for Giulietta, is an affair of moods, of setting three states of mind against each other by way of contrast, whereas the F sharp major Sonata is concentrated throughout upon the expression of one dominating emotion.

Content and form are at once unusual and strictly logical, for Beethoven was the man to persuade himself that the unprecedented could be made reasonable. The musician in love with a countess, and by no means without a chance of requital, was a new thing hardly thinkable before the French Revolution; to the fierce humanitarianism of Beethoven there was nothing unsuitable in it, apart from merely practical considerations. Much less did he hesitate to treat the sonata form, previously approached with a great deference for its conventions, with a proud superiority that put the frank expression of feeling before ceremony. Although the Sonata Op. 78 is not necessarily a conscious confession of

Beethoven's love for Therese, the similarity of his independence in human affairs and in musical construction cannot fail to strike us when we see the name of an exalted beloved on the title-page of a work whose peculiar expressiveness depends to a great extent upon its formal boldness.

Beethoven's daring, which in two previous works, such as the 'Waldstein' and the *Appassionata* Sonatas, had shown itself in a conspicuous enlargement of traditional form, is now seen to manifest itself in extreme concentration. Two movements suffice him. Within each of them a profusion of material is compressed and, what is more remarkable, astonishingly co-ordinated. It is noteworthy that the earlier work, dedicated to Giulietta, was called a *Sonata quasi una fantasia,* and the later, devoted to Therese, simply a Sonata. But the qualification *quasi una fantasia*, now done away with as an apology for formal irregularity, has not become inappropriate to the later sonatas merely because of what is, from the point of view of each separate work, perfect cohesion, since they do not conform to a general pattern any more than the earlier works in question. There is certainly no falling-off in fantasy as work after work tends towards a riper mastery of formal resource placed at the service of invention.

Adagio cantabile—Allegro, ma non troppo.—The *adagio* begins as though it would develop into one of Beethoven's great slow melodies. Indeed, how such a development was to be resisted passes comprehension. At the same time, it is the very fact of its being interrupted in the middle of the fourth bar that imparts to this brief introductory remark its effect of tense expectancy. The music remains suspended on a pause for an instant, then merges quietly into the very moderately paced *allegro.* The first subject, or rather the first strain of a group of short motifs that constitute the first subject, is now stated at once. It is this:

Ex. 212

There is no need to enlarge upon the placid beauty of this melody, and its functional significance will appear presently; but it is worth while drawing attention at this point to Beethoven's subtilization of a time-honoured device—the Alberti bass. Mozart and Haydn, who still applied it almost mechanically at times, or even Beethoven himself in his early days, would probably have written the bass of such a passage in the manner of an accompaniment pure and simple. Here it acquires a melodic significance of its own, almost as though a viola and a cello were contributing independent parts of their own to a quartet. It is very characteristic of Beethoven's piano writing that it should often convey the impression of a consort of instruments. A hint of anything from a string trio to a full orchestra may surprise the ear at this or that moment. Thus, if his piano texture is not ideally adapted to the keyboard instrument, it is at any rate something more rather than something less than sheer pianism.

The first-subject group continues thus:

Ex. 213

The next five bars are a superb example of Beethoven's use of thematic fragments in a manner that is at once purposeful and economical. The three-chord figure marked *c* in Ex. 213 is at first restated in a hesitant way a degree of the scale higher. One of the semiquaver groups in 213*a* is then followed by the opening figure 212*a*, which leads directly into a transitional episode of semiquavers in the right hand and chords in the left. The important point about the passage just described is not, of course, the ingenuity with which it is contrived, but the perfect naturalness with which three thematic scraps are made into an incident that would be beautiful and significant even if its derivation remained unnoticed.

The semiquaverage that follows is again so interesting as a specimen of that concerted instrumental texture implied by Beethoven's keyboard writing that one cannot resist quoting a passage:

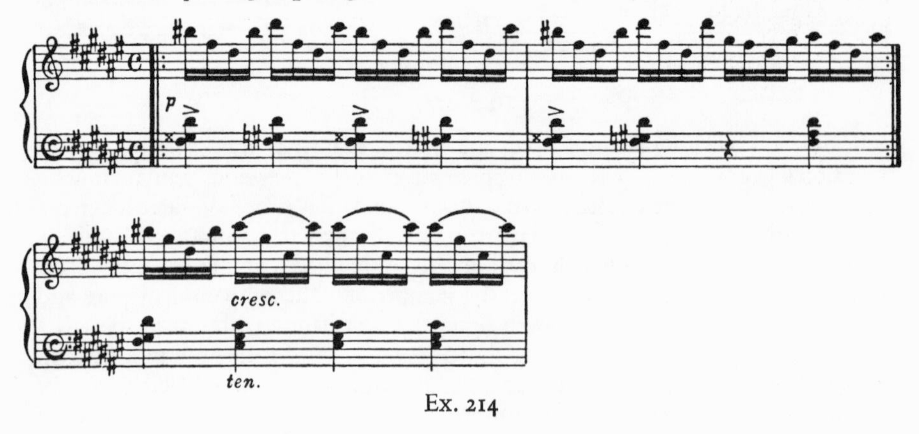

Ex. 214

A competent orchestrator, asked to score this Sonata, would not only reproduce the semiquavers, possibly with a slightly different lay-out, in the violins, let us say, but would also amplify the invisible but clearly perceptible melody by means of another treble instrument—a flute, perhaps—in some such way:

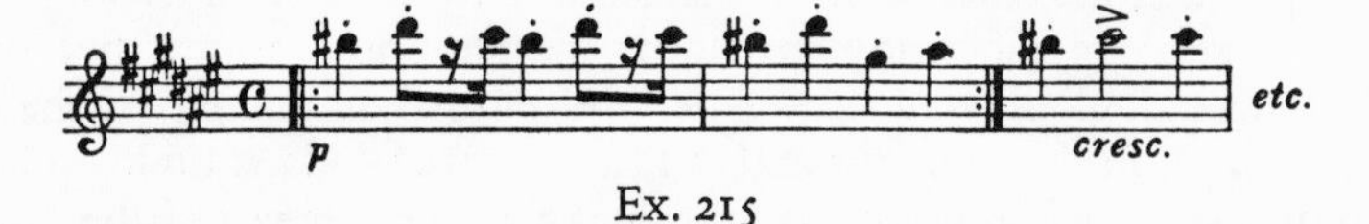

Ex. 215

The transition culminates in an emphatic cadence of C sharp major, in which key the second-subject group opens half a bar later. It will be noticed that Beethoven makes the new departure in the orthodox key—that of the dominant—very deliberately in this instance; as much so, in fact, as the eighteenth-century composers, who often advertised their arrival at this turning-point by a flourish on the dominant that had in itself no musical significance. He compromises characteristically by retaining the emphasis but insisting on significance to the last.

The opening of the second subject is this:

Ex. 216

In its very brief course a new semiquaver figure surges up twice, then descends into the bass to form a bridge passage that leads to the repeat of the exposition from the beginning of the *allegro*.

The concluding bridge passage now takes a turn into F sharp minor, in which key reappears the opening strain of the first subject (Ex. 212*a*–*b*). A bold modulation through A major brings 212*a*–*b* back in G sharp minor, after a first hint at it in the bass. Then the small figure 212*a* alone lends its rhythm, with a different melodic formation, to a stretch of development that leads, through a variety of keys, to the dominant of F sharp major, and so to the recapitulation. The working-out, therefore, has been extremely brief, but then, so is the whole movement, and since Beethoven achieves a remarkable feat of thematic concentration within less than twenty bars of closely reasoned discourse on his first-subject material, he has said all that needed saying at this juncture. His terseness, in fact, combined with unswerving relevance to the main topic, is one of the secrets of his greatness.

The recapitulation is of great interest as conforming to tradition or departing from it just as it suits the inspiration of the moment. The return of the second-subject group is managed in the orthodox manner: the semiquaver transition is reintroduced in such a way as to reach its final cadence, not on the dominant this time, but on the tonic, in which key (F sharp major) the second subject duly reappears with the strain quoted above (Ex. 216). But before this, the transition itself is approached by a startlingly new disposition of the first-subject group. It opens as before (Ex. 212), but the semiquavers (Ex. 213*a*) are so extended that the triplet scale (Ex. 213*b*) is now displaced into the key of E major. The chords 213*c* also are differently managed, for they now appear five times in succession instead of only twice. After the normal unfolding of the second subject (Ex. 216, in the tonic throughout) a very brief coda is built up from the bass semiquavers previously used as a bridge, first to the repeat of the exposition and then to the working-out. Its importance is now emphasized by a passing reference to 212*a–b*. The whole of the second part, like the first, is repeated, an unusual procedure at this stage of the evolution of the Beethoven sonata, but justified by the great concision of the whole piece.

Allegro vivace.—The second movement being also the final one, Beethoven is constrained to use the same key as he did for the first. With great subtlety, therefore, he avoids insisting on it as long as possible, and whether this was done consciously or not, the fact remains that it is a masterstroke. It does not vastly matter in art whether greatness be achieved by or thrust upon genius, and it will not always do to inquire how its most astonishing feats come about. (Eggs in pudding are no less welcome because King John's cook first let them drop into the mixture by accident.) Whether intentionally or by intuition, Beethoven here exhibits one of the most convincing proofs of his technical cunning.

The movement opens as follows:

Ex. 217

The chord of the augmented sixth at the beginning at once aims at ambiguity of key, and until the fourth bar following this quotation the composer sedulously avoids stating the tonic chord in root position. He makes, in fact, a perfect cadence to B major (last two bars of Ex. 217) before he asserts F sharp major. It is with the fluttering semiquavers heard a moment later that the tonic key definitely establishes itself. After a few bars the figuration is changed to rapid, broken pairs of notes in rising steps, distributed between the two hands. Then the main theme (Ex. 217) returns, the impression made being that of restating a rondo subject after the first episode. However, it is not followed by a new incident, as it should be in a regular rondo, but by the same as before, except that the broken two-note figures now descend instead of ascending.

A new notion now comes to the fore, which a glance at the movement as a whole reveals as a definite second subject. Not that this would mean that the piece could not be a rondo; but it does not contain a sufficient variety of episodes to be definitely classed as such, so that it must be regarded as partaking as much of the sonata as of the rondo form, though the feature of a working-out section is lacking. It is characteristic of the concision of this Sonata that Beethoven should have chosen this curious hybrid form for the finale, almost as though he had wished to condense three movements into two.

The second subject, which is in a mixture of D sharp major and minor, begins thus:

Ex. 218

It leads back to the broken figures, which both rise and fall this time, and so to the main theme again, with its phrases now distributed between treble and bass. For some time no new material is used, and the second subject (Ex. 218) reappears in F sharp major and minor. A last return to the chief theme marks the introduction of a short but highly significant coda that admirably sums up the musical argument. The rhythm of the figure marked *a* in Ex. 217 is used a dozen times in a new melodic formation and followed by three unexpected chords that hold up the rhythm, the last broken up into arpeggios. The movement is then rounded off by a brief sentence based on the fluttering semiquavers heard before. Like the first movement it ends abruptly: Beethoven has said all he set out to say as economically as possible and disdains to announce the fact by any merely rhetorical conclusion.

SONATA IN G MAJOR, Op. 79 (1809)

(B.S.S. RECORDS, VOL. XII)

THIS slender work was composed in 1809 and published in December 1810 by Breitkopf & Härtel of Leipzig. In February 1810 Beethoven offered it to the publishers together with the Sonatas Opp. 78 and 81*a*, as well as several other works, with the proviso that they should not be issued before 1st September, as he intended to bring out another edition in London. The present Sonata was, of course, much the least important of the three, and the composer himself entitled it *Sonate facile ou sonatine*. But although the second and third movements are very slight indeed, the first is neither as easy to play as Beethoven claims nor in the least sketchy or even unusually condensed in form. A curious fact is that Beethoven's first sketches for it were in C major.

Presto alla tedesca.—The tempo indication is curious and requires some care in its interpretation. Beethoven's '*presto*,' like that of other classics (e.g. Bach's for *My heart ever faithful*) must not be taken too literally in the sense in which we use it to-day. It simply qualifies the '*alla tedesca,*' which is the tempo of the *Ländler* or early waltz; in fact this 'in the German manner' is the exact equivalent of the *Deutsche* of Mozart and Schubert, whose dances of that type, however, are in a very moderate tempo which Beethoven's '*presto*' is intended to speed up. The compromise between the two terms may be safely made by a reasonable *allegro*.

Much ado about very little, perhaps; but the movement does wear an air all its own, and even if Beethoven's indication should be a jesting contradiction in terms, it conveys something to the interpreter—as much at any rate as Debussy's *Tarantelle styrienne* (as he originally called the early *Danse* for piano) or Erik Satie's *Tyrolienne turque*.

The first subject is this:

Ex. 219

At its first appearance Beethoven's harmony in the fifth bar is as shown in the actual context; but he seems later to have decided not to repeat this dissonant anticipation of the dominant (together with the tonic bass), feeling perhaps that its effect would be attenuated if it occurred more than once. I have indicated the variants in Ex. 219. But, of course, editors who cannot see beyond the length of their blue pencils put down this irregularity to forgetfulness. Some of them do repeat the dissonance and others, worse still, remove it even the first time as a 'slip of the pen.' In any case they restore symmetry at all costs, for which they all equally deserve Sir Donald Tovey's snub, which I cannot forbear to quote. He says that these different versions

. . . are characteristic in themselves and in their discrepancy. To any person, pupil, teacher, or editor, who thinks it a matter of conscience to level them up, we, who take Beethoven's style seriously, can only say: 'Why throw away upon music talents intended by nature so plainly and so exclusively for the more perfectible art of book-keeping by double entry?'

The initial figure of Ex. 219 is of special structural importance and will occur later in the three different forms marked *a*, *b* and *c*. The figure shown as *d* also assumes a certain constructive significance in the future developments, but it must decidedly not be regarded as having influenced the accompanying scales of the second subject:

Ex. 220

The exposition closes with four isolated statements of figure 219*c*, which lead to the repeat of the whole section.

The same figure serves as a bridge to the working-out, but with the addition of two more statements which bring the music into the distant region of E major. In this key the first seven bars of Ex. 219*b* are heard, and then comes a development of figure 219*b* in E major and C major, which covers sixteen bars. 219*b* is so altered as to make its first crotchet into a bass note and the other two into falling thirds played by the left hand over the right. Bars 8–11 of Ex. 219 then reappear in C major, and 219*d* is detached to provide a modulation into C minor. The process just heard is now repeated in C minor and E flat major, and 219*d* again forms a connection with yet another appearance of 219*b* in its modified form. This seems to be in D major, but the intrusion of a C♮ soon shows that it stands for the dominant of G major. In that key the recapitulation begins—and remains. It is so brief that Beethoven adopts the (for him) unusual device of repeating the whole working-out and recapitulation, which the second time, by a new use of figure 219*c*, merges into a coda.

Here the main theme (Ex. 219) appears alternately in the bass and in the treble, the second statement being ornamented with snappy grace-notes. A bass formed of 219*b*, waltzing gently along in tonic and dominant, concludes the movement.

Andante.—The slow movement, in G minor with a middle section in E flat major, is short, simple and easy to play. In character it resembles those songs without words by Mendelssohn which bear the title of *Venezianisches Gondellied*: in other words, it is of the barcarolle type affected by many composers of the nineteenth century, for whom it may be said to have been what the *siciliano* was to those of the eighteenth. This Sonata, in fact, does not look back, but rather forward, in spite of its brevity and simplicity. The main G minor section is repeated note for note after the E flat major episode, but amplified by a three-bar echo of its principal strain and three concluding pairs of chords.

Vivace.—The chief theme of the finale, which is a very condensed rondo, begins thus:

Ex. 221

Paul Bekker points out the melodic resemblance between this and the opening of the E major Sonata, Op. 109 (see Ex. 281, page 225). This observation may as well be dismissed as soon as its truth has been admitted, though it need not be done as rudely as Brahms did it on a similar occasion, when a friend saw a family likeness between a theme in his first and one in Beethoven's ninth Symphony. The coincidence is of no significance whatever, the present work being a mere toy in comparison with Op. 109 and obviously in no sense a study or sketch for the later work. Moreover, a merely melodic similarity of this kind is not nearly enough to constitute a relationship between two works. The differences between these two Sonatas, as those between Schubert's *Heidenröslein* and the little duet for Pamina and Papageno in the first finale of Mozart's *Magic Flute*, are infinitely greater than, for instance, those between Opp. 109 and 110, for all that the latter show no thematic connections whatever. To see any relationship between Op. 79 and Op. 109 because of this one little feature they have in common is as absurd as to say that Abraham Lincoln was like Nero because he had a Roman nose.

The second strain of the main theme:

Ex. 222

is more important than the episodes; we shall see why.

The first episode in E minor and the second in C major are well contrasted and both very brief. A characteristic procedure of this rondo is the linking up of the episodes with the returning main themes by means of passages derived from the latter. Apart from the changed accompaniments shown in Ex. 221, the first return leaves the theme unaltered. At the second and last return its shape is still retained, but the melody soon becomes disintegrated into broken triplets. A short but conclusively phrased coda is then constructed from alternate appearances of Exx. 222 and 221 in various modified forms.

INTERLUDE IX

THE PROGRAMME SONATA

WE shall now come upon a work that is unique among the Beethoven sonatas. It alone shares with the *Pathétique* the distinction of having been given a fancy title by the composer. He called it *Das Lebewohl; die Abwesenheit; das Wiedersehen*, and it will be seen from the notes hereafter why he took exception to the French title of *Les Adieux, l'Absence et le Retour* by which it is generally known to-day. Not even the fact that the composer gave a name to another sonata as well alters its singularity, for it does not mean much more that he called his Op. 13 a *Sonate pathétique* than that a critic associated moonlight with Op. 27 No. 2 or that a publisher insisted on calling the Op. 28 a 'pastoral' sonata. Op. 81*a* alone owes its existence confessedly to an outward event and consciously depicts it in three definite stages. It is the only Beethoven sonata that may, in fact, be called programme music.

Broadly speaking, this was not so very much of a novelty. Programmatic keyboard sonatas had been written before, not to mention sonatas with distinguishing if not characteristic titles such as Dussek's *Le Retour à Paris*, composed about 1807. As early as 1700 Johann Kuhnau, Bach's predecessor at Leipzig, wrote his descriptive Bible histories in the form of six sonatas, and Kuhnau himself refers in his preface to earlier works of the kind by Froberger and others, including one called *La Medica* by a famous electoral director of music, a sonata describing a man's sickness and treatment by the physician, and finishing with a jig described as showing that 'the patient is progressing favourably, but has not quite recovered his health.'

Now it has to be remembered that such works were not sonatas in the stricter sense of the term. They are too early for that. What we understand by the sonata did not exist before Carl Philipp Emanuel Bach or, at the remotest, Domenico Scarlatti, in whom at least rudiments of the modern form are found. Kuhnau's sonatas, for instance, were really suites and could be called *suonate* only in the sense that they were something to be sounded on an instrument. On the other hand, once we have admitted the primitiveness of their form from the sonata point of view, we must also agree to remember that much other descriptive music for the keyboard, and far earlier music, preceded Beethoven's programme sonata. There are Munday's *Weather Fantasia* in the Fitzwilliam Virginal Book and Byrd's battle pieces in Lady Nevell's book, the latter an anticipation of an unworthy successor, *The Battle of Prague*, as Frescobaldi's battle Capriccio also is to some extent. A forerunner of an infinitely more important work, Holst's *Planets*, was written by Buxtehude in the form of characteristic clavier suites, unfortunately lost to posterity. Later composers continued to make the keyboard a vehicle for realism. Couperin's Greuze-like girls' portraits and Rameau's clucking hen, to mention only isolated manifestations of the naturalistic gusto of the French *clavecinistes*, Froberger's Suite depicting the Emperor Ferdinand IV ascending to heaven by way of Jacob's ladder, the farm-yard pieces by Muffat and Bach's *Capriccio on the Departure of a Brother* are true keyboard programme music.

This last work brings us very near to Beethoven again, not in time, but in subject, and it also links him in some ways directly to Kuhnau, whose influence is to be found in Bach's little suite of descriptive and expressive pieces. Kuhnau is far more descriptive than expressive, in Bach the two elements are balanced, and in Beethoven expression immensely predominates over description. But the idea, or the situation, if you like, that gave rise to the Beethoven programme sonata is the same as that which stimulated Bach's affectionate caprice, and even without the link of Bach we can see a connection between Beethoven and Kuhnau. The latter explained in his preface that it would have been impossible to make the hearer see precisely what he intended to outline musically if he had not had recourse to verbal descriptions, in which indeed his biblical sonatas abound. Well, there is a remnant of his method in Beethoven, who wrote the word *Lebewohl* over the opening phrase that serves him as a musical motto, being evidently anxious to make sure that the listener should know exactly what this melodic snatch stood for. Nor must the importance he attached to the descrip-tive titles be overlooked. Nowhere else in the piano sonatas did he do anything of the kind, and he would have laughed the moonlight idea associated with Op. 27 No. 2 to scorn, provided it had not infuriated him too much. It follows that, as he was here explicit for once, he wanted the Op. 81*a* to convey quite unmistakably what it meant to him.

The music itself is clearly affected by the ideas, nay the experiences, of farewell, absence and reunion, as I have endeavoured to show in the notes that follow. The size of the coda in the first movement, if not the slow introduction to it, which is rare though not unique in the piano sonatas; the structural plan of the *andante espressivo*, which has no independent existence apart from the finale because the resignation to absence was all the time accompanied by the certainty of eventual return; the adoption of a slower tempo for the coda of the last move-ment: all this shows how form at certain points yielded to content. And it was not only form that yielded; the theory will be propounded later that certain har-monic audacities explain themselves easily by the tangible ideas that came into Beethoven's mind as he pondered over the parting with his pupil-friend at the same time as over the writing of this vividly expressive work. One does not go even half-way with the pedants who have held that Beethoven's drastic musical procedures must be apologized for and can be excused only because of his programme, for one would then logically have to condemn many harshnesses in the works of the last period that could not be academically explained by a programme, or by anything else, for that matter, unless indeed one took refuge in the crowning folly of making Beethoven's deafness responsible for supposed miscalculations.

Still, in this Sonata one cannot escape seeing some incidents attributable to the outward event that dictated the work. Among them is the suggestion of the horn, the characteristic sound of which was soon to become so prominent in German romantic music. Here, by the way, is another link with Bach's Capriccio, where the fanfare of the posthorn is humorously woven into a little fugue. Beethoven, more serious and more subtle, gives this *Lebewohl* motif itself the disposition of parts that comes up again and again in horn music because it represents the natural intervals of that instrument. Needless to say, the association may have been made quite unconsciously; but there is no necessity for us to make the impossible attempt at drawing distinctions between what, in such a work as this, may be programme music by inadvertence and what by deliberation. It is enough to know that a programmatic incentive was there to give us the right to see musical description and poetic suggestion where we reasonably can.

Here the reader must be warned, though, not to go beyond reason. This work must first of all be regarded as a sonata, a piece of music satisfying as such, just as the Pastoral Symphony should be so regarded. More so, in fact, for there Beethoven did imply a realistic intention by the very warning he issued against its being taken too seriously; he said that the work was *more* the expression of feeling than painting, thus hinting that there was *some* painting in it. In connection with the Op. 81*a* we have no such confession beyond the subtitles and the *Lebewohl* motto to strengthen us in our conviction, upheld by our knowledge of the circumstances, that here is a piece of keyboard programme music. Had Beethoven really intended to reveal events musically incident by incident, he might here have written as bad a piece as *The Battle of Vittoria*—not to say *The Battle of Prague*, which is not so very much worse than his description of Wellington's victory. What he did write was a great sonata, and that because the musician in him, the great shaper of significant form—to borrow Clive Bell's phrase—dominated at every point the deviser of human scenes and the interpreter of human feelings. In that sense the Op. 81*a* was after all a great novelty, for it was the first keyboard work that can be called programme music and is at the same time as highly organized a sonata as Beethoven, and therefore anybody else, ever wrote. Already in Clementi's programme sonata, *Didone abbandonata*, form tended to become disintegrated again. Thus, in the same sense, this work of Beethoven's has remained unique to the present day.

SONATA IN E FLAT MAJOR, Op. 81*a* (1809)
(B.S.S. RECORDS, VOL. IV)

THIS work was composed in 1809 and published in 1811. Its opus number, 81*a*, is curious, but can be explained by the fact that between 1810 and 1812 Breitkopf & Härtel, of Leipzig, published all Beethoven's works marked Opp. 75 to 85, but that Simrock, of Bonn, had already issued an Op. 81 in 1810—the Sextet for strings and two horns in E flat major. It would seem that Beethoven was unwilling to break the chronological order of the Breitkopf & Härtel works and therefore decided to make the less important Sextet Op. 81*b* and to reserve the number 81*a* to a Sonata which he had reason to favour exceptionally. For it is one of the works, all of them of outstanding significance, dedicated to the

Archduke Rudolph, the member of the imperial house of Austria who will again be referred to in the tenth 'Interlude' and in the notes to the Sonata in C minor, Op. 111.

The archduke became Beethoven's pupil at the age of sixteen, and a curious friendship developed between the two. They differed so greatly in position, character and age that no normal relationship either of master and pupil or of prince and courtier was possible between them. The archduke was enough of a musician to defer entirely to Beethoven in matters of art, since it was as a musician that he sought him, and he had the good sense to absolve the fiercely independent composer from all court etiquette. Thus an extraordinary and undisturbed devotion grew on both sides, and when, in May 1809, the French besieged Vienna and the imperial family was obliged to leave the city, Beethoven was sincerely afflicted by the departure of the youth who was at once his pupil, his patron and his friend.

The archduke left on 4th May—none too soon, for the French entered Vienna on the 12th—and Beethoven at once began the composition of the first movement of this Sonata to commemorate the parting. Among the sketches for it is found the following note in ungrammatical German:

> Der Abschied am 4ten Mai—gewidmet und aus dem Herzen geschrieben S.K.H.
> (The Farewell on 4th May—dedicated to, and written from the heart for, H.I.H.)

The three movements of the Sonata were subsequently entitled *Das Lebewohl* (*Les Adieux*), *Die Abwesenheit* (*L'Absence*) and *Das Wiedersehen* (*Le Retour*). The finale was as truly the expression of the composer's feelings on meeting again as the first movement had been of those at the archduke's departure, for its composition was actually deferred until after the conclusion of peace on 14th October 1809 and the return of the imperial family. The slow movement that describes the composer's feelings during his friend's absence was written between May and October.

In a letter to Breitkopf & Härtel dated 2nd July 1810 Beethoven calls the work a characteristic sonata. It is interesting to note that he wished the German subtitles to be used, and that it was the publishers who substituted the French ones, according to the fashion of the day. On 9th October 1811 Beethoven upbraided them in the following manner:

> I have just received Das Lebewohl, etc. I see that you really have other copies with French titles. But why? *Lebewohl* is something very different from *Les Adieux*; the first is said in a hearty manner to a single person, the other to a whole assembly, to whole towns.

To which one might add that *Le Retour*, too, does not mean the same thing as *Das Wiedersehen*.

Adagio—Allegro.—This is one of the five out of Beethoven's thirty-two piano sonatas that begin with a slow introduction, and it has the only such introduction which, apart from the principal thematic material required by the sonata form, contains an important motto theme that enters prominently into the musical structure. It is at once stated by the player's right hand:

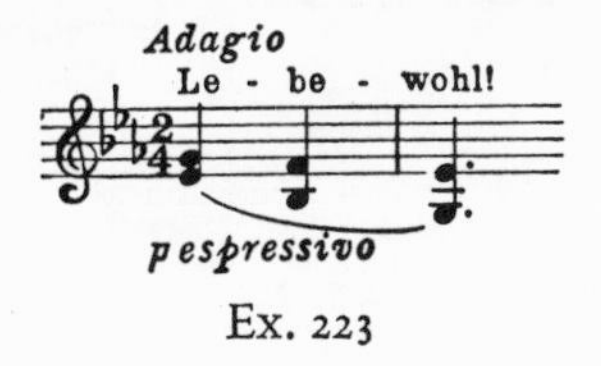

Ex. 223

the left entering to make an unexpected change of harmony. Beethoven makes its meaning quite clear by setting the word *Lebewohl* over it. (As it happens, the English 'Fare thee well' fits the phrase equally well.) An expressive melodic phrase follows, with an echo in the octave above and a cadence dropping back to the motto, which is presented the second time with a poignant harmonic change that removes the melodic sequel into a far-off key. But a series of figures, broken as though by an excess of emotion, lead quickly back to E flat major for the opening of the *allegro* movement. The chord of the sixth with which it opens is three times repeated tentatively and very softly before it suddenly asserts itself as the opening of the first subject:

Ex. 224

It continues with far-flung octaves and then with runs, mostly in contrary motion. Next comes an incident that seems to allude to the motto, also in contrary motion, and introduces a quaver figure (in the second bar below) which becomes a thematic feature of some importance:

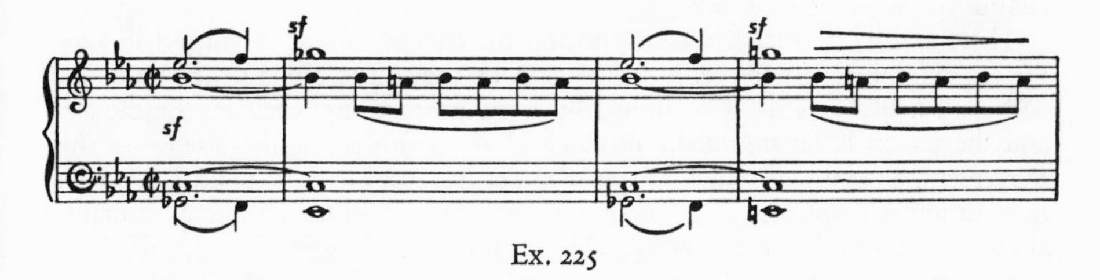

Ex. 225

This figure will be seen to make the inner pattern of the second subject, which also draws on the motto for its treble melody:

Ex. 226

The presentation of the whole expository part is thus, it will be seen, extremely economical in its use of thematic material. The music arrives at the double bar by a rhythmic contraction of Ex. 223, followed by its sudden statement at its normal pace, which leads first to the repeat and afterwards to the working-out section, in this manner:

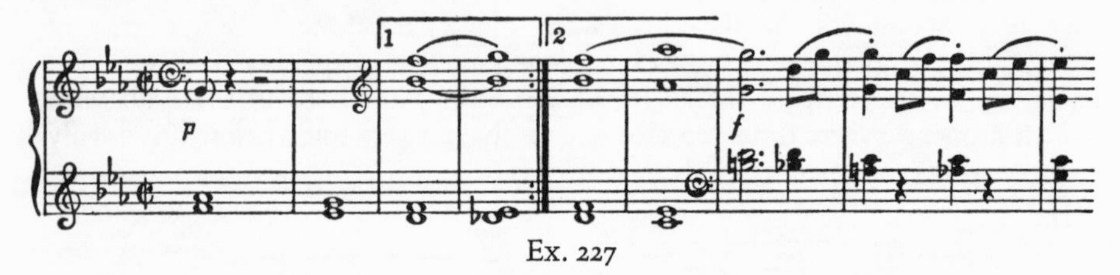

Ex. 227

A wonderful development now follows, matching the exposition in concision, but concentrating an astonishing amount of musical eventfulness into the space of a mere forty bars. They look bare enough on paper at that. We seem to see nothing much beyond a modified statement of Ex. 224 in G flat major that leaps to the eye about the middle of this section. But the ear is enthralled by the most magical transformations of the motto theme, four times reduced to its first two notes without so much as its two-part harmony and interspersed with changing chords to which the figure *a* in Ex. 224 provides the only accompaniment. At last, after the thematic allusion in G flat major, this figure becomes fixed in the bass on octave Cs (with a single deviation to B♮) over which a chain of shifting harmonies leads at last to the recapitulation (beginning with Ex. 224), the recurrent Cs revealing themselves as having driven all the time towards the establishment of its bass note.

There are the normal deviations during the recapitulation, calculated to keep the second subject in the tonic key and to let the music remain there until the coda is reached. This is of unusually large proportions, even for Beethoven, and the reason is no doubt the presence of an extra theme—the motto—of this movement, a feature of which the possibilities have still to be exploited, not only in a structural, but also in a programmatic way. Considerations of structure alone at first absorb the composer. He begins the coda with the transition that had already served for the passage from the exposition to the working-out (Ex. 227), but changes it so that it now leads into F minor, in which key he reverts more or less to the opening of the *allegro*. But soon the motto asserts itself and now becomes significant in relation to the circumstance that gave rise to this Sonata. It is almost throughout fashioned into a duet of two voices: the friends are distinctly heard to call their 'fare thee well' to each other. At first the phrase is made to overlap unaccompanied, then it appears above and below brilliant quaver ornamentations and lastly it becomes rhythmically altered by a new upbeat and for an instant diminished to half its note-values. Perhaps the most eloquent moment comes at the point where Beethoven daringly makes tonic and dominant harmonies clash:

Ex. 228

(The diminution will be seen at the end of the example above.) Needless to say, early editors, who did not understand this passage any more than its famous counterpart in the *Eroica* Symphony, saw fit to correct it. If any excuse can be made for them, it is perhaps that they had no notion of any other thematic function in a sonata than that required by its construction. It did not occur to them to look for a poetic significance in such a device as this, though it is quite plainly the suggestion of the voices of two people mingling as they withdraw from each other.

Andante espressivo.—The slow movement, devoted to the reflections during the friend's absence, is short; in fact it is really an introduction to the finale, for it does not finish on a tonic chord, but leads straight on. The music is noted in C minor, but actually is not more often in that key than in several others, the whole piece being a shifting tissue of phrases which vary in character from wistfulness to tenderness, and from that to emotional fervour. Only the first need be quoted:

Ex. 229

Its opening figure will soon be found to be a governing idea of the musical discourse. The whole statement of the themes is repeated over again, as though the same thoughts insisted on recurring; but the keys are changed the second time and there are differences of distribution on the keyboard, such as octave displacements and doublings. When Ex. 229 recurs a third time, in yet another key, and appears to be leading to the same process of recurrence again, it suddenly rises expectantly and becomes hushed, floating gently upwards in the dominant of E flat major.

Vivacissimamente.—All at once this dominant harmony bursts out in a loud chord: we have reached the joyous finale, expressive of the friends' feelings on meeting again. There are ten bars of a sheer overwhelming rush of sound—dominant-seventh chords broken up into arpeggios, with only a fragment of a thematic feature. Then, after a rising *crescendo* the clear, singing first subject detaches itself quietly:

Ex. 230

The upbeat is at first smothered in the introductory semiquavers, but it will become clearly apparent at the repeat of the exposition, quite apart from the fact that the rhythmic pulse of the music unmistakably suggests it. The phrase quoted above is followed by playful skips; then the theme descends into the bass and there are semiquaver octaves above it which soon afterwards develop into arpeggios and descending scales, tonic and dominant harmony alternating, but the bass remaining fixed in the tonic, a device much favoured by Mozart, but handled in a new way by Beethoven. Even more novel is the passage that follows, a distinctly pianistic one, since it makes use of the pedal to produce an effect quite different from that shown by the written notes. To the eye this is bare octave unison; to the ear it is harmony:

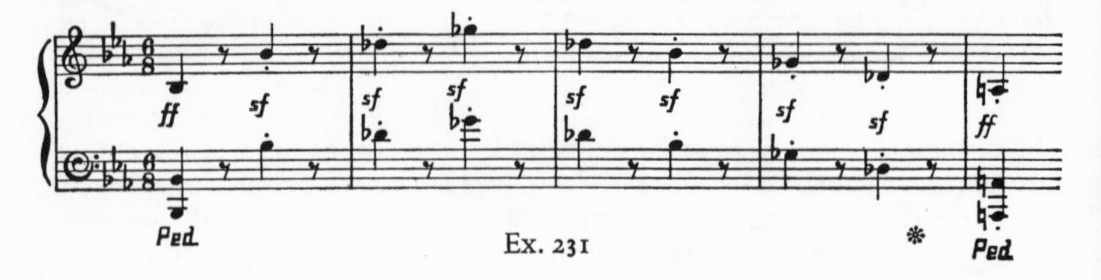

Ex. 231

This repeats itself on the chord of F major, and afterwards the passage is varied in both keys by a soft and skittishly elaborated version. One imagines the gruff Beethoven and the graceful archduke exchanging greetings in the same words, but with different expression.

In the second subject the dialogue is drawn together so that both voices are heard at once. At any rate there are two simultaneous melodies:

Ex. 232

This is developed with great brilliance and leads, after a shake in the left hand, to syncopated passages in which song seems to become unsettled in delirious joy. The exposition is repeated. The working-out then begins with the figure 230*a* in a new lay-out and in E flat minor, followed by a new melodic phrase. 230*a* is repeated in G flat minor, and the new melody is expanded until Ex. 232 starts its twofold song again, this time in B major. It is now seen that its two strains are invertible, i.e., written in double counterpoint, for 232*a* now appears in the bass and 232*b* in the treble. This second subject modulates and then gives way to the first (Ex. 230), which almost imperceptibly merges into the recapitulation. The whole first subject is now presented fundamentally as before, but with new semiquaver figures of accompaniment that enhance the glad rush of the music. Ex. 231, with its nimble variant, appears in two new keys, and then comes the second-subject group, fixing the key of E flat major during its whole extent.

For the coda a slower tempo, *poco andante*, is surprisingly adopted, and here one is again conscious that the poetic idea predominates over the musical scheme. There is no reason why Beethoven should not have kept up the *vivacissimamente* to the end; he could have rounded off the Sonata significantly in a hundred different ways without a change of pace. But obviously at this reunion with his exalted pupil some sober reflection was indicated. Here was a journey ending in no lovers' meeting, but in a manly friendship which after the first enthusiasm of the renewed contact settled down to calm, heartfelt pleasure. This is the expression which the principal subject now assumes in its final presentation. Still, at the very end the considerations of musical balance come uppermost after all: Beethoven resumes the original tempo for the last six bars.

SONATA IN E MINOR, Op. 90 (1814)
(B.S.S. RECORDS, VOL. I)

THIS Sonata adheres to the two-movement form of which we have already had a great example. Op. 90 is dedicated to Count Moritz von Lichnowsky, one of Beethoven's many aristocratic friends, who was at that time engaged to be married. In order, no doubt, to make the work appropriate to the occasion, Beethoven referred to it as depicting 'a contest between head and heart,' regardless of the fact—unless the intention was to perpetrate one of his doubtful jests—that he was thus casting reflections on the count's wisdom and on the suitability of his betrothed. However that may be, commentators have seen restlessness in the first movement and peaceful contentment in the second. Lichnowsky's love affair is now a matter of supreme unimportance, and almost as much so are Beethoven's jokes; all that matters is that we have here two wonderfully contrasted movements which do suggest, in a way applicable to mankind at large, some sort of passionate quest attended by a satisfying discovery, some agitating problem followed by a calming solution.

Mit Lebhaftigkeit und durchaus mit Empfindung und Ausdruck.—By the time Beethoven wrote this Sonata he had reached the phase in which he rejected the Italian directions that had hitherto been current in the music of all nations and insisted on the use of the German language. The piano itself was soon to be called *Hammerklavier* by him, which has led to some curious speculations about the nature of the new instrument for which the last sonatas were supposed to have been written. One of these works, indeed, has retained the name as a special distinction; but, deep-rooted as it is, it had better be discarded as soon as may be. A few years earlier Beethoven would have put at the head of the present first movement: *Animato e sempre con sentimento ed espressione*, and we, were we possessed of a spirit of linguistic intolerance similar to that which took hold of him later, should convert his direction thus: 'Lively, and with feeling and expression throughout.'

The movement opens with a succession of four short phrases, each in a different key, of which the first two are given here:

Ex. 233

The impatience with which Beethoven immediately leaves the tonic key of E minor is characteristic of his later style. With the fourth phrase he has arrived at B minor, but he now continues his first-subject group with a new strain, the first note of which (D) is converted from the third of B minor into the fifth of G major:

Ex. 234

This leads back to a pause on the dominant of E minor, in which key a third motif, based on the rhythm of the first, is stated. Then comes a series of bare, rising octaves which insist on the metrical accent of the first two notes of each of the groups constituting the opening theme (Ex. 233*a*). This is used for some time, with rapid descending scales by way of connecting links. A very interesting modulation, still with this simple rhythm behind it, is worth quoting for its original harmonic scheme:

Ex. 235

The augmented fourth shown at the beginning is turned, by the enharmonic change of B ♭ to A ♯, into a diminished fifth, and presently a chord of the diminished seventh is used as a pivot on which the modulation swings into B minor. This, after some further development, is the key in which the second-subject group is introduced with this agitated theme:

Ex. 236

Note, once again, the new treatment of the conventional Alberti bass. This six-bar phrase is repeated with varied figuration in the right hand and merges into an auxiliary theme with a rising bass scale followed by a cadence.

The working-out begins with a fascinating new presentation of Ex. 233, with far-flung modulations and a wide distribution over the keyboard. After the descent of a chromatic chord sequence over a pedal on G, the bass suddenly begins to rise against the falling treble until the two meet, dissolving into a new statement of Ex. 234, at first in two parts and then with a semiquaver embroidery for the right hand. It is the last of these semiquaver figures which lets this transition flow into the recapitulation in the most wonderful way imaginable. The figure itself is that shown as *a* in the following example, and its transformations are indicated one by one:

Ex. 237

The last of these figures is followed by the opening phrase of Ex. 233, which, it will be seen, consists of the same notes. It is as though we were turning round a corner full of expectation and nothing surprised us so much as the fact that we had really known all the time what was coming to meet us there. Never did Beethoven's inexhaustible gift of managing transitions in a new way manifest itself more simply and astonishingly. The recapitulation proceeds quite normally and the coda is very ingeniously based on the concluding phrase of the second subject, three statements taken from Ex. 233 and a passage from the context of the movement that has not been quoted. As in the Sonata Op. 78, Beethoven closes without the least oratorical ado. He does not even insist on the final tonic chord.

Nicht zu geschwind und sehr singbar vorzutragen.—Beethoven's influence on later composers is manifest enough. The most familiar item of the heritage he left is, of course, the rhythm of the slow movement in the seventh Symphony which, a discovery for casual use to him, was to become almost a mannerism with Schubert. In the second movement of the Sonata Op. 90 we see how a much less likely composer was indebted to him. The following two passages, played rather slowly and sentimentally, can hardly fail to remind one of a later and smaller master so forcibly that it is scarcely necessary to mention his name:

Ex. 238

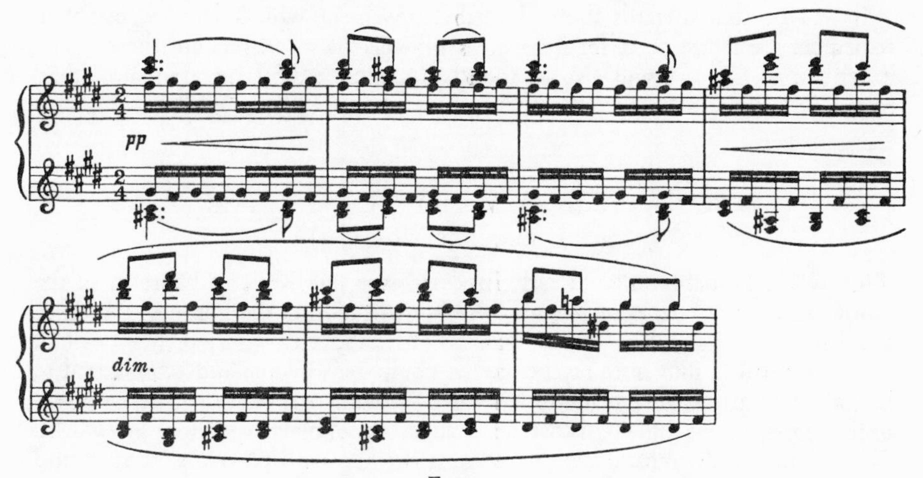

Ex. 239

Fortunately, in this case, the music is neither slow nor in the least sentimental, so that it will not be found a great deal like—the name will slip out after all—Mendelssohn. Nevertheless, that composer's debt to Beethoven is evident enough.

The German direction may be translated into 'Not too fast, and to be played very songfully.' The key is E major. We have seen how in the F sharp major Sonata, Op. 78, Beethoven solved the problem of contrast in spite of his retention of the same key for the second movement; here he makes a change from minor to major and can accordingly afford to insist upon his new key at once. The form of the movement is that of a rondo with a sonata-like closeness of thematic application.

The music opens with the strain quoted in Ex. 238, which is the rondo subject that recurs again and again, often with slight differences of treatment. A second melody, occurring immediately after the completion of Ex. 238 and some time before Ex. 239, must be shown because of the phrase marked *a* at the end:

Ex. 240

This figure will be heard as an important structural feature later on. There is also another theme, coming very soon after Ex. 239 and easily recognized by an accompaniment changed into quaver triplets, that must be mentioned as an organic constituent. It is not necessary, after the many details that have already been given of Beethoven's structural procedures, to analyse this movement step by step. Its development may be quite profitably followed unaided, for the material is used very lucidly and without any hidden allusions.

It will be seen towards the end of the movement why it was important to remember the figure 240*a*, for it becomes unexpectedly conspicuous there. The cadence *a* in Ex. 238 will also be found to assume a vital function more than once.

SONATA IN A MAJOR, Op. 101 (1816)
(B.S.S. RECORDS, VOL. VII)

THIS work, probably finished early in 1816, was published in February of the following year by Steiner of Vienna, with a dedication to the Baroness Dorothea von Ertmann, one of those exalted patrons of Beethoven's whose pretensions had a way of turning into humility before the composer's genius and who ceased to be patronizing on being made to feel his own withering pride. The baroness, unlike most of his other aristocratic friends, was able to perform his works. She was in fact the most distinguished amateur keyboard player in Vienna, and Beethoven thought so much of her musicianship that he called her 'Dorothea Cecilia.' They must have been excellent friends, for the story goes that when she was brought to the verge of insanity by grief over the loss of a child, he saved her reason by playing to her.

It was in connection with this Sonata that Beethoven first took it into his head to invent a German name for the pianoforte. In various letters of 1816 addressed to Tobias Haslinger, whom he appears to have at first had in view as a publisher for this work, he seriously debates the question, going so far as to wish to consult an expert linguist whether the word to be chosen should be *Hammer-Clavier, Hämmer-Clavier, Hammer-Flügel*, or what. 'With regard to the title a philologist must be consulted. . . . The answer must be put before me,' he commands in his peremptory fashion. (No wonder he called Haslinger his 'adjutant,' while he was the 'general').

He was at this time much concerned about the Germanization of the whole musical terminology, as his works of the period, including this Sonata, show. With regard to the pianoforte he felt that, since it was the invention of a German, there should be honour where honour was due. It was not at that time definitely established that the actual inventor of the instrument was Cristofori, not Silbermann or Schröter. Even so, however, what Grove called Beethoven's German fit passed off, and the only two sonatas for which he actually used the term of *Hammerclavier* are the present work and the one in B flat major, Op. 106, which alone is to this day distinguished by that name, for no very good reason, it will be agreed.

As Bekker points out, Op. 101 is quite as much a *sonata quasi una fantasia* as the earlier works which Beethoven actually called so. The reason why he no longer used the term by 1816 is that he came to take the free, fantastic treatment of the sonata form for granted. Bekker is right to suggest that Op. 101 has a great formal affinity with the very first work so designated by the composer, the Sonata in E flat major, Op. 27 No. 1. At least it is true that, here as there, the slow movement is merely an introduction to the finale and that the latter is the most extended and highly developed movement. But spiritually Op. 27 and Op. 101 are as far apart as they are in years. In the later work all is expression, nothing mere display or technical contrivance. There are difficulties demanding brilliant playing, to be sure, and the writing has the ingenuity of the completely self-possessed master; but it is due precisely to this self-possession that Beethoven is now able to concentrate his whole creative mind on emotional expression in the most poetical terms of which music is capable. The means by which this is attained through manipulation of the composer's craft, and put into logical shape by his instinctive knowledge of how to handle and adjust form, came to him quite naturally by this time, provided that he was seized by the fever of irresistible inspiration, as in this glorious work. They had simply become part of the expression itself.

Etwas lebhaft, und mit der innigsten Empfindung (*Allegretto, ma non troppo*).—Although the real, crucial sonata movement in this work is the finale, the first movement, unlike that of other works of the *fantasia* order, is in a regular sonata form. This form, however, is extremely condensed, so much so that if the movement went at the pace of an *allegro* instead of an *allegretto*, it would be over in a flash. There is no doubt that Beethoven was perfectly well aware of this, though perhaps not altogether consciously.

There is a first subject, not a group representing the first subject, as in most classical sonatas. It is ineffably suave and lovely: 'somewhat lively, and with the most heartfelt expression,' Beethoven directs in German. One would like to think that this was the very music he played to the bereaved mother:

Ex. 241

After these four bars the music reverts to bar 1, hesitating slightly and taking a new modulatory turn. For a moment it is hung up on a pause.

And now a remarkable thing happens: Beethoven still continues in the vein of his first subject, but his key-scheme already verges towards the second, for we are no longer in A major, but so to speak obliquely approaching the key of the dominant (E major) through its own dominant. The first and second subjects thus appear to be telescoped, which is exactly what had to happen if the movement was to get over the ground of the sonata form as quickly as the composer intended. He was obliged to take short cuts, in fact, and he took them boldly.

The actual second subject is this:

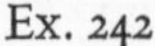
Ex. 242

The rising figure in the bass and the falling one in the treble, with the notes that follow, are free inversions of each other. It will also be noticed that the flowing part-writing of both the examples quoted above resembles that of a string quartet, as indeed the whole of the music so far discussed has done. But presently we come upon a passage that is wholly pianistic and especially noteworthy for the way in which it displaces the accentuated beats by syncopation:

Ex. 243

This serves as a link with the working-out section: in fact it may already be part of it, for again the formal demarcations are deliberately dissolved into each other. The syncopations, periodically hung up on long chords, form an accompaniment to allusions to Ex. 241 that appear in the bass. Presently they mount into the treble, continue for a little while, give rise to some new material and seem on the point of continuing to develop in various keys, beginning with A minor. But no: A major follows, and though the different display of the music at first makes us disbelieve such a fact—again that confusing and overlapping—we are actually in the recapitulation before we know it. It is even more condensed than the exposition, the whole of the first hesitant approach being cut out. Ex. 242 and 243 follow, the latter being made to modulate into a fascinating coda, concerned mainly with Ex. 242 and the rhythmic deception of Ex. 243. It contains two of the loveliest cadences to be found anywhere in the world's music.

Lebhaft, marschmässig (*Vivace, alla marcia*).—The second movement makes an almost startling contrast, with its impatient, ironical, restless succession of jerky figures in dotted rhythms. The whole of the first strain is shown here in melodic outline only:

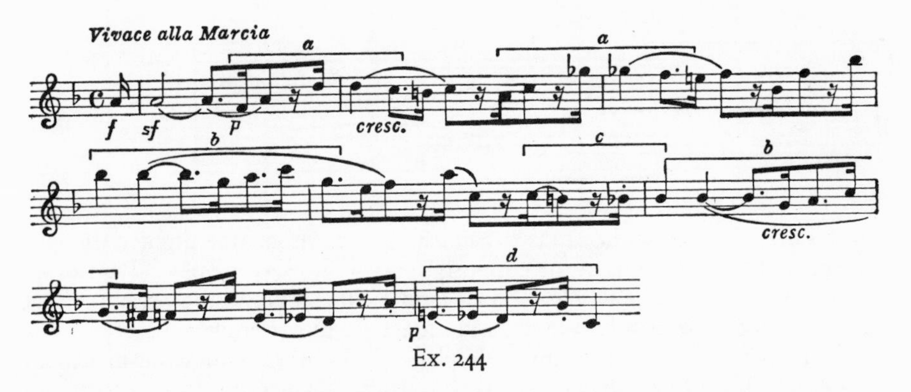

Ex. 244

and the bracketed phrases lettered *a*, *b*, *c* and *d* above will be found to make up practically the whole of this fantastic march. There is, further, a clinching bass figure, *e*, which also has an important function:

Ex. 245

At the end of the first section—i.e. after the first repeat—for example, *e* is heard in rapid alternation with *d*. After a brief interchange of *a* between the two hands, the music diverges to new matter, though not without an allusion to *c* in the accompaniment, and presently *a* returns, becoming elaborately interlinked and a little later treated melodically in the key of D flat major. This is the only episode in the march approaching to something like lyricism, and it loses itself in a mysterious *pianissimo* with a bare, unharmonized treble and bass lying very far apart. A rapid *crescendo* then leads to a new interchange between *b* and *c* and to another new idea laid out in contrary motion, partly for crossed hands, or rather for an imaginary interplay of three hands, the middle as well as both ends of the keyboard being used. The end of the march draws upon *c*, *d* and *e*. The second part, which is much longer than the first, is also repeated.

The trio section is a complete contrast, but not exactly a suave one, in spite of the prescribed *dolce*:

[*Continued*

Ex. 246

It is for the most part written in two-part canon and without the slightest thought whether the combinations of the curiously sprawling, leggy themes fall agreeably on the ear or not. The whole shows a kind of uncompromising reasoning that cares more for truth than for beauty, and certainly will not produce beauty by any kind of falsification of the composer's plan. If he intends to write in canon, then canon it must be, whatever the consequences. The canonic answers sometimes come at the distance of one bar, as above, and sometimes at half a bar, which requires some special manipulation that no doubt made the problem more enticing for Beethoven. The brief appearance of a rhythmically quite new figure, in canon at the half-bar, will not escape notice. Soon afterwards the strict treatment resolves itself for a moment into the falling together of two parts in thirds in the left hand, where the right plays a shake three bars long; but they diverge again at once, and the canon is resumed. However, it resolves itself suddenly into a new and extended presentation of the figure 246*a*, and this unexpectedly gives way to a combination of figures 244 *b* and *c*. It is now obvious that the march is to be heard again, and in fact it is played right through once more without the repeats.

Langsam und sehnsuchtsvoll (*Adagio, ma non troppo, con affetto*).—We have now reached the slow section that is not a self-contained movement, but an introduction to the finale. Nevertheless, it is charged with the most poignant emotion, by no means attenuated by the use of the damping pedal throughout, which gives the whole a kind of subdued tearfulness. Nor does the fact that the music is very closely modelled on the two figures *a* and *b* shown below produce the least dryness of expression:

Ex. 247

Only two short and very expressive strains diverge from this material immediately after the opening quoted here, and there is another leading into the free cadenza at the close, during which the left pedal is released, all the strings being brought into play again to bring about a great surprise. This is nothing less than a quotation of the opening of the first movement, which begins exactly as quoted in Ex. 241, save that there is a pause between the two phrases. That pause is significant. There is clearly some doubt whether the happy mood can really be recaptured. We soon find that it cannot. The music hesitates again. The final figure of Ex. 241 is tentatively repeated. But it engenders a new feeling. It rises upwards three times and grows more emphatic at each repetition. Then there is a rushing descent, arrested on a shake that rises up by three semi-tones. It thus becomes poised on E, the dominant of the principal key of the whole Sonata—A major—in which the finale is now to begin.

Geschwind, doch nicht zu sehr, und mit Entschlossenheit (*Allegro*).—'Fast, but not too fast, and resolutely,' says Beethoven, and in truth we find him in one of his defiant frames of mind. There is much happiness here, but it is not the soft abandonment to bliss of the first movement: it is gladness won by grim determination. Here is the initial strain of the first-subject group (for at last we have a very fully developed sonata movement with first and second subjects comprising a great deal of material):

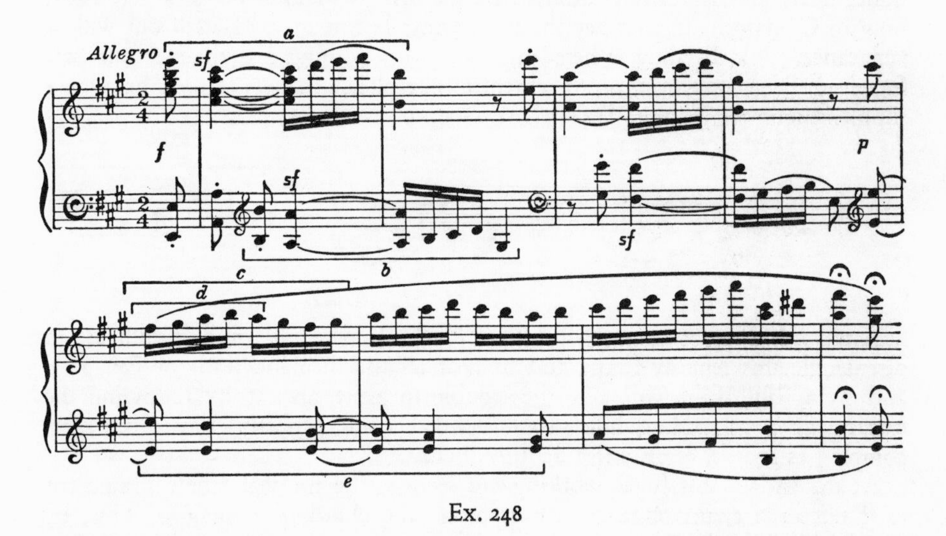

Ex. 248

Figures 248*a* and *b* are now inverted in double counterpoint, i.e. the left hand plays what the right had before, and vice versa. The same happens with the fragments *c* and *e*. A new, more melodious and very cheerful idea intervenes briefly before new elaborations of Ex. 248 carry on the music. A great deal is made before long of the mere thematic scrap 248*d* and various derivations of it. Then again comes a more lyrical theme, acting as transition to the second-subject group, the two main ideas of which are this imitative phrase, plainly akin to 248*a*:

Ex. 249

and the following clinching figure:

Ex. 250

After the latter the whole exposition is repeated.

With a magical touch Beethoven uses this last idea (Ex. 250) to carry him on into the working-out section. But after half a dozen bars the music slackens undecidedly and is abruptly aroused by the first two falling notes of Ex. 248*a*, now in C major. In that key the music now begins to work itself out with a vengeance. For Beethoven here embarks upon nothing less than a four-part fugue on the subject of 248*a*, to which, to complicate matters further, he adds a supplementary strain (Ex. 251*a*):

Ex. 251

Any one listening to a performance of the Sonata will find it difficult to disentangle this lengthy fugue and to hear all the thematic leads of Ex. 248*a* and 251*a*, but if he will take the trouble to assist his ear by following the music with a score, the whole structure will become perfectly clear to him, for, complex as it is, it is also wonderfully lucid.

At the end of this fugal working-out section, the musical tangle straightens itself out in a chain of rising arpeggios on the chord of E major. This, by revealing itself as the dominant of A major, acts as a pivot on which the movement swings into its recapitulation.

This is by no means regular. For one thing, the cheerful melody heard early in the exposition is cut out, for a reason that will appear presently. Then, after the pauses at which the break in this movement occurred earlier, there is a new ingenuity: Ex. 248*a* appears simultaneously in both hands, in contrary motion. Ex. 248*c* is also differently presented, and the elaboration of 248*d* appears in new keys and positions. The second-subject group, on the other hand, comes back without change except that of key from dominant to tonic, no doubt because that in itself is enough to create a sense of newness.

And now comes a very interesting and extended coda to round off this unceasingly enchanting work. The clinching figure, Ex. 250, is heard muttering softly in the bass against derivatives of 248*a*, and then comes again that peremptory drop of its opening figure, repeated softly in what appears to be a new approach to the fugal development. Indeed the fugal entry, Ex. 251, starts up in F major, and we wonder whether the whole process is going to be repeated in that key. But Beethoven knows better: he has reached a stage at which the argument must be brought to its conclusion. Accordingly, he quickly veers back to A major again, and it is now that he makes the cheerful theme he had previously omitted from the recapitulation recur once more. Nothing could suit him better, for it is clear that the Sonata is meant to end in a playful vein. It spreads itself rather more than before, and leads to a final use of the running figures of Ex. 248*c*, the while the chirpy cuckooing of the cheerful tune still continues. 248*c* is then abbreviated to several references to 248*d*. The music softens and slackens; but there is a sudden vigorous outburst of rising A major chords, which at last cut short this engrossing musical discourse.

INTERLUDE X

'*HAMMERCLAVIER*'

It is one of the silliest conventions of musical professionalism to call Beethoven's B flat major Sonata, Op. 106, the *Hammerclavier* Sonata. One might equally well call it *the* pianoforte Sonata, which indeed perhaps it is, since magnitude and profundity cannot fail to confer an outstanding distinction on a supremely well-organized work for the keyboard. What is the word *Hammerclavier* except an attempt on Beethoven's part, during a phase of patriotism, to find a German word for the instrument which people in Vienna, as elsewhere, insisted on calling by a contraction of its earliest Italian designation: '*clavicembalo col piano e forte*'? The habit by which this Teutonic name has attached itself to one particular work, absurd in itself, is made the more ridiculous by the fact that Beethoven actually invented it for the A major Sonata, Op. 101, and that by the time he came to Op. 106 he used it again simply because he had not yet shaken off what Grove called his 'German fit.' If therefore we do not call both these works *Hammerclavier* sonatas it is simply because we cannot call two children by the same name without creating endless confusion. The only acceptable reason, then, why the name of *Hammerclavier* should still be retained for the one child to whom it happens to have become attached is that it is useful for identification. But let us not pretend that it has in itself any more sense than most nicknames.

The Sonata, which is dedicated to the Archduke Rudolph, was composed in 1818–19 and published by Artaria of Vienna in September of the latter year. But in the spring Beethoven evidently tried to get it printed, on as favourable terms as possible, in London, for he had some correspondence about it in April with his former pupil, Ferdinand Ries, who was then living in England.

He was very hard pressed for money at that time and anxious to secure a lucrative engagement in London, which however did not materialize. How great his anxiety must have been to see the Sonata published on almost any conditions, so long as it was well paid for, may be judged from the letter dated 19th April 1819, in which he goes to the length of suggesting that the *largo* introduction to the finale might be cut out, if desired, or even the first movement omitted altogether and the scherzo and slow movement reversed, so that the work would open with the latter, in F sharp minor, and end in B flat major.

That from Beethoven, on whom we are accustomed to look as the most passionately scrupulous of all composers in matters of musical form! His plight must indeed have been a sorry one to bring him to such a pass, and the truth is that it forced him into an equivocal position in more material respects as well, for he was not above contemplating the striking of a double bargain by selling the Sonata to an English and a German publisher at the same time. Perhaps in burdening his conscience thus in one way he lightened it in another, for he must have been anxious that the German edition at least should represent the work exactly as he intended and wrote it. As for the other—well, England was a long way off.

This complaisance in the matter of one of his most tremendous works is the more strange because only three days earlier he had given Ries some very careful directions as to the metronome marks to be added to the manuscript sent to London, and it was in this letter that he asked his disciple to prefix to the slow movement the extra opening bar, containing the rising third A–C♯ (see Ex. 269*a*, page 217).

Among composers' afterthoughts this is the most famous and curious. At first sight it really does not seem to matter in the least whether this rising third is there or not. It does not make any strong link between the two distant keys of the scherzo and slow movement, and the surprise of the F sharp minor chord would not have been more shocking than some of Haydn's wanderings from key to key between sonata or quartet movements, especially if we agree with Sir Donald Tovey that F sharp minor is here merely a convenient notation for G flat minor. However, the initial A of the added bar is the leading note of B flat and it is curious that at the beginning of the finale—the *largo* introduction Beethoven professed to be so ready to sacrifice—we have the same relationship, for the opening F there is, of course, the leading note (E♯) of the concluding F♯ that went before.

But commentators have found more than that. They have noticed that the A–C♯ of this additional bar in Ex. 269 is answered by a descending third of C♯–A in the next bar, and that precisely the same thing happens (on other notes) at the beginning of both the first movement and the scherzo (see Exx. 252 and 262). No doubt they would be happier if the finale too answered to that scheme; but they can at least find the rising third F–A (converted into a tenth) at the beginning of the fugue subject (Ex. 275, page 221), and if it is any comfort to them, there is perhaps no reason why they should not see the answering drop of a third in the figure that follows by looking only at the first and last note (B♭ and G) and shutting their eyes to the intermediate notes. After all, what are five semiquavers?

But whatever annotators say, and whether or not one follows Tovey in feeling that these two opening notes of the *adagio* 'constitute one of the profoundest thoughts in all music,' there is plenty of evidence that Beethoven wrestled like a giant with the overwhelmingly potent material of this Sonata, the composition of which might be called a kind of artistic climbing of Mount Everest, were it not for the difference that he did actually reach the summit. Although the whole of his tremendous effort can only be guessed from the finished result, we have his sketches for detailed evidence. Never had a great master a harder struggle in hewing his material into the shape that satisfied him; but where we have sketches of his to compare with the finished product, we invariably find that the latter is infinitely superior. It has been noticed that among the more frequent improvements in the whole collection of his sketches are additional upbeats, which heighten the eloquence of a theme, and a special care to avoid beginning on the highest notes of the scale covered by the range of a melody. A comparison of the sketch of the opening theme of Op. 106 with the definitive version (Ex. 252, page 205) shows that both these considerations have borne fruit here. Moreover, the theme is rhythmically much more plastic in its finished form than in the following outline:

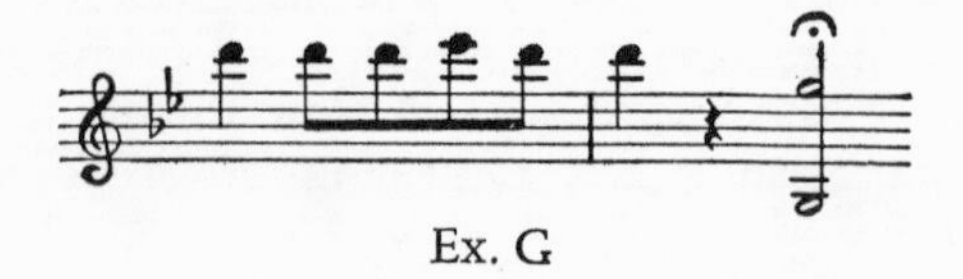

Ex. G

Such close workmanship alone is inspiring. Whether it proceeds from inspiration or engenders it is difficult to say, and we have no right to go for enlightenment to other composers, since Beethoven's creative procedure was unlike that of any master before or since. That the exercise of his skill nourished his inspiration none the less satisfyingly because it often came hard to him cannot be questioned in view of his sketch-books, and there is no reason to doubt that inspiration in turn fired his skill, for that is the way of genius.

His fierce tussle with the actual stuff of music sometimes becomes materially evident in his work, as in the final fugue of the *Hammerclavier* Sonata, where it is reflected in the almost heartbreaking technical effort the pianist is obliged to make in order to keep the texture clear without detracting from the bigness of tone that is required. This has led many people to say that, great as the Sonata is as music in the abstract, it is unsatisfactory as piano music, just as the *Grosse Fuge*, Op. 133, is said to be a marvellous construction but impossible for a string quartet to play. So far as performers are concerned there is, of course, some justification in these strictures; but that is hardly the point. The point is that the pianist, pampered as he is by the wonderfully congenial keyboard writing of a Chopin, a Liszt or a Debussy, must either strain himself exceptionally to reach the highest altitudes of his art or else stay below. He cannot always have everything his own way, nor do those who are capable of understanding this Sonata expect to hear from beginning to end such suavities as could not lend genuine beauty to certain passages for the very good reason that they would rob them of character.

On the other hand it would be preposterous to pretend that there are no beauties of a purely physical, pianistic order in this work, to which in fact some of the greatest masters of keyboard writing are very obviously indebted. The theme of the scherzo (Ex. 262) quite clearly foreshadows Schumann, and at least one ornate passage in the slow movement (Ex. 272) shows that Chopin's highly decorative style did not come out of the blue. That Brahms first called the world to attention with the peremptory rhythm of the *Hammerclavier* opening (Ex. 252) in his C major Sonata, Op. 1, is no less significant, and it is worth remembering that he did use this hint from a work alleged to be unpianistic for a piece of keyboard music.

Grit, in the moral and intellectual sense, being the quality we have learnt to value most in Beethoven as an artist, we cannot only well afford to take his technical grittiness into the bargain, but had better look upon it as essential to our full appreciation of him. That is why Felix Weingartner's orchestral version of Op. 106 is merely an interesting experiment, not a successful substitution. Although it was undertaken because Weingartner honestly felt that it would for the first time fully reveal the meaning of a Sonata that is not playable without superhuman effort, in performance it is found to do nothing of the kind, precisely because one misses an effort that is part of the very stuff and fibre of Beethoven. The interest of this transformation into a symphony, great as it is in a way, remains purely technical and therefore superficial, very much as does that of Wolfgang Graeser's orchestral transcription of Bach's *Art of Fugue*, which many otherwise sane people still declare to be not only unplayable in its original form, but not intended to be played at all.

We must take art as it is given to us, with such limitations and even such defects as it may show. No work is quite flawless, if it comes to that, and art without limitations is unthinkable, as it is undesirable without artificialities. The opening scene of *The Tempest*, for example, is highly artificial on the stage, but although it might be more exciting played in a real storm at sea, with the audience seated in a gale on Brighton pier and the crew in actual danger of their lives, no artist in his senses could think such a presentation desirable or likely to show us the true Shakespeare. Yes, it is for us to accept great works as their creators meant them, and believe in them as they are. That is what distinguishes them from small and casual art.

SONATA IN B FLAT MAJOR, Op. 106 (1818–19)
(B.S.S. RECORDS, VOL. X)

Allegro.—The principal element of the first subject is this imperious gesture:

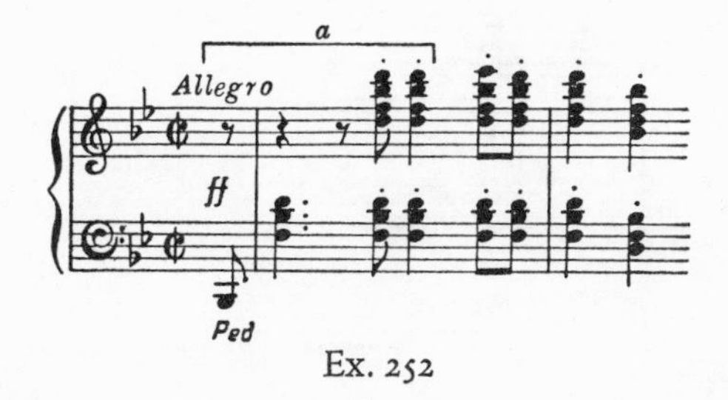

Ex. 252

repeated a third higher but in the same chord position. Nothing could be simpler, nothing more impressive. The figure is stamped on the hearer's mind at once, so that its most elaborate developments later on cannot possibly escape attention. It is Beethoven's masterful way to build his most complex structures out of the most rudimentary material, as earlier and more familiar examples such as the opening themes of the third and fifth Symphonies show quite as clearly as this Sonata.

Equally characteristic is the device of introducing a complete contrast at once:

Ex. 253

This is the kind of theme Haydn and Mozart, supposing that they could have thought of anything so wholly Beethovenish, would most certainly have reserved for a second subject. To them such a drastic departure from the mood set at the beginning, without any sort of transition, would have seemed a glaring error of taste, and even to-day we can only reconcile it with our notions of the classical sonata form by reflecting that Beethoven so convincingly changed many things that taste simply had to change too. So overbearing is genius, fortunately for the continued renewal of art. Ex. 253 is repeated an octave higher, but instead of ending again on a half-close, it leads by an extension to a third salient feature belonging to the first subject-group:

Ex. 254

which returns to the emphatic manner of the opening. (The notes shown in brackets overlap with the close of the preceding phrase.) Passages of thematically subordinate interest, but needing the boldest handling of the keyboard for their pounding octaves and wide skips, next lead to a momentary return of Ex. 252. Its repetition this time does not rise a third, but keeps the B flat major chord with D at the top. There is a reason for this: for one beat that D is heard alone in bare octaves, and this gives a new chord an opening—the common chord of D major, which at once seizes upon its chance to assert itself.

This assertion is not made without a purpose. On this D, transferred to the bass, the rhythmic figure 252*a* is reiterated, and the music thus passes into a long transitional passage harmonically based on D as the dominant of G major. For it is in this key that the second subject is to appear, although according to classical precedent it ought here to stand in F major, the dominant of the main key. However, it is not so far removed in relationship to B flat major as may at first appear, for G minor would be the latter's nearest relative on the minor side of the family, and G major, being as close as possible to that, may be said to be first cousin, or perhaps better a step-brother, to B flat major.

Here is the principal strain of the second-subject group, the small notes shown being, in the first place, the close of the transition into which it thrusts itself in the bass and, in the second, mere harmonic filling:

Ex. 255

Never did an important theme glide into its place so unobtrusively. Without this special demonstration on paper it would be as difficult for the eye as it is for the ear to tell at exactly what moment it takes shape and what, so to speak, belongs respectively to the tadpole and the frog stage of the music, if a ridiculous comparison may be employed to illustrate a sublime topic.

It is perhaps worth noting, although no one can say whether it is more than a coincidence, that the rhythmic cut of this subject is very much like that of the strain quoted as Ex. 253, which lends more substance to the notion that an earlier classic would have used that as a second subject. Can it be that Beethoven himself was aware of this and deliberately modelled his real second subject on it?

Ex. 255 reappears in the treble and then lends itself to a series of descending sequences, followed by this new idea:

Ex. 256

The interlocked figures, Ex. 256*a*, soon afterwards present themselves in three different keys, appearing a fourth higher each time. Next come three vigorous groups based on a rhythm derived from the last two bars quoted in Ex. 255 (left hand):

which is not far from this rhythm of the first subject (Ex. 252):

and may be intended to let us expect the imminent repeat of the exposition. This, however, is delayed by the appearance of yet another theme belonging to the second-subject group:

Ex. 257

Here the principle of the Alberti bass may once again be seen rejuvenated into new pianistic devices suited to a particular purpose and not merely applied as a stock resource, and there is also one of those interior shakes which belong specially to Beethoven's later piano music and still remain almost his exclusive property. Other composers have perhaps felt that they do not sound beautiful enough to justify their technical difficulty; but Beethoven looked as much for character as for beauty, and they are as representative of his thought as anything could be.

After a syncopated theme akin to that quoted as *b* in Ex. 259 below, the exposition closes thus:

Ex. 258

The key of B flat major having been re-established with no less ingenuity than abruptness, the recapitulation, beginning with Ex. 252, joins straight on to the extract shown above.

The recapitulation changes at the end in the following manner, the first two bars quoted below being identical with those at the beginning of Ex. 258:

[*Continued*

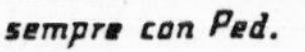

Ex. 259

This is an unusually long quotation, but then this opening of a working-out section of extraordinary magnitude and concentration is of exceptional interest and well worth analysing in detail. It will be seen that the rising figure of three notes (*a*) had already occurred at the end of the exposition (see Ex. 258), but that there it turned G major into G minor for the purpose of using the B flat as a pivot on which to swing back into the key of the tonic. Here, at the second appearance of this figure, it is kept in G major, a key which Beethoven does not intend to leave immediately. He clearly wishes to make quite sure that modulation should not coincide with the transition from recapitulation to development; in other words, that we should not be startled by too striking a point where he can astonish us enough by producing two sufficiently arresting ones.

The three notes rise two steps higher, and now the key of G begins to lose its independence, being made to serve as the dominant of C minor. The syncopated figure already mentioned (*b*) is used for that purpose and, rising in sequential steps, turned into the dominant of E flat major. In that key the three rising notes appear again, differently displayed each time (Ex. 259, bars 13–16), whereupon the rhythm with which the chief subject opens (*c*) returns as at the end of the exposition, save for a change of key. E flat major is retained for the beginning of a fugal section which produces about as close and logical a working-out as could well be imagined. The figure *c* is extended into that shown above as *d* and thus brought, it will be seen, into closer relationship with Ex. 252. The texture of this episode is that of a double fugue, the new figure *e* being dealt with like a counter-subject, and what is more, the material is at once treated in close canon—in other words, Beethoven cuts out the usual leisurely initial presentation of the fugue material voice by voice and contracts it immediately by means of strettos, as Bach occasionally does (e.g. *Well-tempered Clavier*, C major Fugue, Vol. I, No. 1). Complex as the various combinations are, the thematic entries are made so clear that the whole fugal fabric sounds astonishingly lucid. Note that *e* is sometimes turned upside down, as in the bass of the following passage, which also contains two canonic entries of *d*:

Ex. 260

Technical ingenuity rises to still greater heights where three parts are increased to four and each entry of the canon is made by two voices simultaneously, two octaves and a third apart:

Ex. 261

Gradually the web of parts becomes simpler. They sort themselves out into conjunct motion of thirds and sixths, and presently this fugal development ceases, to be followed by a series of modulations which make use of nothing but the predominant rhythm (Exx. 252*a*, 259*c*) linked up, it is true, by groups of gently falling quavers which lend variety to all this hammering away at the same metre, done not for crude emphasis, but doubtless in order to fix the hearer's interest for the moment on the ceaseless harmonic transformations without new melodic or rhythmic distractions.

When the figure has been reduced to bare octaves, there is a sudden upward jerk from D to D♯, and it is only less surprising to hear the suave subsidiary theme Ex. 257 in this context than to find it standing in the very distant key of B major, with an admixture of minor. Its final phrase is beautifully echoed an octave lower and the same thing happens when that phrase has been repeated in a version loosened into quaver runs. So far Beethoven, who is fond of such tonal ambiguities, has used the key signature of B minor for this episode, in spite of its major inflections; but he now changes to five sharps for a new outburst of the prevalent rhythm that appears to prepare us for another fugal episode. This expectation is not realized, however, for no sooner has the theme No. 252 been used four times in canon than it is reduced to its opening figure (252*a*), which Beethoven shapes into a transitional passage leading straight into the recapitulation.

A far from normal recapitulation it is, though. At the very outset there is a change, for Ex. 252 now appears with a new left-hand part against it continued at the return of Ex. 253, the cadence of which, newly harmonized, again ends on a pause.

And now Beethoven already makes for the new regions of tonality demanded by the eventual reappearance of the second subject in the tonic key. As that second subject had previously been heard so far afield as G major, the new transitions to a more normal position involve greater modulatory adventurousness. Hence these early vagaries in what according to orthodox rules ought to be a simple restatement for the whole duration of the first subject, though older masters—notably Haydn, who can be very unconventional indeed—had no scruples about disregarding these rules when it suited them.

What happens here is that the second half of Ex. 253 is developed by means of upward sequences, so that Ex. 254 appears, after some delay, in G flat major. It arrives at its end to find itself drastically manipulated into taking one of Beethoven's characteristic short cuts through the circle of keys. Having arrested the music on D♭ as the dominant of G♭, he changes the former enharmonically into C♯, thus making it into the dominant of F♯, which of course is the same thing on the piano and means a change only for the eye. But almost instantly that F♯ becomes in turn the dominant of B, and so it is in B minor that Ex. 252 reasserts itself, very emphatically, but only once in its original form. The upbeat of its rhythm is then used separately, much as before, and we soon have the transition to the second subject running into B flat major and remaining on the dominant of that key until the subject itself (Ex. 255) turns up in the tonic. There is nothing new to be said about the restatement of the whole of that group, in which Exx. 256, 257, and 259*b* return to their former order.

The coda, on the other hand, though short for a late Beethoven work on so vast a scale, is full of new significance. At first the figures quoted at the beginning of Exx. 258 and 259 are more extensively used, preparing the ground for another wayward reappearance of that incalculable theme from the second-subject group (Ex. 257), which further astonishes us by taking yet another shape and ending with a formal $^{6}_{4}$ chord topped by a shake, as though a cadenza were to be expected. Indeed, the free runs that follow, and the fantastic new uses of the rhythm 252*a* in alternations of loud and soft tone, might have the effect of such an extemporization were it not that the music remains strictly in time and proceeds inflexibly in a perfectly logical clinching of the argument. Ex. 252 in fragmentary forms then starts a series of falling chordal figures in B flat major harmony, curiously discoloured by passing G♭s in the bass. The end is like the rumblings of a receding thunderstorm, followed by a parting crash.

Scherzo : assai vivace.—Beethoven had not had a scherzo in a piano sonata since Op. 31 No. 3, and even that was a scherzo in name and nature rather than in form and style. The present specimen begins in a much more normal vein, but becomes curiously wayward later on, very much as Beethoven's humour sometimes did. It would be difficult to think of any movement that represents him more strikingly in his capriciously playful mood, in which he is never far from sudden accesses of anger and rudeness.

That, however, is only the surface impression of the music, which, for all its fitfulness, is technically an impeccable feat of organization. It is indeed in movements such as this that the student who has cultivated some insight into musical structure most admires the classic in Beethoven, who could be as extravagant as any romantic composer in expression, but never allowed himself to present that expression untidily. The miracle here is that he conveys a feeling of oddity without letting himself get out of hand as a craftsman.

The scherzo begins thus:

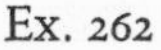
Ex. 262

and contains a second important strain:

Ex. 263

There is no other material, and these two elements are exploited by repetition in such a way that traces of the two formal sections of the old minuet are still discernible here, though nothing is restated so exactly that the duplications could be indicated by repeat marks.

Much the same is true of the trio section, which stands in B flat minor. Here we have two quite distinct periods, built on this kind of material:

[Continued

Ex. 264

but the restatements, though exact, exchange the theme and the accompaniment between the two hands, thus:

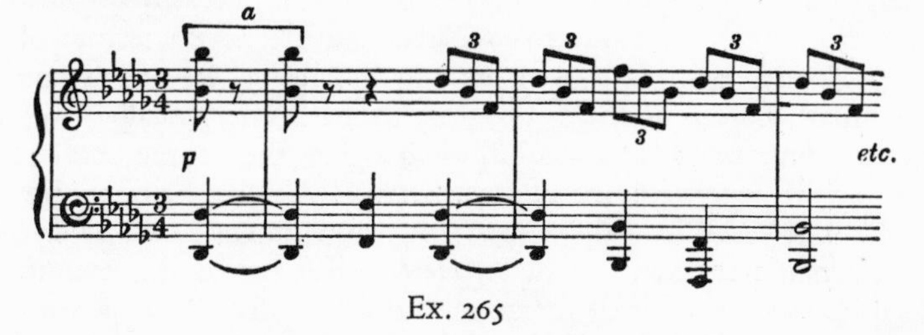

Ex. 265

All this is straightforward enough. But now comes the surprise: Beethoven's quick change of temper, if you like. The following impertinent little tune suddenly bursts in, played in unharmonized octaves at first:

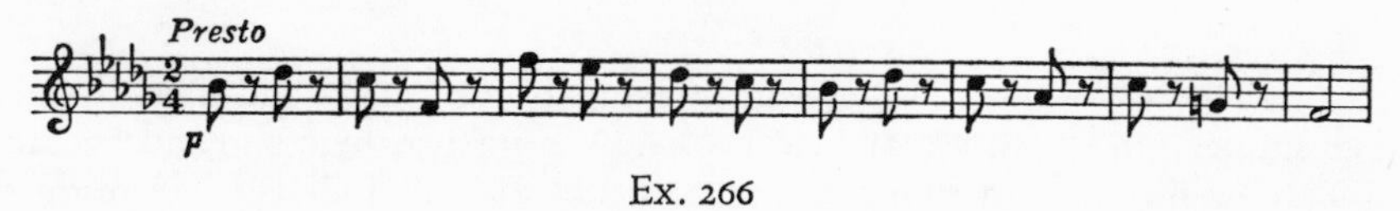

Ex. 266

An answer in the bass, and in a different harmonic position, is slashed through by syncopated chords above and swells to *fortissimo*, whereupon Ex. 266 crashes in again in full harmony and with an accompaniment of broken octaves. The final chord tumbles violently down through five octaves, and this is followed by a cadenza of a scale rushing up the whole of the keyboard (at any rate Beethoven's keyboard) and incidentally preparing a return to the major key. Then, with the resumption of the initial tempo, comes a broken chord of the dominant minor ninth which is so curious that it must be quoted:

Ex. 267

A more freakish return to the main section of a scherzo could scarcely be imagined; but the *da capo* itself is so normal as to restore the balance, though the music does not reproduce its first appearance quite identically. There are tiny interpolations such as the syncopated F in the following example:

Ex. 268

and the bass of the second strain takes the alternative form shown in small notes in Ex. 263. The final phrases, too, are different. The two detached quaver octaves on B♭ which conclude the scherzo and are also a feature of the trio (see Exx. 264*a* and 265*a*), instead of proving conclusive, are quietly contradicted by two similar octaves on B♮. B♭ reasserts itself energetically. B♮ answers back, and this time B♭ slyly returns disguised as A♯, the leading note of B minor, in which key the opening figure of the scherzo (Ex. 262*a*) haltingly tries to gain a foothold. But the B♮s again return, softly and intermittently at first, only to break into a hammering riot of noise, *presto*. But just as this extraneous note seems to have established itself for good and all, it slips down a semitone and becomes B♭ again after all. This is the signal for the close, which is effected very simply by three final statements of the initial figure (262*a*), rising up through as many octaves.

Adagio sostenuto.—The slow movement is one of the longest and most elevated in all music. In length it may be exceeded by Bruckner, who also endeavoured earnestly to match it in sublimity—so earnestly that his followers are ready to accept intention for achievement. However, there is no sense in seeking occasions for disparaging one composer when another is under discussion, and I have, in fact, not dragged in Bruckner's name for that purpose, but because he naturally comes to mind as a creative musician on whom the influence of Beethoven's spaciousness has had its effect, no matter whether with wholly satisfactory results or not. A composer who can keep a slow movement going for twenty minutes or more performs so rare a feat as to be worth attention for the mere attempt, and those who consider, not without justice, that Bruckner's music meanders and progresses clumsily had better bear in mind that much the same has been said of Beethoven's, though in that case without any justice whatever. The truth is that patience to follow the present *adagio* is a listener's virtue which has to be cultivated and that no one should approach such music lightly; but it is equally true that a better return for patience than the full appreciation of this movement is difficult to imagine and that music on an epic scale is the apt reward of those who come to it in a heroic frame of mind.

The vastness of Beethoven's material, let alone his structure, strikes the annotator more forcibly than ever when he finds that it is quite impossible to quote any theme from this slow movement in its entirety within such space as musical examples ought not to exceed. Here, for instance, is the first paragraph of the first subject (the movement is in sonata from), shown in addition to the famous opening bar (marked *a* below) already discussed in the article preceding these notes (see page 203):

Ex. 269

But this grandly expanding melody goes on for no less than another twenty-two bars—and twenty-five bars of such slow 6–8 time, equivalent to fifty bars of slow triple time, mean music that gives the illusion of a cosmic scale.

The end of the first subject is a broken cadence (Ex. 270*a*), which wonderfully produces the effect, not of cutting anything short, but of making what follows appear inevitable. It is as though a dramatist made a character on the stage pause expectantly in order to make it strikingly apparent to the spectator that a second personage is about to appear:

Ex. 270

This is not yet the second subject, for apart from its being still in the tonic key (F sharp minor), Beethoven's vast plan does not allow such a sudden turning round the corner into a new region after so expansive a first subject. He therefore interposes a transition of no less than eighteen bars, only the first four of which are shown above (not counting the broken cadence, 270*a*, belonging to the first subject). An elaborated version of its first three bars follows, and then the music begins to modulate over rising steps in the bass, which for a moment become fixed on A and then begin to wander again, only to decide finally on that A as the dominant of D major. The trio-like treatment of a new thematic idea in three polyphonic upper parts should be noticed.

The second subject at last arrives in D major:

Ex. 271

The magical effect of that deep, bell-like melody tolling in the bass and ringing in answer above is heightened by a fascinating variation that has a triplet for a new feature, and this triplet idea, already suggested by the accompanying figures, now seems to seize Beethoven's imagination irresistibly—and the process of composition is often seen to be such an engendering of a great notion by what was at first a merely incidental or purely technical feature—for he continues the second subject with a rich texture of inner parts of triplet runs in contrary motion and so produces a passage of translucent beauty. The second subject is virtually as long as the first. When the triplets cease it will be noticed that the music goes through a series of modulations that can only be described, in non-technical terms, as a kind of harmonic drooping. The effect is poignantly lovely. The close of the second subject is at the same time a link with what is to follow.

What does follow is an elaborate working-out section. We are still in D major, in spite of the drooping modulations, which did not seem to have the strength to draw the music elsewhere. In that key the four opening bars of the first subject (Ex. 269) reappear with some modifications other than the change of key. But almost at once we get into C sharp major—so near and yet so far—and here the two figures of the theme are exchanged in double counterpoint. Three notes descending in thirds are afterwards detached from the theme and so transformed rhythmically that they constantly change their position in the bars, their duration being the equivalent of four quavers, while the bars have room for six. This figure is used again and again in a series of drastic modulations which take a long roundabout way to F sharp minor.

In this key the recapitulation begins with the first subject (Ex. 269) in its complete form, but elaborately disguised by a right-hand demi-semiquaver embroidery. The deception, however, is more complete to the eye than to the ear. Looking at the printed page at this point, we need special attention to detect the melodic formation; but on listening we discover that its salient notes disengage themselves from the rich figuration quite naturally.

For the second half of the theme the demi-semiquavers are abandoned, although the lay-out of the music still remains more lavish than it had been at first. The transition (Ex. 270) is very much altered, both in tonality and figuration. As to the latter, I cannot resist showing an extract to illustrate the point concerning Chopin made in the introductory article (page 204). (I use the octave sign for convenience, though Beethoven does not, and merely sketch in the harmonic basis, which he breaks up into an accompaniment similar to that shown in Ex. 270):

Ex. 272

This might appear in a Chopin nocturne. The difference is that while it would be an extraneous decoration there, more or less in the nature of a cadenza, with Beethoven it is strictly part of the whole formal organization.

The second subject appears in the tonic major (F sharp), with no alteration at first beyond transposition into the new key, but with some subtle little changes in the passage containing drooping modulations. These changes are worth noting, for they show with what infinite care Beethoven considered the importance of details in passages he wished to be duplications of something that had gone before, but not note-for-note repetitions.

The passage that had formerly led to the working-out now merges into a coda which may well be regarded as a further development, both of the first and the second subject. They are brought quite close together, as though they had to be compensated for the enormous distance they were previously compelled to keep. Ex. 269 is alluded to first; Ex. 271 spreads itself at greater length in its varied form, with the triplet figure; then a condensed form of 269, interspersed with what appears to be a recollection of the mere rhythm of 271, brings this long and sublime movement to a peaceful conclusion in F sharp major.

Largo.—In order to pass convincingly from his contemplative slow movement to his titanically energetic finale Beethoven inserts an introduction in the nature of a free fantasy, which, apart from effecting a transition of mood, also has the purpose of making the contrast between the keys of these movements, F sharp minor and B flat major, less violent. Not that it is easy to see why the sudden drop from F♯ to the F of the introduction should be very much less so; but somehow our ear tells us that there is logic behind it, and if the ear fails, Sir Donald Tovey's explanation will serve. For other reasons, too technical to be given here, that great scholar holds that the slow movement, though written for convenience in F sharp minor, is really in G flat minor, and that the F at the beginning of the introduction to the finale is the leading note of that key, which after many modulatory convolutions becomes—to cut a long story short—the dominant of B flat major.

That long story of the introduction may be briefly summarized by saying that there are five changes of key signature and that these do not indicate all the changes of key, to which may be added that for some unfathomable reason Beethoven makes his second signature that of B flat major and then writes music in G flat major after it, with the extra accidentals in front of each note. The opening passage may be quoted as perhaps the most curious-looking in all Beethoven's music and the most difficult for the sight-reader:

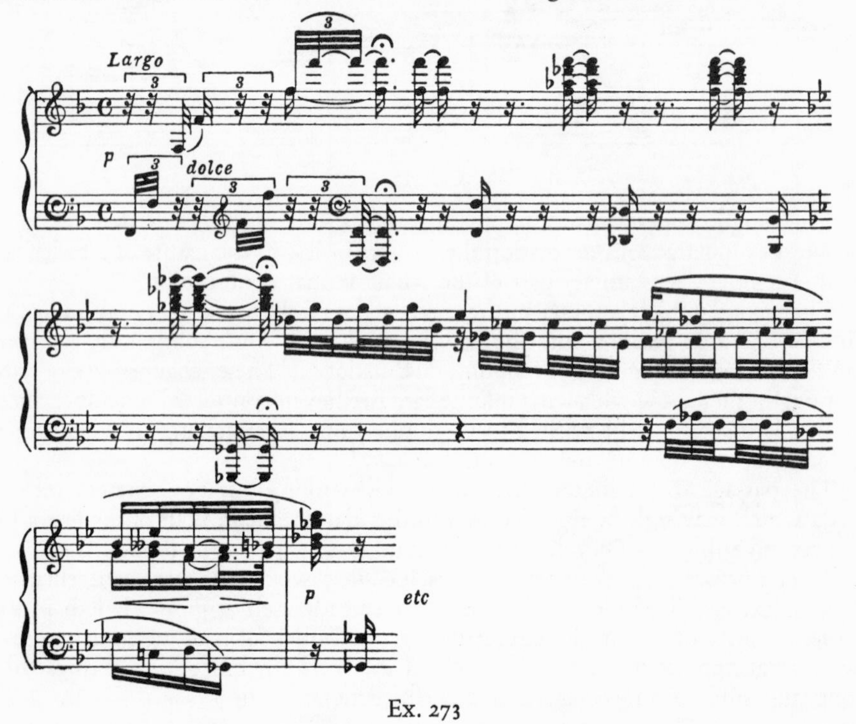

Ex. 273

Indeed Beethoven feels obliged to give a special direction in his quaint Italian as to how the passage should be counted: '*Per la misura si conta nel Largo sempre quattro semicrome.*' The whole strange introduction recalls, if anything, the fantasies Bach prefixed to some of his organ fugues, which have much the same exuberant fancy and ornateness. The following almost gives one the physical sensation of listening to Bach's organ:

Ex. 274

Was Beethoven, by some trick of unconscious association, drawn into writing such an introduction because he too was about to write a fugue? For a fugue it is to which all this preparation leads.

Allegro risoluto.—There are five bars of adumbration on the dominant of B flat major, and then begins what Beethoven calls a '*fuga a tre voci, con alcune licenze.*' The three voices are scrupulously adhered to for the most part, and the liberties for which he prepares us are quite rare: some extra notes in chords now and again and the addition of a fourth 'voice' in at any rate one place. All the same, this is by no means an academic fugue, and it would be ridiculous to pretend that Beethoven handled counterpoint with perfect ease. For all that, this movement is one of the most gigantic and significant fugues in existence, comparable only with his own *Grosse Fuge* for string quartet, Op. 133, all things considered. As to its so-called violations of text-book counterpoint, it is as well to remember that Bach's own fugal writing is so full of them that pedants are constantly obliged to account for them as the exceptions which a great man, unlike a student, may permit himself; and Beethoven's alleged clumsiness had better be accepted without demur if it is found to produce music of a grandeur and profundity which unimpeachable masters of fugal writing such as Kirnberger or Cherubini never even envisaged.

Here is the opening of the fugue subject:

Ex. 275

The answer comes in the dominant and in the right hand. It has a new counter-subject running against it:

Ex. 276

The reason for this is not difficult to see: Beethoven clearly wishes to avoid the overlapping of semiquaver figures at this stage of the proceedings, partly perhaps because they are very difficult to fit into playable keyboard passages, but chiefly because, with that difficulty in mind, he is aware that they will be a splendid means of climax later. So here the fugue becomes a double fugue, and although a pundit who did not happen to know that this movement had been written by a great master would be sure to say that if a double fugue was intended, it should have been a double fugue from the beginning, those who have ears to hear will be perfectly satisfied with the expedient. Every genius is ready with such dodges, and the difference between them and the fumbler's subterfuges is merely that they make their point and are often striking in themselves as well.

When the material has been sufficiently treated in two-part counterpoint, the third 'voice' enters with the subject in the bass. Here a second counter-subject containing the following figures comes into the scheme:

Ex. 277

while elements from both Exx. 275 and 276 are used simultaneously. The three-part writing continues for some time, for the occasional doubling of the bass in octaves need not be regarded as one of Beethoven's 'licences.' [1] It is the closing phrase of Ex. 276 that comes in for this treatment. A moment later the chief subject (Ex. 275) enters delayed by a beat, so that the whole series of accents becomes shifted and the music appears as if seen from a new angle. It must be left to the reader to discover some of the thematic combinations for himself, preferably with the aid of the printed page, which makes listening to a fugal movement much clearer. To point out every one of the composer's ingenuities would be to discuss the movement bar by bar, which is neither possible nor desirable.

A new episode now starts, treated elaborately in double counterpoint, viz. with parts that can be exchanged between top and bottom and will go equally well together in both positions. It is in G flat major.

[1] No organist would regard himself as guilty of interfering with Bach's part-writting in a fugue because he uses octave couplers for the bass.

The next arresting incident is the augmentation, into notes of twice the duration, of the main subject (Ex. 275, figure *b* and what follows), and after that, more striking still, we have figure *a* combined into a stretto by simultaneous augmentation and inversion, with the even quaver figure of Ex. 276 added immediately afterwards.

The episode heard a little earlier then returns, now in A flat instead of G flat major. The next thing that will attract attention, and had better be shown in music type, is this formation:

Ex. 278

It looks new at first sight, but the shake at the end has a familiar air. The reader suspects something; but if he needs further help, he is advised to read this quotation backwards. He will then see that an exact reproduction of the first three bars of Ex. 275 emerges, except that the music is transposed a semitone higher. The theme has in fact been turned back to front, a procedure for which the technical term is *cancrizans* (crabwise), and it is now used fugally in this new way, not without an admixture of other elements of the composer's material. Not content with this ingenuity, Beethoven here adds a new counterpoint to his texture, a melody that must not be allowed to escape attention:

Ex. 279

Hans von Bülow took pains to point out that this new lyrical element was infinitely more important than the clever reversal of the theme, which he felt to be a 'pedantic triviality.' But it is a mistake to regard this device as no more significant than the riddle canons and other technical conundrums with which the Flemish masters of the fifteenth century amused themselves and each other, for the very effort Beethoven was obliged to make, and now and again betrayed in a particularly harsh or angular passage, does much to account for the immense intellectual vitality and integrity of this gigantic finale.

After many developments that cannot possibly all be described in detail, but will not escape attentive readers or listeners, we find the chief subject again, this time inverted instead of reversed. In this upside-down position it is developed with some of the auxiliary figures shown in Exx. 276 and 277. A huge climax is then reached, with a pause after two 'licentious' chords of A major.

All of a sudden there is utter stillness, and yet another theme appears, quietly and songfully, to be fugally developed in the smoothest and most beautiful counterpoint, as if to show that rough treatment was not Beethoven's only polyphonic resource:

Ex. 280

A mere episode, you think. But behold! the key of B flat major is re-established for the return of the principal subject, and now, miraculously, this new theme (Ex. 280), which seemed as though it could only have been invented spontaneously for the sake of beauty, is found to fit in wonderfully with the thorny fugal material. The lamb lying down with the lion, indeed.

The next outstanding event is a stretto in which the subject combines with itself, with very close entries, both in its normal position and inverted. Later other thematic features, notably Ex. 276, become prominent, but although one could go on endlessly pointing to thematic complications, an end must be made at last, as Beethoven himself decides to do even in his longest sonata the moment he feels that he has said all he had to say and has completed one of the vastest of his tonal structures.

The design cannot be left without a crowning feature, however, and so there is a page of coda. It is no longer strictly fugal, but nevertheless relevant, just as a pediment may not be technically a necessary part of a Greek temple, yet a thing without which that edifice would be without balance and style. This coda opens with a convenient landmark for the hearer: a series of right-hand arpeggios over a deep left-hand shake. Above these low rumblings there is a last flicker of thematic allusions, and then the movement ends with the grandest peroration, made out of the runs and shakes of the fugue subject.

SONATA IN E MAJOR, Op. 109 (1820)
(B.S.S. RECORDS, VOL. II)

THIS work, composed in 1820, was published in November 1821. The dedication is to Maximiliana von Brentano, one of the children of the Senator Franz von Brentano of Frankfort and his wife, *née* Antonie von Birckenstock, a Viennese noblewoman whom Beethoven had met before her marriage.

The Sonata is most unusual in form even for a late Beethoven work of the kind, though each of the last sonatas obeys only rules drawn up for its own purpose. First we have a fast and a slow movement dovetailed, then an agitated piece in 6–8 time that could by no stretch of imagination be called a scherzo either in mood or in form, and last a set of very elaborate and at the same time free and fantastic variations on a slow melody.

The interlocking of two differently paced sections in an initial sonata movement was by no means unprecedented, and Beethoven himself resorted to the device more than twenty years earlier, in the *Pathétique* Sonata. But it is to be noted that he makes an innovation here in so far that he begins with the quick movement and that this is never developed in accordance with the classical sonata pattern. In earlier cases of intersection the slow portion had always come first, and though it may have occurred again in the middle of the fast movement, it retained the character of the conventional slow introduction, remaining subordinate to a larger animated portion in sonata form. But here, while the sonata form is disintegrated in the *vivace*, the *adagio* assumes at least equal importance.

The variation form had, of course, been used by Beethoven long ago in the piano sonatas—in the middle movement of Op. 14 No. 2, for instance, and in the first movement of Op. 26. But here it is for the first time employed in a finale, as it was to be used again in the last Sonata, Op. 111. It is true that even this was no entirely new departure: in the string Quartet Op. 74 (1809), the so-called 'Harp' Quartet, for example, we already find a variation finale; but the point is that Beethoven had not before filled the variation form with a significance that made the movement cast in it unmistakably the peak of a whole work. The quartet finale in question is still the musical diversion on a given theme with which musicians of the eighteenth century used to entertain their hearers and themselves, a relaxation, so to speak, after the intellectual effort demanded of the composer and the listener by the first movement and the emotional stress of the slow one. The finale of Op. 109, on the other hand, is both emotionally and intellectually the most exacting movement in the work besides being much the longest and most complex. Compared with it the earlier movements are in the nature of introductions, obviously designed to rouse expectation and to create a mood in which the variations may come to us both as a surprise and a solace.

Vivace, ma non troppo—Adagio espressivo—Tempo primo—Tempo secondo—Tempo primo.—The theme of the *vivace* appears to be merely a series of broken figures, more apt to a study or prelude than to a sonata, as the following specimen of the opening bars will show:

Ex. 281

But enwrapped in the figuration is continuous melody. A second glance at this example will reveal that a definite tune (G♯, B, E, G♯, C♯, E, F♯, G♯) stands out, even for the eye, and much more for the ear, provided that the symbols of musical notation are properly interpreted. Almost before we have grasped the composer's intention, however, the music has swung with a sudden harmonic jerk into the *adagio*, which begins thus:

Ex. 282

It takes harmonic turns of the utmost unexpectedness, yet without going far from the neighbourhood of the principal key. After the first three bars shown above the texture is one of elaborate embroidery. The impression is almost that of a cadenza, strangely superficial in appearance after the highly emotional opening (Ex. 282). But it will not do to judge until we know the whole story: Beethoven has another great slow melody in store for us, and it is by the most acute artistic insight or instinct—one hardly knows which—that he decides to suppress any show of deep feeling for the present.

At the return of the *vivace* the figuration is at first exchanged by the two hands, the left having the melodic line, which now takes a downward turn and thus forms a new thematic feature that is presently taken up and developed by the right hand. The broken semiquaver groups continue throughout as an accompaniment. The music soars higher and higher until Ex. 281 returns on the crest of a climax in the upper reaches of the keyboard. The next six bars lead to the return of the *adagio*, now placed a fourth higher, but otherwise reproducing Ex. 282 fairly accurately. The scheme of modulation, however, is even more audacious this time, the music being suddenly thrust into C major and as quickly and unexpectedly back into E major. For the last time the *vivace* is resumed, interrupted for a moment by a passage of crotchet chords with a lovely cadence at the end, which is the only break in the incessant motion of broken semiquavers. This, however, closes the movement.

Prestissimo.—The restless, nervous second movement in E minor flashes past in a very short time. But for all the impression it gives of a fleeting instant—a true *moment musical*—it is very closely constructed. The opening exposes a pair of equally important phrases, one in the treble, the other in the bass:

Ex. 283

Beethoven's direction to mark the bass well contains a hint that it had better be noticed as an organic factor, and we shall see before long how important it is to act upon it. Close upon a continuing strain another vital figure arises, at first in the bass alone:

Ex. 284

and then, after slight hesitation, the music rushes on in the original tempo and rhythm. Soon the metrical pattern becomes slightly distorted by syncopation, as though dishevelled by the whirlwind pace of the music, and presently, with a sudden *piano*, comes a kind of scattering of the musical material, all but a little fluttering motif detaching itself over an arpeggio bass:

Ex. 285

This leads to yet another salient feature, again heard in the bass:

Ex. 286

but immediately afterwards transferred to the top of the keyboard, while the ascending scale which at first rose above it is given to the left hand.

A new version of Ex. 283 then brings with it an elaboration in canon of its bass (Ex. 283*a*). It is first placed over a new pedal bass, which rises a semitone after nine bars, and then twisted round in various ways until a halting, questioning presentation of it is answered very emphatically by a return of Ex. 283 in its original form. But presently the hands exchange their parts, which are thus seen to make double counterpoint.

Next the figure shown in Ex. 284 is considered at greater length. Exx. 285 and 286 recur, second-subject fashion, in new keys but otherwise unaltered, except that the latter is attended by a group of three notes (dominant, dominant, tonic) which lends itself to the building of a very short but most eloquent peroration with Ex. 286 as a bass.

Gesangvoll, mit innigster Empfindung: Andante, molto cantabile ed espressivo.—The theme on which the complex variation-finale is built is one of the greatest slow melodies ever devised, by Beethoven or any one else, and, with the *cavatina* in the Quartet, Op. 130, or the slow movement of the Trio, Op. 97, one of the most characteristic and beautiful things of the kind he wrote in all his career. All three of these contain, as it happens, an ascending passage representing what Ernest Newman calls Beethoven's 'fingerprint.' In the present instance it occurs in the last bar shown below:

Ex. 287

The texture, it will be observed, is not especially pianistic, but rather that of a string quartet in which each lower instrument sings its own part instead of merely accompanying the top melody. Beethoven reserves pianistry for the later elaborations of his tune, some of which, such as that of the second variation, are eminently congenial to the instrument. The key is E major again after the excursion no farther than to E minor for the preceding movement.

The first variation is no less expressive than the theme itself; but it is melodically different, while the harmonic scheme is left untouched. The left hand now has a true keyboard accompaniment, mostly in chords on the second and third beats preceded by a bass note on the first. Played much too fast and with a kind of frivolous elegance, this section would be not unlike a waltz by Chopin. As it stands, however, it is purest Beethoven.

The second variation, marked *leggiermente*, breaks up the melodic line into brilliant semiquaver figures and then presents another, less restless allusion to the theme, as though two variations were to be crowded into one section. This second idea is then embroidered after the manner of the opening in order to bring about a reconciliation of these contrasts, and thus a similar treatment of the second half of the theme is approached. It is not easy at a first hearing to detect the resemblance of this variation to the tune, but it remains quite recognizably attached to the thematic basis.

The hearer may be rather taken aback by the *allegro vivace* of the third variation and fail to see the slightest connection with the theme in this movement, written in two parts which are invertible by double counterpoint. Nevertheless, the general plan of the subject in hand is again closely followed and even the melodic formation, especially of the second strain, remains perceptibly outlined.

The fourth variation, which is much slower again, is approached without a break. It is in 9–8 time and obliterates nearly every trace of the theme while still retaining its harmonic outline. The musical fabric is at first woven very closely from two rhythmically distinct phrases, which are beautifully interlinked in various ways, but the second part is almost entirely harmonic and melodic, though the latter only incidentally, so to speak, melody being inherent in and subservient to the harmony.

The fifth variation, *allegro ma non troppo*, shows a fugal texture without being in any strict sense a fugue. Its subject, it is true, appears in various voices (at one point inverted); but it is not brought in voice by voice at the opening, as it should be in any well-behaved fugue. Beethoven cares nothing about manners as such and so does not hesitate to let us plunge into the middle of a fugal discussion without any attempt at a formal introduction to the disputants.

Again there is no break between this variation and the next—the sixth and last. This opens in the tempo of the theme itself and in fact reintroduces it in very much its original form, though with a repeated B in the top part which forms an inverted dominant pedal. Now Beethoven proceeds to lay out his material in all sorts of different ways, decorating the thematic allusions very lavishly with difficult pianistic figurations, but always making them strictly relevant to his main topic. His double shakes in the middle parts and the very extended shake on the dominant, first in the bass and afterwards in the middle again, are highly characteristic of his late pianistic style. Towards the end notes which adumbrate the theme are heard gently dripping above the rippling accompaniment. The music droops and softly melts into a restatement of the theme itself, heard almost exactly as at the opening of the movement. The Sonata thus ends with the utmost simplicity after all the intellectual strife it has gone through. In a collaboration of head and heart the mind has been in hard pursuit of truth and beauty, but it is the heart which is allowed the last word.

SONATA IN A FLAT MAJOR, Op. 110 (1821)
(B.S.S. RECORDS, VOL. III)

In the year 1821 Beethoven completed only a single work—the present Sonata, which bears the date of Christmas Day. (It was published by Schlesinger of Berlin and Paris in August the following year.) But this is not to say that he was relatively idle during that time, which was much occupied by the *Missa solemnis*, while the ninth Symphony was also slowly shaping itself in that laborious, trial-and-error manner of working that is so characteristic of Beethoven.

It is curious that so deeply personal a work as this Sonata should bear no dedication. This, however, was not Beethoven's original intention. He at first planned to inscribe one of the last three sonatas to Ferdinand Ries, who was in London and had done him many useful services there. However, no sooner had he come to a decision than he sent Schindler the following peremptory command: 'The two Sonatas in A flat and C minor [Op. 111] are to be dedicated to Frau Brentano *née* von Birkenstock—Ries nothing.' But even that was not decisive, for the last sonata was eventually offered to the Archduke Rudolph, while the work in A flat found no dedicatee.

There was also a question of something being dedicated to the wife of Ries, in return for which, Beethoven wrote, 'the only thing I will accept is a kiss, which I am to receive when I come to London.' But none of these exciting things came to pass. Ries wrote a Concerto, entitled *Farewell to London*, which so offended Beethoven that he not only withdrew his offer of these dedications (including, presumably, the kiss), but was with difficulty prevented from writing a letter to the *Musikalische Zeitung* in Leipzig publicly ordering Ries no longer to call himself his pupil. The reason was apparently that he considered Ries to have plagiarized him. At any rate, Schuppanzigh said that 'Ries steals too much from Beethoven. All steal, but Ries by handfuls.'

Moderato cantabile, molto espressivo.—Beethoven is much more explicit in his directions in this late Sonata than in the earlier examples. The less he was able to hear, it seems, the more anxious he grew to let the player know how his music should sound, not only in the matter of tempo and dynamics, but in that of meaning. Not content with making it clear that this movement is to be songful and expressive, he also adds, as will be seen in the quotation below, that it should sound amiable. And truly, it is one of the gentlest things he ever wrote. For all its dark colour, it has an inexpressible warmth, like a summer evening after sunset. There has been thunder, we know, but we are not asked to remember it here. It will be time enough for that in the next, and last, sonata.

The sonata form, though this first movement clearly conforms to it, is curiously softened, its main features smoothed and its connecting links rounded so that its divisions melt into each other almost imperceptibly. It is no longer possible to say quite decisively how far the first- and second-subject groups extend and what is in the nature of transition.

The opening motif is structurally of the utmost importance:

Ex. 288

Its second clause is followed by a rest on a shake, to which succeeds a limpid, singing phrase poised in syncopation over a simple accompaniment of repeated chords. Thematic features then disappear, giving place to harp-like demisemiquaver passages which sweep lightly all over the keyboard with a slender support of chords in the left hand.

A transition is now made to the key of the dominant (E flat major), which indicates that the second-subject group is reached; but there is actually no phrase that can be quoted in preference to any other, for here is a whole cluster of significant incidents which between them go to make up an important scene, much as though a number of characters were upon a stage together, each contributing to the trend of the drama, but none taking a leading part.

There is no repeat of the exposition, in fact nothing in the nature of a double bar at all. The passage from this section to the next is deliberately blurred. The music merely comes to a head on a chord of E flat major, which dissolves into bare E♭ octaves that sound like a close and yet let the ear expect a continuation. What happens is that the bare octaves simply drop to D♭, thus at once driving the music forward and turning it into a new key. That key, for the moment, is F minor, and we find that in it the initial motif (Ex. 288) is brought back. We are thus in the working-out section. The theme is first set over the accompaniment previously used for the second strain, then over scales, modulating farther afield.

The merging of the working-out into the recapitulation is as surprising as anything in this movement. Ex. 288, which has not ceased for a moment, reappears in A flat major, as at the beginning, but now over an accompaniment made out of the harp-like demi-semiquaver figures and transferred to the left hand. The continuing (syncopated) strain appears in D flat major, transformed into the minor by an enharmonic change (C sharp minor) that brings the demi-semiquaver arpeggios into E major, a procedure that seems to take the music strangely far from the predominant key-centre, but becomes perfectly clear when one accepts the explanation of Sir Donald Tovey, to whom we all owe so much for technical elucidation of things that ought to be perfectly obvious to all—with the only difference that he sees them while others do not. Beethoven, Tovey points out, simply uses a more convenient notation for F flat major, which is not far removed at all, being the relative major of the subdominant (D flat) minor.

After a modulation from E major back to A flat major the second-subject group is stated, with some small modifications, in the latter key.

The division between recapitulation and coda, again, is deliberately obscured by Beethoven in his anxiety that this movement should be all of a piece, and not all in pieces. Instead of letting the close of the exposition, which was in E flat major, simply repeat itself in A flat major, he changes it back half-way to E flat, which, however, is now quite definitely felt to be the dominant of A flat and therefore remains inconclusive, leaving us in suspense for what may come next. What does come is a magical transition passage, with accents displaced off the first beat, that leads back once more to the arpeggios, now heard in the tonic key. They are followed by a simple but ethereally lovely close in which the rhythm of Ex. 288 is enfolded as though the composer were reluctant to part with his theme.

Molto allegro.—The scherzo is much in the style of Beethoven's later *Bagatelles*—terse, witty, sharp-tempered and a little uncouth in expression. These small piano pieces, though not among his most important compositions, show him at his most characteristic. To hear one of them is like reading one of his letters, with their rough-and-tumble humour, indeed almost like being addressed by him with some growling remarks in which it is difficult to distinguish between fun and abuse.

The music opens stealthily in F minor, and is at once abruptly answered in C major:

Ex. 289

A second section continues at first in much the same vein, but also introduces a far more definitely melodic phrase that rises up through the first three degrees of the A flat major and F minor triads.

The trio, in D flat major, is on the other hand kept melodically quite featureless: it is mere harmony, disintegrated, so to speak, into rapid figuration with passing chromatics. The left hand plays isolated notes, mainly on the second beats, rising periodically over the right into the treble. The effect is curiously unlike what it appears to be on paper. In the following passage, for example, we see very clearly a leap over two octaves which strikes the eye as an outstanding incident:

Ex. 290

but what we actually hear is this:

Ex. 291

The scherzo returns exactly as before, save for one small but significant change: the first part now has its repeat fully written out because Beethoven marks the second recurrence of Ex. 289 *ritardando* for the first four bars and *a tempo* for the other four. It is as though he led us to expect some coming change and then took mischievous pleasure in cheating us by going on with an exact reproduction of what had been heard before. There is, however, a final addition—a short coda formed merely of minim chords intersected by minim rests, which would be as simple a final cadence as possible but for the fact that the rest is omitted after the last chord of the scherzo proper and again between the final pair of chords, so that we have a vague feeling that a syncopated rhythm has suddenly dislocated the regular four-bar periods. The final chord clears into F major.

Adagio, ma non troppo.—This slow section, nominally in B flat minor, but actually in that key only for a moment at the beginning, is not an independent, fully rounded-off movement, but a prelude to the fugue that is to follow, leading from the key of F major, in which the scherzo closed, and which acts as the dominant for B flat minor, back to the main tonality of A flat major. It is, however, far too important to be considered a mere introduction, and in order to make quite sure that it will be regarded as a fit substitute for a separate slow movement, Beethoven has the astonishing notion of quoting an important part of it later on, in the course of the finale.

The opening is rather like the orchestral introduction to some dramatic piece. Sure enough, there follows a recitative, *più adagio*, opened by a rising arpeggio. It is hardly a singer's recitative, however, but more of a free violinistic interpolation. Those repeated high As, swelling up and dying down again, can, in fact, hardly be imagined, if one looks at them on the printed page, in anything but the tone of a violin. It remains a matter for dispute to this day how Beethoven expected the pianist to play such groups of two tied notes as and . Sometimes they are repeated, no doubt for the reason that it is hard to imagine why he should have written them in pairs, had he wanted them to sound as single quavers and semiquavers respectively. Where they occur in string music, as for example in the *Grosse Fuge*, Op. 133, it is surely permissible to say that they were intended to be played with a change from up-bow to down-bow, but with the least possible effect of repetition, and from that may perhaps be deduced that the proper way for the pianist to play them is to make a change of fingering on the key, but without striking it again more than almost imperceptibly the second time.

The third recitative phrase leads into a bar and a half of *adagio, ma non troppo*, introductory to the *arioso dolente* which for the first time sets a definite melody going, but now an astonishingly extended, passionate and beautiful one—indeed, one of the finest of those long-drawn slow tunes in Beethoven's late manner:

Ex. 292

This is only the opening of a line that continues without interruption for another twelve and a half bars. The semiquaver accompaniment continues throughout. At the end there is a very quiet cadence in A flat major, unharmonized.

Allegro, ma non troppo.—Here begins the long and elaborate fugue that forms Beethoven's finale, an intellectual climax of the most bracing kind to a work in which imagination and contrivance conspire throughout towards perfection. Except at the close, the fugue is strictly in three voices, for octave doublings do not constitute a fourth voice in a piano fugue any more than the use of octave couplers means an additional part in polyphonic organ music. The subject is this:

Ex. 293

The counter-subject in even quavers should be noticed as an important structural feature. It is impossible to describe the development of the fugue in all its details, but the appearances of the subject in one voice or another will always be perfectly clear, both for the ear and the eye. Attention must, however, be drawn to the way in which Beethoven uses the counter-subject, sometimes in the lower parts and sometimes above (double counterpoint), but much more often with remarkable freedom than strictly. For he is not in the least inclined to write a paper fugue to satisfy the pedants; he writes music that is vital in every bar to please himself and those who may be sensible and sensitive enough to take joy in such glorious liberty. If the scholars cannot be that, it is their loss; at the same time, few can be quite so churlish, since after all there is nothing whatever technically wrong with Beethoven's fugue writing. His instinct for what is clean and logical always guides him, which proves that genius is in the last resort the better legislator than the most learned of professors. The difference is that each great master makes laws valid only for himself, while the professors are left to devise much narrower codes for the small people who think it necessary to assume the responsibility of creation.

Beethoven's late fugues do not make a point of being beautiful. Some, like the finale of the Sonata Op. 106 or the *Grosse Fuge*, often sound curiously against the grain; others, like the 'Et vitam venturi saeculi' in the *Missa solemnis*, are above all directed towards some very definite impression. The present example may be said to be the most suave, the most sensuously appealing of them all; but even here beauty is not attained of set purpose so much as conjured up by a concentrated mental effort. T. S. Eliot has said in effect, as one of his reviewers pointed out, that Dante was never 'poetical,' and that all the beauty of his words was absorbed in what they have to tell us. Much the same might be said of the mature Beethoven's fugues: they do not seek poetry by making conscious flights of fancy, but grow into beauty by an intellectual harnessing of the imagination to a hard task such as is congenial only to creators of the highest type—the Dantes and the Beethovens, in fact. And it achieves, correspondingly, the highest form of beauty.

The *arioso* returns as a perplexing interruption of the fugal texture, but as a dramatically very satisfying contrast. It is now in G minor and the melodic line is curiously broken, as though it had gone through a shattering emotional experience.

The key is now G major, and in it the fugue is resumed. But the composer now introduces the subject upside down, beginning with an entry in the middle voice, followed in turn by one in the treble and one in the bass. Then, as the music drifts into G minor, Beethoven resorts to a rare and astonishing technical device—a diminution that makes the theme not twice as fast, as usual, but three times. It will be seen here in that diminished form in the bass, while the treble shows it augmented to twice its normal duration:

Ex. 294

Needless to say, this contraction and expansion produced an entirely new disposition in the relation between the parts.

The next feature is a slackening of the pace (*meno allegro*) which has however the reverse effect of acceleration, the note-values being now halved. The indication of a slower tempo merely results in not making the pace as much as twice as fast. The fugue subject is still more tightened by appearing in semiquavers and with two of its notes cut out, thus:

Ex. 295

Two bars later an augmentation appears in the middle voice, inverted and with its intervals as well as its note-values enlarged. Then the theme returns in its normal form and key in bass octaves. For the last page or so Beethoven unexpectedly abandons counterpoint and achieves a final climax that is as glorious as it is surprising by letting the theme sing out fully in harmony over a running accompaniment. The effect may perhaps be likened to the floodlighting of the main features of a great edifice, which are enhanced to the sight by judicious decoration, though it must be done with the warning that Beethoven should not be suspected of anything quite so flashy. He maintains the gentle, harmonious glow that distinguishes this Sonata to the last.

SONATA IN C MINOR, Op. 111 (1822)
(B.S.S. RECORDS, VOL. I)

THE Op. 111 was dedicated to Beethoven's patron, friend and pupil, the Archduke Rudolph of Austria. It is the last sonata written by Beethoven for the piano, which, after endowing it with so much sublime music, he suddenly decided to regard as 'after all an unsatisfactory instrument.' This did not prevent him, however, from writing for it later the longest set of piano variations in existence (on a theme by Diabelli) and a last set of *Bagatelles*. His denunciation need thus not be taken any too seriously. The truth is that for him no instrument or combination of instruments was wholly satisfactory. He had a way of asking impossible things from all of them at times, especially in the later years, when his deafness made him conceive music, one is sometimes inclined to think, as wholly detached from its material means of embodiment. Hence, some think, his frequent awkwardnesses and harshnesses; hence certainly his spirituality.

The last Sonata sums up the whole experience gathered by Beethoven throughout all the sonata writing that had occupied him on and off for twenty-six years. In the few sonatas preceding this final work we notice above all two remarkable technical acquisitions, one affecting texture, the other form. He had developed, for one thing, a leaning towards fugal writing, as exemplified especially in the colossal fugue (*con alcune licenze*) that forms the finale of the *Hammerklavier* Sonata in B flat major, Op. 106, and, for another, a liking for the variation form, which distinguishes the Sonata in E major, Op. 109. In the present work we find both these experiences exploited with the greatest skill and subtlety. The first movement, though in sonata form, is very largely a free fugal fabric, and the finale (again there are only two movements) is the utmost refinement imaginable of a highly developed variation form.

Maestoso—Allegro con brio ed appassionato.—The directions, it will be observed, are now Italian again. The adoption of German may have been but a wave of chauvinism; but it is equally possible that Beethoven's growing international fame had something to do with his reverting to what was then, and still is, the musician's universal language.

The slow introduction is thematically unconnected with the *allegro* that follows, but nevertheless prepares it admirably. The very first bar screws expectation up to the highest possible pitch by making a start on a diminished-seventh formation that leaves it undecided in which key the movement will settle down. We know it, of course, as we know the end of *King Lear* before the curtain has risen; but that does not make the contrivance of suspense any the less remarkable from the creative point of view. Assuming ignorance, then, we may expect the diminished-seventh chord, which Samuel Butler once described as a musical Clapham Junction, to lead us to any conceivable station of tonality. In the second bar, however, the music settles down to C minor by means of a perfect cadence. But only a beat later it is torn out of the key again, and the tearing is emphasized by a widespread arpeggio. And so the music goes on ranging over the byways of a variety of keys, until the dominant of C minor, with a calm melody turning round its axis, prepares the way for a definite establishment of the tonic, and so to the *allegro con brio*, which is the sonata movement proper. A rumble of demi-semiquavers in the bass is reduced to notes of half the value at the change to double the pace, so that it actually retains the same motion. The end of this slow shake, turning up to the tonic, then forms the opening of the first subject in this manner:

Ex. 296

For six bars after this the left hand goes on doubling the right in octave unison. Then comes a harmonized version of the theme, followed by a full close, and this in turn is attended by an elaborate fugal development. The three notes 296*a* form its basis, but there are two new figures, rhythmically rather than melodically derived from 296 *b* and *c*:

Ex. 297

The composer's method here is that of double counterpoint: that is to say, he freely reverses the positions of the parts, at one point placing the motif and the runs into the left hand and the octave quaver figures into the right.

The second subject is extremely brief, but stands out by strong contrast to the stormy violence of the first. It opens thus:

Ex. 298

This suave phrase is attended by a kind of coloratura cadence that disintegrates the rhythm and winds into the second statement of the theme itself. A transition to the repeat of the exposition (and the second time to the working-out) then follows. It is a development of the material belonging to the first-subject group.

The working-out, starting with Ex. 296*a*, including the upward run, given out in octave unison and, a moment later, treated fugally with 296*b* and a new counter-subject. Afterwards it is stated in chords by the right hand with arpeggios in the left.

Now a very remarkable thing happens. The semiquaver runs shown in Ex. 297 just begin to reappear as though ready to complicate the working-out, when we discover that they merge into a return of 296 *a* and *b* in their original sequence, though much abbreviated, and almost before we are aware, we find ourselves in the middle of a very condensed recapitulation. Cutting out nearly all the discussion of the main theme as first heard in the exposition, no doubt for the very good reason that we already had a repetition of it all, Beethoven proceeds directly to a rearrangement of his fugal transition in a new order of keys and so to the return of the second subject (Ex. 298) in the tonic (C) major. But now, having given his first theme rather short shrift in the recapitulation, he lets it spread itself once more, though not before the second subject has been given a much ampler development this time, the thematic balance being thus restored.

The very brief coda has an entirely new melody, or at any rate a melodic cadence, three times repeated with a change at the end. This organically disconnected feature would be impossible to understand, were it not for the movement that follows, towards which it is a definite reaching-out. The contrast between the stormy first movement and the world-removed variation-finale would have been too great but for some sort of preparation, and so Beethoven, with a supreme stroke of genius, contrives to suggest a sudden appeasement of mood without giving us the feeling of the least wrench, and he closes his movement very quietly in the tonic major, thus already establishing the key of his second and last movement.

Arietta : Adagio molto, semplice e cantabile.—To write about this farewell to the sonata for the piano (that unsatisfactory instrument!) is to come as near an attempt at describing the indescribable as any one can possibly be faced with.

One cannot even extract musical quotations from it. No idea can be given of the theme on which Beethoven bases his variations except by writing out the whole of it; but it may as well be listened to or looked at in the score. The hearer, after a second or third attempt to come to grips with this movement, which can be formally analysed but is extremely hard to assimilate spiritually, may find it profitable to keep the theme in front of him while the variations are progressing: this will show him how closely Beethoven adheres to its outline for a time, in spite of his growing lavishness of decoration.

The name borne by the theme, *Arietta*, will not mislead the layman, for whom it will mean simply a song on a small scale; but those who know a good deal of music will have to guard against the implication of lightness and flippancy which the term carries. Ariettas in eighteenth-century operas were usually frivolous little songs sung by soubrettes. This interpretation will not do here: Beethoven's theme is a short song, certainly, but neither light nor gay. Still, a song, and one of the most hearteasing ever sung by a musical instrument.

Both the theme and the first variation are written in the unusual 9–16 time. For the second variation the time-signature is changed to 6–16, but the value of the beat remains exactly the same. So it does when the third variation, marked 12–32, doubles the pace of the rhythmic figures of the second, without, however, affecting the duration of the thematic basis.

The fourth variation, again in 9–16, with a steady, broken triplet figure in the bass and a syncopated disintegration of the melodic line, is remarkable for the fact that the two halves of the theme, each of which has hitherto been repeated note for note, are now fully written out with a different treatment for each recurrence. But although on paper there appear to be no repeats, the theme is still retained fundamentally in its original form.

There is no visible sign of the join at which the actual variations cease and the more independent coda begins; but once the theme has been clearly impressed on the hearer's mind, the point can be detected by the ear, or failing that, found by counting thirty-two bars from where the 9–16 signature is resumed. The coda at first continues exactly in the vein of the fourth variation, and then begins a marvellous free fantasy that definitely departs from the theme, yet remains strictly relevant to it. At first there is a continuous chain of shakes over which broken thematic fragments appear, then the material is scattered by syncopation. This portion passes through various keys; then C major is re-established and the *Arietta* returns to its original melodic form, though without repeats and poised over a new accompaniment. To this succeeds another meditation that keeps closely to the theme.

Almost the whole of the concluding section is played, with an ethereal softness, under and over a long shake on G. The first strain of the *Arietta* seems to be evaporating gently into space. An array of soft triplets in thirds and sixths, a sudden swelling up on descending scales, a brief exchange of the falling opening figures of the theme between tonic and dominant, and one of the most complex and difficult movements in the whole range of piano music has ended in utter simplicity—the simplicity which only a child or a master-mind dare express with the perfect assurance of being understood.

POSTLUDE

SUMMING-UP

WE have now studied the mechanism of all the thirty-two Beethoven sonatas usually published and, I hope, seen many things we had not noticed before. I certainly did, though I may have failed to bring this or that point home to the reader, or to make it seem worth his attention. But has all this dissecting and analysing brought us any nearer the secret of the essential greatness of Beethoven? That is the vital question and, I am afraid, one that must remain in the last resort unanswered. We have arrived at some knowledge of Beethoven as a master-builder, no doubt, and as far as that goes these notes may have been of some use. But that his buildings are imposing, beautiful and perfectly satisfying in style, proportion and decoration we all knew before. What we ask ourselves now is whether we are any the wiser about the mystery of where exactly these great qualities lie. Those who play or listen to Beethoven frequently may have found some help in these annotations: that is the most one can hope for; but it would be to delude oneself sadly to imagine that formal analysis of a sonata explains its greatness—or for that matter its mediocrity in a case far enough removed from Beethoven.

For it is quite possible to show in this way that some sonata or other may satisfy every possible formal requirement and yet to discover, on hearing it, that the music is not alive. It will be even less likely to have the spark of true inspiration if it is not structurally sound; but such soundness is only the first condition for a work of genius, which must have some kind of acceptable shape, even if that shape, dictated by an uncommon kind of imagination, turns out to conform to no laws but those established for its own sake. Form, however, is not only an indispensable attribute of a work of genius; it is the only attribute that is analysable. Thus any writing about music that is not merely the record of a personal reaction, that seeks to offer information about a composer's procedures objectively, is bound to drift into formal analysis; and since that kind of expounding has its uses, well and good, so long as we do not pretend that it explains everything.

What it does not explain, I repeat, is the difference between competence and genius. In other words, it does not reveal the secret of what is the real wonder about such music as Beethoven's sonatas, any more than astronomical observations can tell us why one sunset is more beautiful than another. (Or shall we say a sunrise? That metaphor seems more fitting.) Then what is the writer to do? He can, of course, fasten on to some historico-aesthetic question and, according to his knowledge and taste, make something more or less interesting of that. But, apart from the constant danger of falling into a recital of subjective reactions which may not appeal to his reader, he will then be apt to talk all round music instead of about it.

However, as analysis alone will certainly not do, an attempt must be made to consider Beethoven's keyboard sonatas from another point of view in spite of such perils. It has been made before in these intersecting essays; but here, for the last time, something must be said, however diffidently, about some aspects at least of these beautiful and historically important works of art.

The most obvious point at which to begin is the beginning, and as I shall also have to come to an end presently, let us take the start and the finish together for a survey of Beethoven's development from 1795 to 1822, that is from his twenty-fifth to his fifty-second year. The differences between the Sonata in F minor, Op. 2 No. 1, and that in C minor, Op. 111, are enormous, as great as the advance made by Wagner from *The Flying Dutchman* to the year in which he completed *Siegfried*, to choose for comparison a development that took about the same time. But Beethoven, mainly because he occupied himself with all kinds of composition, not with one species alone, and because he advanced by a constant process of much trial and little error, reached his maturity far less spasmodically than Wagner. The whole series of the sonatas—to confine ourselves rather arbitrarily to that branch of his art—shows a very gradual approach to that last enigmatic manner of his which still seems so obscure to those who are too shy to cultivate intimate familiarity with it.

What is to be noticed about this gradual change, if we follow it step by step, is that it is by no means one from lucidity to obscurity, as even experienced musicians are far too often inclined to think. It may be one from explicitness to mystery, if one likes to put it so; but that is another matter. Beethoven's obscurity, if one must call it that, is never due to any lack of clarity, for the later sonatas are planned quite as logically and express his thoughts quite as directly as the earlier ones, to say the least. No, it is due to the fact that the thoughts themselves have acquired a depth not easily penetrated by the superficial listener. If Beethoven was ever given to obscurity, that showed itself first, in his earliest works, and there it was due only to a beginner's inability to find precisely the right forms and terms of expression for what he wished to say. If any of his sonatas refuse to show their meaning clearly, they are those of his boyhood, which have remained almost completely unknown, not because they are bad, but because they actually often mean nothing. As soon as he had acquired mastery his music clarified itself. The difficulty with the later works is only that his ideas became, so to speak, less and less immediately communicative and communicable. And since he always fitted form to matter perfectly, the later formal schemes seem to the unprepared listener of necessity as vague as the thoughts seem obscure, though in actual fact neither judgment is true.

The unprepared listener must prepare himself—that is all; and no better preparation for the later sonatas can be thought of than the playing through of the whole collection in chronological order, now that it is available as a complete series in Artur Schnabel's gramophone records made for the Beethoven Sonata

Society.[1] When this has been done, perhaps not once but a dozen times, the differences in Beethoven's style (or the three styles, if one likes to keep to that conventional classification) will not only be better understood: they will in the end be noticed less than the similarities. For, greatly as he changed with the years, he was always very much himself. His manner of expression changed with him, but as it was at any time of his career ideally suited to what he had to say to the world in this or that phase of his intellectual and artistic development, the impression is from beginning to end that a man, a whole man, stands in front of us. Even in the earliest sonatas, which are not included in the current editions or discussed in the foregoing notes, we see a personality, and if they do not in this case show a man, it is only because Beethoven was still a boy when he wrote these works. A few words may be said about them here for the sake of a complete record.

The two easy little Sonatinas in G and F major, which we have all practised in our childhood, may be dismissed, as it is not certain that they are by Beethoven. They might indeed just as well be by Diabelli. But the three Sonatas dedicated to the Elector of Cologne, written at the age of eleven and published when the composer was thirteen, though unripe in form and callow in expression, are of immense interest to those who like to study a great man's development.[2]

The first, in E flat major, begins like the orchestral *tutti* of some conventional eighteenth-century concerto or other, and suggests by its rudimentary form that the youthful composer knew more about Carl Philipp Emanuel Bach than about the mature works of Haydn and Mozart, though even at this early age he is not as dry as C. P. E. Bach. His perfunctory way of telescoping the working-out section and the recapitulation with no clear idea of the proper function of either is to be encountered in the earliest Haydn also; but it is not likely that Beethoven knew that master's first works of twenty and more years earlier when he ignored the example of the mature middle-period symphonies and sonatas. What is much more probable is that he was brought up on formally weaker models: the Mannheim school, Schobert and—we can tell from matters of texture—Clementi. The *andante* and rondo are only very superficially Mozartian: in other words, they employ certain turns of phrase which Mozart himself borrowed from the common stock of contemporary composers, any of whom, if we only knew their music well, these movements might just as well be found to resemble.

The F minor Sonata, with a slow introduction that reappears in the working-out of the first movement, is in many ways the most interesting and characteristic of the three, though in its keyboard writing it too often resembles an arrangement of an orchestral work—a symphony by Stamitz or some other Mannheimer, perhaps. The opening of the finale, however, is the most Beethovenish theme we can discover in this immature group:

---

[1] Not strictly in the order of opus numbers: it is recommended that a beginning should be made with the two small Sonatas, Op. 49, which represent the early style most adequately and very likely *are* earlier than Op. 2.

[2] They are published by Breitkopf & Härtel in the complete edition of Beethoven's works and also separately in the Urtext edition.

Ex. H

The third Sonata, in D major, which has a set of variations on a minuet in the middle and a finale which is the only thing that comes near a Haydn vein, is very awkwardly written and much more difficult to play than its effect warrants, but has a first movement that is distinctly interesting in spite of a number of solecisms.

Its promise is to a great extent fulfilled in the unfinished C major Sonata of 1792, dedicated to Eleonore von Breuning (with characteristic haste before completion). Here the maximum of effect is obtained from a technically always easy manner of writing, the Clementi-like texture is always airy and lucid, and the sonata form has been mastered astonishingly. There is a distinctly striking working-out section with truly Beethovenian drastic modulations, and the false start made by the second subject in the recapitulation, immediately corrected by its reappearance in the right key, gives the impression of a dramatic *trouvaille*, not of a tentative subterfuge. It is a pity that this Sonata was broken off towards the end of the second movement, which was later completed by Ferdinand Ries, for it already points unmistakably towards the achievements of Op. 2.

That Beethoven knew Haydn's work well by the time he wrote Op. 2 would be obvious even if we did not know that he became that master's pupil and had not the testimony of his dedication of these three Sonatas to him. But until he met Haydn at Bonn in 1790, he is likely to have known more of Mozart, whom he visted in Vienna when he was seventeen (1787). Even then the three 'Elector' Sonatas had already been in existence for some six years, and although they are in the idiom of the day, we have seen that in their general character they resemble neither Haydn nor Mozart. To call Beethoven's 'first period' Mozartian has always seemed to me wildly fantastic, incidental resemblances notwithstanding. I have tried to show in the notes on the G major Sonata, Op. 79 (see page 180), that thematic resemblances are of no significance, even within the work of one single master, when the context of the music as a whole is different, not to mention its spirit. And of course, in spirit Beethoven inhabits a world that is not Mozart's; neither a better world nor a worse—it is simply that the twain do not meet soul to soul, for all that sometimes, materially, they happen to see eye to eye.

J. Arthur Watson in an interesting article on 'Beethoven's Debt to Mozart,' [1] has shown a number of passages in the younger master's music (mainly the chamber works, as it happens, but one might look elsewhere with as much success) where he seems to have hit, by accident or choice or unconscious

[1] *Music and Letters,* Vol. XVIII, No. 3, July 1937.

memory, on very much the same notions as Mozart. But there is no suggestion that Beethoven 'copied' Mozart or that any of the works in question are in the least alike in any way that would detract from Beethoven's greatness as a creative individuality. In fact Mr Watson, in order to show quite clearly how little importance he attributes to this indebtedness in that respect, quotes a couple of sentences from Marion Scott's book on Beethoven which make the true situation admirably clear: 'Beethoven by the alchemy of his genius made everything into his own gold. The more one sees of his debt to other men, the more entirely Beethoven he appears.'

That is in fact true of Mozart himself when he wrote in something like the vein of Johann Christian Bach or Piccinni or Schobert, true indeed of any great master. Purcell is not less Purcell because he takes a good deal from Lully or Corelli; Bach not less Bach because he is influenced by Buxtehude, Reinken, Pachelbel, Vivaldi and a dozen others; Handel not less Handel because he follows in the footsteps of Keiser or Alessandro Scarlatti or Steffani; and so on. Beethoven is so much himself that even when another master's influence is very clearly marked in a work of his, as Cherubini's is in *Fidelio*, for instance, we think of the other's share in his creative make-up as a kind of unconscious anticipation rather than as a contribution. A smaller composer like Cherubini, at any rate, simply seems to have caught one of those currents that are in the air at certain periods of artistic history, a current that was in reality intended to flow to another connection. Admittedly that is not quite fair to Cherubini and his like, for minor artists with distinctive personalities often do contribute something vital to new evolutions; only ultimately the development remains in the hands of the strongest, to whom most of the credit legitimately goes.

In the case of an equal like Mozart it is different. Each great master goes his own way, once he has absorbed what is useful to him in the art of smaller men. When Beethoven's music happens to be like Mozart's for a moment, the resemblance is not of the same kind as that which links him to Cherubini, who could be imitated because he was not inimitable in the sense that a supreme genius like Mozart is. Thus, as Mr Watson has shown, we find thematic coincidences between Mozart and Beethoven that do not affect the spirit of the latter's music, but look like deliberate quotations. There is a good instance in the D major Sonata, Op. 10 No. 3. The passage leading up to a pause before the recapitulation in the first movement reminds one so irresistibly of one in Mozart's *Don Giovanni* that one can only suppose Beethoven to have thought of Leporello's 'ma in Ispagna' and quoted the incident with some humorous afterthought of his own. Here is his version:

Ex. I

and here is Mozart's original:

Ex. J

Such glimpses of Mozart, or whomsoever else, are of course always liable to be caught in Beethoven. The point is that they either give the impression of having become wholly Beethoven or of being reminiscences deliberately introduced. In either case Beethoven's style remains pure: the other composer's idea either blends with his invention to perfection or it remains merely on the surface as a foreign intruder. Such is the independence of absolute mastery: it absorbs everything from outside that can serve its own ends and keeps everything that will not do so quite distinctly in its own place. And that is the kind of mastery we have been studying with the aid of these annotations, I hope. But long after we have grown tired of writing and reading about Beethoven's sonatas, we shall go on playing and hearing them with ever-accruing interest and profit.

BIBLIOGRAPHY

BEHREND, W., *Ludwig van Beethoven's Pianoforte Sonatas.* Translated from the German by I. Lund. (London, 1927.)

Bekker, Paul, *Beethoven.* Translated from the German by M. M. Bozman. (London, 1925.)

Broel, Wilhelm, *Die Durchführungsgestaltung in Beethovens Sonatensätzen.* (Brunswick, 1937.)

Coviello, Ambrose, *Difficulties of Beethoven's Pianoforte Sonatas : an Analysis of Common Faults in Performance, with Suggestions for their Cure.* In progress. (Oxford and London, 1925, etc.)

Heer, Josef, *Der Graf von Waldstein und sein Verhältnis zu Beethoven.* (Leipzig, 1933.)

Johnstone, J. Alfred, *Notes on the Interpretation of Twenty-four Famous Piano Sonatas by Beethoven.* (London, 1927.)

Kalischer, A. C., *Die 'unsterbliche Geliebte' Beethovens.* (Dresden, 1891.)

Kastner, Rudolf, *Beethovens 32 Klaviersonaten und Artur Schnabel.* (Berlin, 1933.)

Laisné, H., *Le Message de Beethoven*, 2 vols. (Paris, 1933.)

La Mara, *Beethoven und die Brunsviks.* (Leipzig, 1920.)

Leichtentritt, Hugo, *The Complete Piano Sonatas of Beethoven : Analytical Notes.* (New York, 1936.)

Lenz, W. von, *Beethoven et ses trois styles.* New edition. (Paris, 1909.)

Lowe, C. E., *Beethoven's Pianoforte Sonatas : Hints on their Rendering, Form, etc.* (London, 1921.)

McEwen, John B., *Beethoven : an Introduction to an Unpublished Edition of the Pianoforte Sonatas.* (Oxford and London, 1932.)

Mersmann, Hans, *Beethoven : die Synthese der Stile.* (Berlin, 1922.)

Mies, Paul, *Beethoven's Sketches : an Analysis of his Style based on a Study of his Sketch-books.* Translated from the German by Doris L. Mackinnon. (Oxford and London, 1929.)

Milne, A. Forbes, *Beethoven : the Piano Sonatas* (selection of twelve), 2 vols. (Oxford and London, 1925 and 1928.)

Nagel, Wilibald, *Beethoven und seine Klaviersonaten*, 2 vols. New edition. (Langensalza, 1923.)

Newman, Ernest, *The Unconscious Beethoven : an Essay in Musical Psychology.* (London, 1927.)

Prod'homme, J.-G., *Les Sonates pour piano de Beethoven* (Paris, 1937.)

Riemann, Hugo, *Beethovens sämtliche Klavier-Solosonaten*, 3 vols. (Berlin, 1919–20.)

Rolland, Romain, *Beethoven the Creator*, Vol. I: *From the 'Eroica' to the 'Appassionata.'* Translated from the French by Ernest Newman. (London, 1929.)

Salisbury, Janet, *A Concise Analysis of Beethoven's Thirty-two Pianoforte Sonatas.* (London, 1931.)

Schering, Arnold, *Beethoven in neuer Deutung.* Vol. I. (Leipzig, 1934.)

——, *Beethoven und die Dichtung.* (Berlin, 1936.)

Scott, Marion M., *Beethoven.* (London, 1934.)

Shedlock, J. S., *Beethoven's Pianoforte Sonatas.* (London, 1918.)

Tovey, Donald F., *A Companion to Beethoven's Pianoforte Sonatas.* (London, 1931.)

INDEX

ADAM, ADOLPHE, 25
Albrechtsberger, 4, 10, 21, 23
Anschütz, Heinrich, 156
Arnold, Samuel, 24
Artaria, publisher, 25, 202
Attwood, 24
Auber, 24

Bach, 1, 170, 177, 178, 181, 182, 244
  Art of Fugue, The, 205
  Capriccio on the Departure of a Brother, 182, 183
  Fugues for organ, 221, 222
  Well-tempered Clavier, The, 1, 6, 108, 211
Bach, Carl Philipp Emanuel, 2, 171, 181, 242
Bach, Johann Christian, 2, 244
Bagehot, Walter, 4
Balfe, 25
Beethoven:
  Adelaide, 141
  Andante favori, 148, 153
  Bagatelles, 103, 231
  Battle of Vittoria, The, 183
  Concerto for piano, B flat major, 67
  Concerto for piano, C minor, 79
  Concerto for piano, E flat major, 169
  Country Dances, 112
  Fidelio, 23, 80, 91, 92, 148, 244
  Grosse Fuge for string quartet, 204, 221, 233, 234
  Leonora Prohaska, 94
  Leonore Overture No. 3, 17, 89
  Missa solemnis, 229, 234
  Preludes through all the keys for piano, 162
  Prometheus, 80, 93, 112, 141
  Quartet for piano and strings (early), 5, 16
  Quartets:
    Op. 18, 79, 112
    Op. 74, 156, 157, 225
    Op. 95, 169
    Op. 127, 79
    Op. 130, 228
    Op. 135, 169
  Quartets for strings, 63, 79
  Quintet (Op. 29), 112, 123
  Ritterballett, 148
  Rondo, G major, for piano, 108, 110
  Septet, 63, 79–81, 88, 144, 146, 147

Beethoven—*continued*
  Sextet (Op. 81*b*), 183
  Sonata for horn and piano, 79
  Sonatas for piano:
    Op. 2, 21, 25, 144, 242, 243
      No. 1, **4–9**; 16, 64, 88, 241
      No. 2, **10–15**; 3
      No. 3, **15–20**; 144
    Op. 7, **26–32**
    Op. 10, 81
      No. 1, **32–9**; 46
      No. 2, **39–44**; 54, 91, 138, 147
      No. 3, **44–51**; 88, 244
    Op. 13, **56–62**; 44, 55, 67, 90, 120, 181, 224
    Op. 14, 23, 156, 169
      No. 1, **67–74**; 65, 66, 91
      No. 2, **74–8**; 225
    Op. 22, **81–90**; 63, 79–81, 110, 112, 169
    Op. 26, **93–101**; 90–3, 102, 147, 148, 225
    Op. 27, 90, 113
      No. 1, **102–7**; 65, 194, 195
      No. 2, **107–12**; 91, 112, 113, 120, 140, 172, 173, 181, 182
    Op. 28, **112–18**; 140, 141, 163, 172, 181
    Op. 31, 147
      No. 1, **123–31**; 80, 122
      No. 2, **131–6**; 58, 155, 157, 158
      No. 3, **136–41**; 56, 80, 113, 170, 213
    Op. 49, 125, 242
      No. 1, **141–3**
      No. 2, **144–7**; 80, 81, 88
    Op. 53, **147–54**; 93, 159, 163, 173
    Op. 54, **159–62**; 91, 142, 158, 159
    Op. 57, **163–7**; 54, 80, 81, 120, 155–7, 159, 173
    Op. 78, **172–7**; 58, 121, 170, 177, 192, 193
    Op. 79, **177–80**; 243
    Op. 81*a*, **183–9**; 54, 55, 58, 169, 177, 181–3
    Op. 90, **190–4**; 169
    Op. 101, **194–201**; 24, 113, 169, 202
    Op. 106, **205–24**; 79, 113, 136, 157, 169, 194, 202–5, 234, 236
    Op. 109, **224–9**; 29, 65, 180, 225, 236
    Op. 110, **229–36**; 113, 180
    Op. 111, **236–9**; 58, 90, 91, 159, 169, 184, 225, 241

Beethoven: Sonatas for piano—*continued*
C major (early, unfinished), 5, 243
D major (early), 5, 242, 243
E flat major (early), 5, 242
F minor (early), 5, 58, 242
Sonatas for violin and piano:
Op. 12, 21
Op. 23, 112
Op. 24, 112
Op. 47, 24
Sonatinas (early), 5, 242
Symphonies, 58
No. 1, 63, 169
No. 2, 51, 63, 112
No. 3, 80, 92–4, 147, 169, 187, 206
No. 5, 46, 164, 206
No. 6, 157, 183
No. 7, 72, 192
No. 8, 80
No. 9, 91, 169, 180, 229
Trios:
Op. 1, 5
Op. 9, 33, 81
Op. 11, 144
Op. 97, 169, 228
Variations on the Theme by Waldstein, for piano duet, 148
Variations on a Theme from Mozart's *Magic Flute,* for cello, 112
Variations on a Waltz by Diabelli, for piano, 90, 236
Variations on *Vieni amore*, for piano, 24
Beethoven, Caspar, 141
Beethoven Sonata Society, v, 4, 54, 241, 242
Bekker, Paul, 86, 180, 194
Bell, Clive, 183
Bellini, 25, 87, 118
Bennett, Sterndale, 25
Berg, Alban, 22
Berlioz, 24, 25
Berton, 24
Bishop, 24
Bittner, Julius, 22
Boccherini, 7, 8, 24
Boieldieu, 24
Bouilly, J. N., 23
Brahms, 180
Sonata for piano (Op. 1), 204
Braun, Baroness von, 68, 74
Braun, Peter von, Baron, 68
Breitkopf & Härtel, 67, 177, 183, 184, 242
Brentano, Antonie von, 224
Brentano, Franz von, 224
Brentano, Frau von, 229
Brentano, Maximiliana von, 224
Breuning, Eleonore von, 243
Breuning family, 148
Browne, Count von, 33, 81
Browne, Countess von, 33, 81
Browning, 23
Bruckner, 216
Brunswick, Franz von, 163, 164, 172, 173
Brunswick, Josephine von. *See* Deym
Brunswick, Therese von, 112, 163, 164
Bülow, Hans von, 223
Butler, Samuel, 237
Buxtehude, 181, 244
Byrd, Battle Pieces, 181

Callcott, 24
Cappi, publisher, 93, 123
Carroll, Lewis, 168
Catel, 24
Cervantes, 156
Cherubini, 23, 24, 91, 221, 244
Masses and Requiem, 24
Cimarosa, 21, 24
Clementi, 2, 22, 24, 63, 171, 242, 243
Didone abbandonata, Sonata, 183
Gradus ad Parnassum, 24
Sonata, G minor (Op. 34 No. 2), 58, 90
Cologne, Elector of. *See* Maximilian Friedrich
Corelli, 244
Couperin, 1, 181, 182
Cranz, publisher, 113, 117, 163
Cristofori, 194
Crotch, 24
Czerny, 23, 156, 158

Dalayrac, 24
Dante, 235
Dargomizhsky, 25
David, Félicien, 25
Debussy, 11, 65, 178, 204
Deym, Josephine von, 163, 164
Diabelli, 90, 236, 242
Dibdin, 24
Dittersdorf, 23
Donizetti, 24
Duncker, 94
Dussek, 2, 22, 24, 63
Retour à Paris, Le (*Plus ultra*), Sonata, 124, 181
Sonata, C minor, 2, 56, 57
Sonatas (Op. 39), 22

Eberl, 23
Eder, publisher, 56
Einstein, Alfred, 155
Eliot, T. S., 235
Ertmann, Dorothea von, Baroness, 194

Eschenburg, 157–9
Euripides, 157
Eybler, 22, 23

Fétis, 168, 171
Field, 22, 24, 86, 87, 108
Fioravanti, 24
Flotow, 25
Förster, Aloys, 21
Francis II, Emperor, 21
Franz, Robert, 25
Frescobaldi, Battle Capriccio, 181
Froberger, 181, 182

Gaveaux, 24
Léonore, ou l'amour conjugal, 23, 148
Gazzaniga, 24
Gelinek, 23
Giustini, Lodovico, 43
Glinka, 25
Gluck, 23, 92
Goethe, 156, 157
Gossec, 24
Graeser, Wolfgang, 205
Grétry, 24
Greuze, 181
Grove, Sir George, 141, 144, 194, 202
Guglielmi, 23
Guicciardi, Giulietta, 107, 108, 110, 112, 172, 173
Gyrowetz, 23

Halévy, 24
Handel, 244
Haslinger, publisher, 194
Haydn, 4, 5, 18, 21–3, 30, 54, 68, 112, 171, 173, 203, 206, 212, 242, 243
Masses, 23
Quartets, 8
Sonata, D major, 2, 3
Sonatas for piano, 1, 2, 22, 26, 53
Symphonies, 57
Symphony, G major (Military), 8
Welsh Airs (arranged), 22
Haydn, Michael, 23
Heller, 25
Henselt, 25
Hérold, 24
Hiller, 25
H.M.V. Gramophone Company, v
Hoffmann, E. T. A., *Undine,* 25
Hoffmeister & Kühnel, 81
Holst, *The Planets,* 181
Homer, 156
Hummel, 22, 23, 25

Ibsen, 156

Jackson (of Exeter), 24

Keglevics, Babette von, 25
Keiser, 244
Kelly, Michael, 24
Kirnberger, 221
Korngold, Erich, 22
Kozeluch, 21–3
Kreutzer, Rodolphe, 24
Kuhnau, Biblical Sonatas, 181, 182

Lanner, 25
Léhar, Franz, 22
Lenz, Wilhelm von, 65, 168–71
Leopold II, Emperor, 21
Lesueur, 24
Lichnowsky, Carl von, Prince, 5, 57, 93, 102, 148
Lichnowsky, Moritz von, Count, 190
Lichnowsky, Princess von, 108, 110
Liechtenstein, General Field Marshal Prince von, 102
Liechtenstein, Josephine Sophie, Princess von, 102
Liszt, 25, 65, 121, 168, 204
Lobkowitz, Prince, 79
Loewe, 23
Lortzing, 25
Lully, 244

Macfarren, 25
Malfatti, Therese von, 157
Marschner, 23, 25
Maximilian Friedrich, Elector of Cologne, 5
Mayr, 24
Méhul, 23, 24
Mendelssohn, 25, 102, 108, 179, 193
Mercadante, 24, 25
Meyerbeer, 23, 25, 92
Monsigny, *Le Déserteur,* 24
Mozart, 3, 6, 9, 14, 21–3, 28, 54, 67, 102, 171, 173, 188, 206, 242, 245
Clemenza di Tito, La, 92
Deutsche, 178
Divertimenti, 8
Don Giovanni, 7, 24, 244, 245
Idomeneo, 92
Magic Flute, 22, 112, 180
Masses, 23
Serenades, 8
Sonatas for piano, 26, 53, 89
A major (K. 331), 52, 90
D major (K. 284), 52, 53

Mozart—*continued*
  Symphonies, 57
    D major ('Prague,' K. 504), 52, 53, 56
    G minor (K. 550), 5
Mozart, Constanze, 22
Mozart, Leopold, 5
Muffat, 182
Müller, Wenzel, 22
Munday, *Weather Fantasia,* 181
Mussolini, 157

Nägeli, 122–4, 128, 136
Newman, Ernest, 29, 228
Nicolai, 25

Pachelbel, 244
Paer, 24, 94, 98, 99, 147
  Achilles, 91–3
  Eleonore, ossia l'amore conjugale, 148
Paisiello, 24, 25
Paradis, Marie Therese von, 22
Pearsall, 25
Persuis, 24
Piccinni, 23, 244
Pleyel, Ignaz, 24
Potter, Cipriani, 24
Puccini, 11
Purcell, 244

Raimondi, 24
Rameau, *La Poule,* 182
Reeve, 24
Reichardt, 23
Reinken, 244
Rellstab, 108
Reutter, 23
Ries, Ferdinand, 23, 102, 123, 156, 202, 203, 229, 230, 243
  Concerto, *Farewell to London,* 230
Righini, 24
Rossini, 24
  Barbiere di Siviglia, Il, 25
  Otello, 25
Rudolph, Archduke, 184, 202, 229, 236

Saint-Saëns, 140
Salieri, 21, 23, 24
Sarti, 24
Satie, Erik, 178
Scarlatti, Alessandro, 244
Scarlatti, Domenico, 1, 43, 181
Schenk, Johann, 4, 5, 21–3
Schering, Arnold, 58, 155–9
Schikaneder, Emanuel, 22
Schiller, 155, 156
Schindler, Anton, 70, 74, 131, 155–8, 229
Schlegel, 157, 158
Schlesinger, publisher, 229
Schnabel, Artur, v, 54, 241
Schobert, 242, 244
Schröter, 194
Schubert, 18, 21, 23, 102, 108, 192
  Deutsche, 178
  Heidenröslein, Das, 180
  Symphonies, 25
  Wanderer, Der, 25
Schumann, 25, 96, 121, 204
  Variations symphoniques, 94
Schuppanzigh, 21, 230
Scott, Marion M., 56, 57, 137, 244
Seyfried, 23
Shakespeare, 122, 131, 155–9, 205
Sharp, Cecil, 22
Shaw, Bernard, 156
Shedlock, J. S., 67
Shield, 24
Silbermann, 194
Simrock, publisher, 123
Smith, John Stafford, 24
Sonnenfels, Joseph von, 112
Spohr, 23
  Concerto in modo d'una scena cantante, 25
Spontini, 24, 92
Stadler, 23
Stamitz, Carl, 23
Stamitz, Johann, 242
Steffani, 244
Steibelt, 23
Steiner, publisher, 194
Stendhal, 4
Stevenson, R. L., 8
Strauss, Johann, jun., 37
Strauss, Johann, sen., 25
Strauss, Richard, 14
Stravinsky, 121
Süssmayr, 22, 23

Tayber, Anton, 21, 22
Tovey, Sir Donald, 54, 70, 81, 131, 141, 144, 162 165, 167, 178, 203, 220, 231

Umlauf, 23

Verdi, 25
  Aida, 92
Viotti, 24
Vivaldi, 244
Vogler, 23

Wagner, 4, 14, 25, 45, 113, 241
  Fliegende Holländer, Der, 241
  Rienzi, 92
  Siegfried, 85, 86, 241
  Tristan und Isolde, 113
Waldstein, Ferdinand von, Count, 147, 148
Wallace, Vincent, 25
Wanhal, 23
Watson, J. Arthur, 243, 244
Webbe, 24
Weber, 23, 25
Weigl, 21, 23
Weingartner, Felix, 205
Wellington, Duke of, 183
Wesendonck, Mathilde, 113
Wesley, Samuel, 24
Willmann, Magdalene, 112
Winter, 23
Woelfl, 22, 23, 29
  Sonata, *Ne plus ultra,* 124
Wranitzky, 22

Zelter, 23
Zingarelli, 24
Zumsteeg, 23

Blom, Eric
Beethoven's pianoforte sonatas
discussed